The Catholic Church and the Protestant State

For my mother Ellie Rafferty (née Hassan)
1924–2007

90 0790221 2

THE CATHOLIC CHURCH
AND THE
PROTESTANT STATE

Nineteenth-century Irish realities

OLIVER P. RAFFERTY

FOUR COURTS PRESS

Set in 11 on 13 Ehrhardt for
FOUR COURTS PRESS LTD
7 Malpas Street, Dublin 8, Ireland
e-mail: info@fourcourtspress.ie
http://www.fourcourtspress.ie
and in North America
FOUR COURTS PRESS
c/o ISBS, 920 N.E. 58th Avenue, Suite 300, Portland, OR 97213.

© Oliver P. Rafferty 2008

ISBN 978–1–84682–084–7

Printed in England by
MPG Books, Bodmin, Cornwall

Contents

Abbreviations

Add. MS	Additional manuscript
AAA	Archives of the Archdiocese of Armagh
AAB	Archives of the Archdiocese of Baltimore
AAW	Archives of the Archdiocese of Westminster
ADDC	Archives of the Diocese of Down and Connor
AICR	Archives of the Irish College, Rome
APF	Archives of Propaganda Fide
ARCAT	Archives of the Roman Catholic Archdiocese of Toronto
AUND	Archives of the University of Notre Dame
BL	British Library
BLO	Bodleian Library, Oxford
CSORP	Chief Secretary's Office Registered Papers
DDA	Dublin Diocesan Archives
FPR	Fenian Police Reports
FO	Foreign Office
HC	house of commons
HL	house of lords
HO	Home Office
IHS	*Irish Historical Studies*
NAI	National Archives of Ireland
NLI	National Library of Ireland
PAHRC	Philadelphia Archdiocese Historical Research Center
PRO	The National Archives, Public Record Office
PRONI	Public Record Office of Northern Ireland
SOC	State of the Country Papers
UCA	Ushaw College Archives

Preface

Many individuals and institutions have assisted me in various ways in the preparation of this volume. In particular I would like to thank the College of the Holy Cross, Worcester, Massachusetts for granting me a fellowship beginning in August 2006. My teaching duties were such that I had ample time to work on the essays in this volume. I would like to record my gratitude both to the history department and to the Centre for Religion Ethics and Culture, in particular to Tom Landy who has been a splendid host throughout my time at Holy Cross. I must also mention in this regard Jim Hayes SJ and Thomas Worcester SJ for much kindness and encouragement. Jim Corkery SJ made various observations not all of which appear in this volume. I would also like to thank Simon Smith SJ for help with proof reading.

Two individuals at Four Courts Press have eased the process of production in a remarkable degree and deserve special mention. Michael Adams brought his editorial skills to bear on a somewhat unwieldy typescript, and Aoife Walsh, has been efficient and courteous through-out. Ray Gillespie played a crucial role in seeing the typescript safely to the publisher.

For advice and comments on individual essays I would like to thank: Owen Dudley Edwards, Ian McBride, Elva Johnston, Gerard O'Brien, John Kelly, John Regan, Brendan Bradshaw, Ruth Harris, Patrick O'Sullivan, Catronia Clutterbuck, Roy Foster, Ambrose Macaulay, Gearóid Ó Tuathaigh, and John R. Walsh. The dedication is to my mother who taught me a good deal about history and many other matters.

Extracts from or versions of a number of these essays have appeared in various guises as follows: No. 2 Gerard O'Brien (ed.), *Derry and Londonderry, history and society* (Dublin, 1999); No. 3 *Recusant History*, 21:3 (1993); No. 4 *Bullan: an Irish Studies Journal*, 4:2 (2000); No. 6 Eileen Murphy and William Roulston (eds), *County Fermanagh: interdisciplinary essays on the history of an Irish county* (Dublin, 2004); No. 7 *Recusant History*, 22:4 (1995); No. 8 *Bullan*, 4:1 (1988); No. 9 Oliver Rafferty (ed.), *Reconciliation: essays in honour of Michael Hurley* (Dublin, 1993); No. 10 Lindsay Proudfoot (ed.), *Down: history and society* (Dublin, 1997).

No. 1 began as a paper read in the old house of lords in the Bank of Ireland building in Dublin in May 2000 to mark the bi-centenary of the Act of Union. The conference was organized by Brendan Simms on behalf of the

British Irish Association. An earlier draft of No. 5 was read to a meeting of the History Society at the National University of Ireland, Galway in the autumn of 1998. William O'Reilly was an amiable and attentive guide on that occasion. I wish to thank all those who asked questions and made comments on these papers at those meetings.

Introduction

For most individuals in the post-modern world, given the social and cultural environment of the early twenty-first century, it is at times difficult to appreciate how in the not very remote past religion played a decisive role in the way in which individuals and nations saw themselves. It is impossible to understand the dynamics of Irish society in the nineteenth-century without having some grasp of the operations and functioning of the various churches and religious bodies in the country. Of these the most important was the Catholic Church which by the 1840s commanded the allegiance of about eighty percent of the Irish people. This reality has led one prominent historian to remark that 'Irish Catholicism is the very heart of Irish culture. Within this rubric, the colonial relationship of England and Ireland is perceived largely as a footnote to the great *volta voce* in western history; the Protestant reformation.'[1] For some observers of the Irish scene, Catholicism is to be viewed simply as a social phenomenon,[2] but this is to neglect the fact that its social manifestation is predicated on what it perceives as transcendental realities. And it is these which give shape to its forms and expressions in Irish history.

The context for the essays in this book is provided by the activity of the Catholic Church in nineteenth-century Ireland in a political and social milieu not always favourable to the presence of the church. The body of the book considers Catholicism's role in Ireland under various guises from the beginning of the nineteenth century until 1870. Allusion is made in individual essays to the periods before and after these termini by way of illustration of certain trends in church attitudes to both the state and the internal cohesion of the Catholic body considered as a whole. Some of the essays are concerned with implications for both church and state of the great constitutional issues of the day such as the Union and the disestablishment of the Church of Ireland. Others discuss the problems posed by Fenianism as both government and churchmen grappled with the need to contain the revolutionary propensities among some of the church's adherents. Several localized studies present the church's experience across a range of issues touching on

---

1 D.H. Akenson, *Small differences: Irish Catholic and Irish Protestants, 1815–1922: an international perspective* (Dublin, 1988). Akenson is drawing on ideas expressed in Patrick O'Farrell's 'idiosyncratic and spikey' work, *England's Irish question: Anglo-Irish relations, 1534–1970* (London, 1971). 2 Marianne Elliott's *The Catholics of Ulster* (London, 2000) is a perfect illustration of such an approach.

its devotional and moral life, and consideration is also given in these contexts to relations with other Christian denominations.

Catholicism's experience in Ireland was neither uniform nor mono-faceted. In particular, its existence in Ulster brought it face to face with Protestant Ireland with a greater immediacy and intensity than was common in most of its cultural day to day experience elsewhere in the country. Some of the contours of that encounter are delineated with the help of that acute observer of the Irish Catholic experience, William Carleton. Although somewhat romantic and misguided and offering too-skewed a view on Liberal policy on Ireland, J.L. Hammond many years ago provided a penetrating and classic study of Gladstone's flirtations with an Irish policy.[3] No such work has been attempted for that other protean figure who so dominated the Victorian political landscape, Benjamin Disraeli. A richly textured and illuminating piece by J.P. Parry no more than alludes to some of the points which would have to be addressed in such a study,[4] and the essay in this collection is a brief preliminary sketch of the terrain which seeks to set Disraeli's views on Ireland within his general attitude to Catholicism, going beyond his well know and dismissive parody 'potatoes one day and the pope the next'.

Despite having so much in common, at least in the early part of the nineteenth-century, there was surprisingly little direct attempt by the Catholic hierarchies in England and Ireland to coordinate common ecclesias-tical responses to the problems facing the church in both countries. Perhaps one of the reasons for such neglect is the cautionary tale provided by the example of the misdirected outlook of one notable figure in the English Catholic Church, Nicholas Wiseman. His interventions and schemes for Catholic social advancement in England occasioned an enormous and infamous anti-Catholic outpouring in mid-century, and his politico-religious views met with a great deal of coolness on the other side of St George's Channel. Some aspects of his general outlook and polices are here examined, especially his role in attempts to establish diplomatic relations between the court of St James and the court of Rome.

One ironic feature of the background of the operations of Catholicism in post-Union Ireland was an intensification of sectarian hostility. Despite the aim of the Union proposals to reconcile Catholic Ireland with Protestant Britain and to give Protestant Ireland a great sense of security within the parameters of the United Kingdom, the uncertainties of the social position of each community ensured lingering hostility at a time when, ostensibly, the reasons for such hostility had been removed. Arguably, sectarian conflict had

3 J.L. Hammond, *Gladstone and the Irish nation* (London, 1964). 4 J.P. Parry, 'Disraeli and England', *Historical Journal*, 43 (2000), 699–728.

been a prominent feature in Irish society since the late Tudor conquest, but it was given a greater edge when, for the first time since the seventeenth century, Catholicism emerged as a political force, first with the political concessions to Catholics in the early 1790s, then with the United Irish rising in 1798 and finally with the long awaited arrival of Catholic emancipation in 1829. Catholicism was seen as a political threat as well as a detestable system of belief. Indeed, despite political union, the functioning of Catholicism in Ireland, 'both allied Ireland with Europe and pitted her against England'.[5]

It is possible to read the history of Catholicism in Ireland in the eighteenth century and in most of the nineteenth century as a story of the church's attempt to control the lives of its adherents in their social context. This is especially true with regard to specifically religious practices and in particular in relation to abuses in such things as wakes and patterns and the grosser superstitions connected with popular practice of Catholicism.[6] But where it was feasible, the church sought to exercise its influence even in the directly political sphere. It would be a mistake, however, to suppose that Catholicism had a clear political agenda per se. Indeed, despite the fact that the Protestant state in the post-union period for the most part no longer persecuted or obstructed her operations, Catholicism developed no satisfactory intellectual framework about how the church was to relate to the state.[7] The question of its external relations with the state were also complicated by a lack of coherence in developing strategies to deal with difficulties which it faced *ad intra* in Irish society as a whole. Perhaps one of the most important challenges for institutional Catholicism was how to direct and control the impulses of those of its lay members who sought to have some say in the internal operations of the church. As early as 1792 Bishop Patrick Plunkett of Meath could complain to one clerical correspondent that 'some symptoms in our laity indicate an inclination to become our masters, and to dictate to us even in the line of our profession'.[8] Lay people often demanded a say in how the local congregation was organized and even who would serve as the pastor for the parish. The many disputes to which these tensions gave rise all serve:

> [t]o make clear the conviction of Irish Catholics that they had a legit-
> imate role in the affairs of their church down to almost the lowest levels

---

5 Clare Carroll, 'The nation and post-colonial theory' in Clare Carroll and Patricia King (eds), *Ireland and post-colonial theory* (Cork, 2003), p. 3.   6 Jim Smyth, 'Manning the ramparts: Ireland and the agenda of the Roman Catholic Church', *History of European Ideas*, 20 (1995), 683.   7 C.D.A. Leighton, 'Gallicanism and the veto controversy: church, state and Catholic community in early nineteenth-century Ireland', in R.V. Comerford *et al.*, *Religion, conflict and co-existence in Ireland* (Dublin, 1990), p. 138. 8 A. Cogan, *The diocese of Meath ancient and modern*, 3 vols (Dublin, 1870), iii, 171.

of society, a fact which assists considerably in accounting for the genuinely popular nature of the reaction to proposals which were depicted as threatening to diminish that role.[9]

We are accustomed in Irish historiography to see and think of the eighteenth century in terms of the 'Protestant elite', 'Protestant patriotism' and 'Protestant nationalism',[10] but it is also true that for most of the nineteenth century we can with conviction and certainty talk of the 'Protestant state' in Ireland. The country was controlled and administered, despite the efforts of the Catholic Church in alliance with the Catholic middle classes, largely in favour of the Protestant ascendancy and the emergent Presbyterian venture capitalists. By 1870, some, but by no means all, of the vestiges of the Protestant state have been swept away. If, however, we revert to old-fashioned Marxist terms we can see that the real power in Irish society, given its economic base, was still felt and exercised in the Protestant interest for some considerable time into the future even after partition, both in Northern Ireland, as one might expect, but also in the Irish Free State. This Protestant influence was experienced in a variety of ways. Even by that time in the nineteenth century when the state did not officially inhibit Catholic participation and prosperity, 'informal sectarianism proved almost as effective a ban to Catholics in public life as had the penal laws'.[11] Of course, sectarianism was a two-way street, and when they could Catholics were at times just as exclusivist as Protestants. Equally, as is clear from even a cursory glance at the relationships between the communities, not all contact was either exclusionist or hostile.

Ranged against the Protestant state, in all its manifestations, was the Catholic Church. More effectively than the state itself Catholicism touched the lives of the majority of the Irish people in their social, political and religious aspects. Much of the history of Ireland from the Union can be read in terms of the interaction of these two great forces of the state on the one hand and Catholicism on the other. In many of its operations, the state presented a decidedly Protestant face, and therefore the interaction between Catholics and the state was in many instances occluded by the confrontation between at times mutually hostile branches of Christianity. But even here the inter-relationship between Catholics and Protestants was not simply read in religious terms. The quality of Catholic-Protestant relations can be measured on a spectrum by which Catholicism was perceived as a political threat to the

9 Leighton, 'Gallicanism', p. 149. 10 Jim Smyth, 'The making and undoing of a confessional state: Ireland, 1660–1829,' *Journal of Ecclesiastical History*, 44 (1993), 507. 11 Ibid., 512.

ascendancy and to the status quo. The less powerful and the less threatening to established Protestant influence, the more tolerance there was for Catholicism. But when social Catholicism began to change, relations were fraught and violence ensued. This was true in the country as a whole, but it was more acute in Ulster, where there was greater proximity between the communities, and above all in towns such as Belfast where the occasional and sometimes 'recreational riots' of the early part of the nineteenth century gave way to vicious sectarian acrimony and violence as the century wore on.[12]

In the early decades of the period the Catholic bishops, despite their support for the Union, were politically wrong-footed *vis-à-vis* the Catholic community at large by government's determination 'to maintain protestant privilege in Ireland'.[13] Despite much misreading of their intentions at the time and subsequently, the Catholic bishops did not expect or look for emancipation as a result of their support for the Union. When, however, the political circumstances become less favourable to the church as the first decade of the century unfolded, a greater weariness can be detected even in the most loyal Catholic adherents of the governing powers. John Thomas Troy, archbishop of Dublin, a keen unionist who, for all his genuine efforts to uphold the prerogatives of the state, could in the face of the veto controversy of 1808 express his sheer exasperation with the lack of government understanding of the problems facing Catholic Ireland. The ambiguity and difficulties facing prelates such as he in their attempts to reconcile loyalty to the institutions of the state, on the one hand, and control of the demands for redress of grievances on the part of the more vociferous members of their flock, on the other, led to much self-obsessed agony. Comparing the situation in 1799 which he had carefully managed, with that which now confronted him, he firmly declared:

> In the former we were called upon, pending the Union question, by an Administration supposedly friendly, and holding out the prospect, if not an implied promise, to consider the measure as the condition of Emancipation. At the present our hopes have not only been blasted, but a No Popery Administration declares in both Houses of parliament that we are to expect nothing more.[14]

Perhaps, however, the real difficulty lay in Troy's ultimate inability to play the political game skillfully enough. His problem was that he was too much a

---

12 Elliott, *The Catholics of Ulster*, p. 325.　13 Oliver MacDonagh, 'The politicization of the Irish Catholic bishops, 1800–1850', *Historical Journal*, 18:1 (1975), 41.　14 See Bernard Ward, *The eve of Catholic emancipation*, 2 vols (London, 1911), i, 145–6.

bishop and not enough of a politician, unlike his contemporaries at the court of Rome who within a few years, as a result of skilful diplomacy, were able to wrest the Papal States almost entirely intact from a reluctant Europe, including Protestant Britain, following the collapse of Bonapartism.

Catholicism faced the nineteenth century by turns euphoric and fearful, but nevertheless determined to maintain its position in the affections of the majority of the Irish people. On the whole, in purely ecclesiastical terms, the Irish Catholic Church lived under a benevolent, if Protestant, government which interfered much less in its life than any European government in the life of its sister churches. When, however, the government, for whatever reason, did choose to act in a way that seemed to restrict the freedom of Catholicism, as in the veto controversy in 1808 or the Charitable Bequests Act of 1844, the consequences were disastrous for both Catholicism and the state. Churchmen were quickly disillusioned and were moved from a position of acquiescence in Protestant government to self-indignant hostility to the operations of the state. This resulted in a cynicism about political intentions which could be, and was, exploited by the more politically advanced members of the community. De Tocqueville's justly famous and much quoted passage about his encounter with the bishop of Kildare and Leighlin and his dinner guests on 20 July 1835 neatly sums up the position of churchmen at that stage of the century. The conversation on the state of the country evinced feelings which were

> extremely democratic. Distrust and hatred of the great landlords ...
> Bitter memories of past oppression. An air of exaltation at present or
> approaching victory. A profound hatred of the Protestants and above
> all of their clergy. Little impartiality apparent. Clearly as much the
> leaders of a Party as the representatives of the Church.[15]

Despite the air of expectancy it is also clear that church leaders did not appreciate either the benefits of Union or the political progress of O'Connellism as constituting important gains for the Catholic Church or community. Even in the aftermath, then, of emancipation in 1829, Catholics still remained disenchanted with government policy. Furthermore it could be argued that when the benefits of the political nation were not forthcoming in the post-1829 era, Catholics became more not less alienated from the state.[16] Of course, there were reasons other than government policy for Catholic

---

15 Alexis de Tocqueville, *Journeys to England and Ireland*, ed. J.P. Mayer (London, 1958), p. 130.   16 Oliver MacDonagh, 'The age of O'Connell 1830–45', in W.E. Vaughan (ed.), *A new history of Ireland, v: Ireland under the Union I, 1801–70* (Oxford, 1898), p. 158.

skepticism. De Tocqueville again recorded the comments of one disgruntled lower class Catholic: 'Emancipation has done nothing for us. Mr O'Connell and the rich Catholics go to Parliament. We die of starvation just the same.'[17]

Equally, emancipation could not be nor was it designed to be a panacea. Ultimately, as a concession it was forced from a reluctant crown and parliament lest something worse convulse Ireland than merely the peaceful political O'Connellite campaign. Emancipation was not in any sense a dismantling of the Protestant settlement of Ireland, still less that of the United Kingdom. The acts of settlement and succession remained in place. Furthermore, the concession of political emancipation notwithstanding, the relief act of 1829 placed certain restrictions on the full operation of Catholicism in the United Kingdom. Catholics remained excluded from some offices of state, especially, but not exclusively, those connected most immediately with the government of Ireland. Religious orders were, strictly speaking, forbidden to operate in the country, and the wearing of religious garb in public was prohibited. Although widely ignored, these provision were appealed to as late as 1908 to inhibit some of the activities connected with the London Eucharistic Congress that year. The prime minister, Herbert Asquith, whom Churchill branded as a lifelong anti-Catholic, appealed at the last minute to the archbishop of Westminster to cancel a parade of the Blessed Sacrament through certain London streets, on a route which had been previously agreed with the police and the home office. The 1829 act was duly invoked as justification for this bizarre incident.[18] If 1829 did not fully produce in the United Kingdom the European liberal ideal of a free church in a free state, it does represent an instance in which, as L.P. Curtis remarks in another context, 'the forces of Catholic "democracy" could effectively combine to discomfort the representatives of the Protestant Ascendancy'.[19] Irresistible Catholic force had met, in this instance, the movable Protestant object.

Reference has already been made to the fact that the church lacked a clear political agenda. Indeed, one can adduce evidence to suggest that churchmen were, in many ways, content to acquiesce in the political status quo. Individuals such as Daniel Murray, archbishop of Dublin, were and remained essentially products of the *ancien régime* in their deference to British authority

---

17 Quoted in K. Theodore Hoppen, *The mid-Victorian generation, 1846–1886* (Oxford, 1998), p. 132.   18 A parade did go ahead without the sacrament. Monks and friars were ordered not to wear their habits. The details can be followed in *Report of the nineteenth eucharistic congress held at Westminster from 9 to 13 September 1908* (London, 1909), pp 572–8. Press reaction is reproduced on pp 615–35.   19 L.P. Curtis, 'Stopping the hunt in 1881–82: an aspect of the Irish land war' in C.H.E. Philpin (ed.), *Nationalism and popular protest in Ireland* (Cambridge, 1987), p. 351.

and their suspicions of Roman interference in Ireland.[20] But even those who
had come of age in the hierarchy in the post-emancipation era could take an
attitude to the great issues of the day which is far removed from the caricature
of the marriage of Catholicism and nationalism which we are assured by
some historians was the norm. Thus Laurence Renehan, president of
Maynooth, could write in 1848, 'I believe the Act of Union to have been most
corruptly, unjustly, iniquitously procured' and yet 'after so long an acquiescence I would be *conscientiously* afraid to ... treat it ... as a nullity'.[21] When
Paul Cullen arrived on the Irish scene in 1850, his views in fact were not
entirely dissimilar to those of either Murray or Renehan. Under his
leadership there was some continuity in the church's contingent political
outlook. At an organizational level its politics were determined by what it
took to be the essentially religious elements in the great questions of the day,
such as education, the dismantling of the last symbols of Protestant ascendancy and, when confronted with the Parnell débâcle the upholding of public
morality (under pressure it must be said, in this ironic instance, from English
evangelicals).

   That institutional Catholicism should have supported both the union and
emancipation was so much as a means to an end. It wished to secure its
position in Irish public life by seeming to have its cake and eat it. When needs
be, it veered to deference to government wishes and alternatively would put
itself at the head of great popular movements. But its *modus operandi* was not
solely determined by the circumstances of its role in the United Kingdom.
Given its position as part of a multinational, if largely European, religious
empire, the Irish Catholic Church could not but be affected by the currents
of ideas in the church at large. A remarkable phenomenon, however, with
respect to Irish Catholic experience in the period covered by these essays, is
that by international standards it was among the most liberal, not to say
radical, components of European Catholicism. Its liberalism, however, must
be read in terms of the emerging Liberal mindset of British political liberalism. It nevertheless had European cognates in the views of individuals such
as Laocordaire, de Lamennais and even perhaps Döllinger. But unlike the
latter the liberalism of Irish churchmen was social and political rather than
theological.

   Among the intriguing paradoxes of the church's interaction with the
British political establishment in the nineteenth century was the fact that the
sentiments and ideas which British liberal statesmen praised in continental

20 MacDonagh, 'Politicization' p. 51.   21 See Donal A. Kerr, 'Priests, pikes and
patriots' in S.J. Brown and D.W. Miller (eds), *Piety and power in Ireland, 1760–1960:
essays in honour of Emmet Larkin* (Belfast, 2000), p. 31. Emphasis in original.

Europe they reprobated in Ireland. Often under pressure from such politicians, the papacy intervened to correct, chastise and inhibit in Ireland, precisely the tendencies English liberals praised in continental radical circles.[22] Not all liberal or radical activity was acceptable even to Irish churchmen, still less to the British Protestant state. There was a symbiotic eliding of interest between the hierarchy and government over the issue of violence, both rural and urban, from what-ever source. In the crucial periods of 1798, 1848 and 1867 the church set its face resolutely against the men of violence and upheld Catholic doctrine on the inadmissibility of revolutionary violence. Here the issues were, however, not simply questions of principle. Uncontrolled violent tendencies could be turned as much against the church as the state, as some eighteenth-century Whiteboy activity indicates. Furthermore, the church's experiences in France in the 1790s made clear it was part of the established order which could easily be undone in circumstances of total revolution. Pius IX's own experience during the Roman revolution of 1848 lent further weight, at an ideological level, to the resistance Irish churchmen expressed to all manifestations of revolutionary fervour, in particular in the Fenian area of the 1860s. The basic sentiments of the hierarchy are well illustrated by Archbishop Murray in 1848, and his views serve as a template for the attitude of the Irish hierarchy throughout the century:

> Fifty years ago I witnessed the miseries which a convulsion ... inflicted on the political, social and moral condition of this unhappy country. Can anyone be surprised that a thrill of horror should rush through my soul at the thought of the recurrence of such a calamity. May God in his mercy advert it.[23]

The circumstances and ideology of the 1798 rebellion were even then beginning to fade from memory. The problem was that for most of the Catholic body their experience of living under the Union had transformed their political expectations and attitudes. This had reached its apogee by the end of the O'Connell era when by then, as Donal Kerr has observed,

> A new generation of Catholics had emerged, grown confident in the wake of O'Connell's great campaigns and no longer willing to accept all that eighteenth-century Catholics had accepted. They could, and did, contemplate more forceful means to remedy their grievances.[24]

22 See for example J.F. Broderick, *The Holy See and the Irish movement for the repeal of the union with England, 1829–1847* (Rome, 1951) *passim*. 23 *The Tablet*, 12 Apr. 1848. 24 Donal A. Kerr, 'Dublin's forgotten archbishop: Daniel Murray, 1768–1852', in

Although at an official and public level most members of the Irish hierarchy sought to restrain the more forceful aspects of demands for redress of grievances, the fact also remains that churchmen were not completely immune from the radicalizing process that had gone on in Ireland in the period between the Union and the end of O'Connell's repeal campaign. To take but one example: James Coulter draws attention to the fact that in August 1789 the Catholic bishop of Derry, Phillip McDevitt, and some of his clergy walked in procession to mark the centenary of the relief of the city by the forces of William of Orange. By contrast, in 1846 the then bishop, Edward Maginn, had a country-wide reputation as a political agitator against the rule of Protestant government in Ireland. Coulter asks, 'What had caused the revolution, because that is the only word that adequately describes the change?'[25] It is to this issue and its attendant questions about the role of the Catholic Church in Ireland that the rest of this introductory essay will be devoted. Of course, one component in the matter is: Does Maginn's position represent that of Irish Catholic churchmen as a whole in the period between the Union and the disestablishment of the Church of Ireland? Bearing in mind, as has already been noted, that the church tended for the most part to have only pragmatic rather than programmatic attitudes to the issues that confronted it in nineteenth-century Ireland, it would, perhaps, be a mistake to expect that the 'revolution' in ecclesiastical dispositions to the state affected all clergy equally and in the same direction. But it is perhaps best to consider an overall approach to the problems faced by the church in Ireland under a variety of discrete but related headings. In the first place it will be necessary to examine the church as a political institution, then the religious and social realities of Catholicism in the period and finally questions of conflict between church and state.

II

One of the results of the failure to grant emancipation at the time of the Union was the fact that O'Connellism and hence growing Irish nationalism became more clearly allied with institutional Catholicism than would otherwise have been the case. The issue of political rights became an issue for Catholicism which led in turn to the association between institutional Catholicism and the Repeal movement. The touchstone and trigger for O'Connell's abilities to engage in mass politics was not, however, by appeal to political issues as such, but rather to the more emotive resonance of religion.

James Kelly and Dáire Keogh (eds), *History of the Catholic diocese of Dublin* (Dublin, 2000), p. 267.   **25** James A. Coulter, 'The political theory of Edward Maginn, bishop of Derry, 1846–9', *Irish Ecclesiastical Record*, 48 (1962), 104.

It was from religion rather than in the ideology of Repeal that O'Connell derived his power over the great majority of his followers.[26]

By the same token, however, the attempts on the part of the church to translate such a symbiotic relationship between Catholic identity and popular agitation into direct political action, as with the Cullen inspired National Association of the 1860s, was a failure as the results of the 1865 general election make clear. Later attempts such as those of the lord mayor of Dublin, Peter Paul McSwiney, to exploit the O'Connell centenary for sectarian purposes in 1875, also went disastrously wrong for those pursuing a purely Catholic agenda. 'Our religion from Rome our politics from home', although not an absolute guide to Irish Catholic realities in the nineteenth century, is a cliché possessing enough veracity to caution against a univocal assertion about the power of institutional Catholicism in politics.

One of the significant political differences between Britain and Ireland in the decades between the Union and the foundation of Fenianism was in the nature of representative politics. Partly because of O'Connellite mass agitation, there evolved in Ireland what Larkin has perspicaciously noticed as an emergence of popular as opposed to parliamentary sovereignty, a perspective on the constitution quite at variance with prevailing Victorian constitutional theory. The Irish had 'opted for a radical rather than a liberal view of the nature of consent as being declamatory rather than representative'.[27] This ties in with the Fenian view, later abandoned, that revolution could only be staged with the consent of and on behalf of the people. British politicians were fully aware of the potential for mischief that the alignment between populist demands and Catholicism could bring about in Ireland. Thus Peel warned the Irish chief secretary in 1846: 'the spirit of Popery, and its alliance with democratic feelings and institutions will constitute a very formidable combination against the Peace of Ireland, and the maintenance of cordial union with this country'.[28] The priestly involvement in popular mass politics ran counter to the hierarchal nature of much of the theology and ideology that was instilled in the average Maynooth product. Mass political mobilization was for the most part in the nineteenth century an O'Connellite phenomenon, and clerical support for popular agitation did not long survive O'Connell's demise,[29] although it was to be resurrected in various guises in subsequent decades up to 1918.

26 Brian Girvin, 'Making nations: O'Connell, religion and the creation of political identity' in Maurice O'Connell (ed.), *Daniel O'Connell political pioneer* (Dublin, 1991), p. 22. 27 Emmet Larkin, 'Irish political tradition' in Thomas E. Hachey and Laurence McCaffrey (eds), *Perspectives on Irish nationalism* (Lexington, 1989), p. 101. 28 See Donal A. Kerr, *Peel, priests and politics* (Oxford, 1982), p. 5. 29 James O'Shea, *Priests, politics and society in post famine Ireland: a study of County Tipperary, 1850–1891* (Dublin, 1983), p. 237.

The problems posed by the involvement of priests in politics perturbed not only successive governments but was also a worrying matter for the church authorities in Rome. In a number of instances in the nineteenth century Rome rebuked the Irish hierarchy and clergy over the issue, especially when pressurized to do so by the British government.[30] The problem of priestly involvement in politics became more pressing when political agitation gave way to direct violence although even peaceful political activity carried with it subterranean violent threats. What's more in purely ecclesiastical terms the relative independence of the operations of the Irish hierarchy from Roman oversight led Rome to fear that the Irish were not as deferential to the decrees of the Holy See as they ought to be.[31] This was especially true in relation to political affairs. On several widely publicized occasions, the Irish hierarchy either ignored or rejected Roman directives on Irish socio-politic matters on the grounds that Roman clergymen simply did not understand the circumstances under which the Irish church operated. This, coupled with the fact that the state rarely intervened in the operations of the church, ensured that Irish bishops had a measure of independence which was the envy of Catholic Europe, and churchmen in Ireland were determined to guard such privilege.[32]

The basis of much political agitation was the legitimate complaint that Catholics were treated in Ireland as second-class citizens. The Union had guaranteed the continued monopoly of power by Protestants in Ireland[33] and under increasing pressure from Catholic agitation that power was gradually wrested from their grasp. Cardinal Cullen's religio-political policy was precisely to intrude Catholics into the centres of governmental and social power and he used every means he could to bring this about. Time and again government did make concession to Catholic opinion especially regarding political and judicial office.[34] This then gave the false impression that in certain circumstances the effective political agenda in Ireland was somehow linked to the designs of senior Catholic churchmen. Protestant fears were, thereby, heightened concerning Catholic dominance of all aspects of political life should the country ever be separated again from London rule.

Thus the Protestant archbishop of Armagh, George Beresford, playing in this case the role of a Jeremiah, had in the 1820s warned that political conces-

30 Oliver MacDonagh, *States of mind: a study of Anglo-Irish conflict, 1780–1980* (London), p. 93.   31 John H. Whyte, 'The appointment of Catholic bishops in nineteenth-century Ireland', in *Catholic Historical Review*, 48 (1962–3), 15.   32 Donal A. Kerr, 'Under the union flag: the Catholic Church in Ireland, 1800–1870' in Robert Blake (ed.), *Ireland after the Union* (Oxford, 1989), p. 28.   33 A.T.Q. Stewart, *The shape of Irish history* (Belfast, 2001), p. 151.   34 Steven R. Knowlton, *Popular politics and the Irish Catholic Church: the rise and fall of the independent Irish party, 1850–1859* (New York, 1991), p. 151.

sions to Catholics would involve a transfer of power, bring to an end the Protestant ascendancy, and mean the abolition of the 'Protestant nation'.[35] It would take the rest of the century for these implications to be worked out, and by then the ascendancy would begin to reassert itself in the Protestant hegemony of north-east Ulster. By the 1830s the Catholics, and by extension the church, had become a formidable power in the Protestant state. Their political activities represented a serious challenge to the settlement enacted in 1800, and although the failure of Repeal and the horrors of the Famine modified the nature and extent of Catholic power, its fundamental character was not altered. Not that this amounted to priestly domination of political life as a whole. Indeed, where the laity was sufficiently literate, wealthy and organized, there was little or no priestly involvement in the political process.[36]

The period between 1801 and the Famine represented the crucial test for the Union. Britain proved itself unequal to the challenge,[37] thereby creating something of a political vacuum that was filled to some extent by O'Connell, but this was made possible only in conjunction with ecclesiastical forces, and thus the Catholic Church was thrust to the fore of national political life. Subsequently Cullen's ultimate suspicion of independent opposition and the Irish Tenant League, coupled with outright hostility to Fenianism,[38] conditioned Irish response to the political problems of the mid-century. Even in the early years of the Home Government Association, Cullen could hardly contain his antipathy, but here the issue was one of Protestant leadership. This was matched in Protestant circles by a thoroughly anti-democratic and indeed anti-modern ethos which saw most Irish Protestants linking themselves with the most conservative and reactionary elements within British society. For the most part, as a community they harkened after the pre-modern days of the rotten borough and the ascendancy, and refused to engage with the democratic sentiments of the majority. Rather than seek accommodation with emergent democracy, as a community Protestants insisted on the privileges of the oligarchy predicated on religious affiliation, and this became the *leitmotif* for exclusivist, and indeed what would be viewed in other contexts as racist and religious, supremacy.

Ultimately, of course, the failure of the Protestant nation was a matter of demography. At the same time we can see that those Protestants who were prepared to place themselves at the head of the emergent nation had their leadership accepted, and past errors of political judgment were obliterated from the collective memory, as in the case of Isaac Butt. The acceptance of

35 Stewart, *Shape of Irish history*, p. 151. 36 Jacqueline Hill, 'Nationalism and the Catholic Church in the 1840s: views of Dublin repealers', *IHS*, 19 (1975), 373. 37 Boyce, *Nineteenth-century Ireland*, p. 53. 38 A view shared by many Irish priests. See O'Shea, p. 136.

Protestant political leadership, incidentally like that of Catholic priests, was contingent upon the fact of leading the Catholic nation in the direction it wished to go. Furthermore, such leadership was supported despite the distrust of some religious leaders such as Cullen. Nevertheless, for all the inconsistencies and irony about the involvement of Catholic priests and bishops in politics, one can perhaps conclude that the church's 'interaction with nationalist politics lead to the creation of a stable, liberal-democratic political system in nationalist Ireland'.[39]

III

Although there are disagreements about the exact contours of the phenomenon, no one disputes the massive transformation in Irish Catholicism in the period after the Famine. We are now more keyed to the fact that the Famine was as much an accelerator of change as a catalyst. Without doubt, however, the situation for the church was changed almost beyond recognition. This was the case not only in the explicitly religious aspects of Catholic community life such as the practice of the sacraments and the move from the home to the chapel as the locus for religious life, but also in the more amorphous area of identity. In the absence of other identifying marks such as language and cultural patterns, Catholicism came to occupy the vacuum in identity created with the very process of modernization in nineteenth-century Ireland. Indeed, one could argue that the church itself was one of the instruments in that process. Questions of religious identity are also inextricably linked with issues of cultural identification,[40] and, as in much of Europe as a whole, with the emergence and foundation of modern nationalism. This is not to say that there was no explicit 'Irish identity' before the nineteenth century, nor is it to imply that there was a ready and easy equation between Irish nationalism and the profession of the Catholic faith. There is, however, a sense in which modern Irish nationalism predicated, at least in some circles, on both Catholicism and a sense of separatism, develops and grows in the century. But it was neither as innovative nor as exclusivist as some historians have suggested. Furthermore, as is clear, to be Catholic in the United Kingdom was *ipso facto* to be separate from the prevailing Protestant culture.

Emmet Larkin has pointed out that the fusion of concepts such as 'Catholic' and 'Irish' in the modern period was circumstantial rather than

39 Nigel Yeats, *The religious condition of Ireland 1770–1850* (Oxford, 2006), p. 74.
40 Christine Kinealy, 'Economy and society in Ireland' in Chris Williams (ed.), *A companion to nineteenth century Britain* (Oxford, 2004), p. 489.

deliberate. As the church became the most important institutional element in Irish life in 'sustaining Irish identity after the collapse of the autocratic Gaelic order, it was inevitable that Irish and Catholic over time would be virtually interchangeable terms'.[41] But even here that interchangeability was never as complete or as exhaustive as even this judicious analysis seems to imply. We see this in the ideology of Young Ireland and Fenianism, and from the political leadership of a later generation provided by Butt and Parnell. However, the nature of what constituted Irish nationalist identity changed over time – from the revolutionary egalitarianism of 1798, to a Catholic version of 'Protestant nationalism' under O'Connell, essentially revived but modified in the 1870s and 1880s, to the separatist ideology of Fenianism and the Gaelic-Ireland ideas of the early twentieth century. For its part, the church hierarchy had to develop its own thinking to take account of these changes. The astonishing thing is not the rigidity of its position but its flexibility and lack of fixed ideological perspective as it accommodated itself to the undulations of the Irish political landscape, from unionism to separatism. As J.H.C. Bernard, Church of Ireland archbishop of Dublin, was to observe, harshly but accurately in 1918, 'the dominant motive governing the actions always of the Roman hierarchy is the desire to keep control over their people'.[42] That desire was not always realized but it was nevertheless the motivating factor in the various social and political circumstances the church faced in Irish society throughout the century, and it explains much of its posturing and apparent contradictions. Equally, the ambiguity of the church's political maneuverings was not unique, and priestly political fluctuations were a reflection of the fact that 'the great majority of their flocks shuttled, in precisely the same fashion as themselves, between sets of contradictory impulses'.[43]

If political and national identity was changing, the initial catalyst for this was provided by the Union itself. The creation of the United Kingdom inaugurated a period of altered identity, in both the British and Irish contexts. This clearly had implications even for the relations between the two countries, and gave rise to a surprising conundrum. As Terry Eagleton has pointed out there was implicit in the British–Irish relationship a failure 'to find the balance point between identity and non-identity, [Britain] at once treated Ireland differently and not differently enough'.[44] The altered state in national identity so far as it concerned Ireland was, furthermore, carried on

---

41 Emmet Larkin, 'The Irish political tradition' in Thomas E. Hachey and Laurence McCaffrey (eds), *Perspectives on Irish nationalism* (Lexington, 1989), p. 103.   42 Quoted in D.W. Miller, *Church, state and nation in Ireland, 1898–1921* (Dublin, 1973), p. 408.
43 MacDonagh, *States of mind*, p. 90.   44 Terry Eagleton, 'Changing the question', in Claire Connolly (ed.), *Theorizing Ireland* (Basingstoke, 2003), p. 81.

hand in hand with the growth in Catholicism of ultramontane ideas and the formalization of belief and ecclesiastical practice in a way more recognizably Tridentine. The factors that led to an identification of an individual with Catholicism were being altered. It was no longer a mere question of self-identification, but rather an issue of formal practice and a more profound knowledge of the tenets of the faith. This operated at varying levels for both priests and people. Even at a theological level priests were having to come to terms with new ideas – some agreeable to them, such as those of Joseph de Maistre represented by his *Du Pape* (Lyon, 1819), others not so commodious, such as the views of the Maynooth professor Louis-Gilles Delahogue, who, according to the Augustinian priest John Furlong, spread 'a detestable doctrine ... that Protestants who were in good faith could be saved'.[45]

Much ink has been spilt on the question of whether or not before the 'devotional revolution' Irish Catholics actually practised their religion. Emmet Larkin's latest thoughts confirm, for the most part, his earlier views. He also remains convinced that prior to the Famine, given the constraints under which Catholicism laboured, 'the level of devotional expectation in regard to religious practice was consequently modest'.[46] Those expectations were met by the 'Easter duties' of confession and communion. Perhaps more importantly, Ray Gillespie has cautioned that too much emphasis on public manifestation runs the risk of merely evaluating religious adhesion in terms of issues of power relationships. Perhaps it is more helpful to see the operations of the church both before and after the Famine as a question of a cultural exchange between official religion and the religious needs of individuals.[47] Such needs were met and expressed in more informal circumstances such as patterns and stations. Even the more unorthodox manifestations such as in the various games at wakes, for example, can be seen in one sense as meeting social and perhaps even spiritual needs. But it is precisely the ability of individual believers to hold in tension certain vestiges of folk religion with official Catholic doctrine and practice that was the most striking component in Irish Catholicism by the mid-century. Sissy O'Brien, writing in 1875 contrasting the Catholicism, she encountered at her convent school in Bruff, Co Cork with that of the maids at her parents farm, could remark of them: 'although they were thankful for holy days and went to Mass they were really more interested in an old Irish world where fairies, witches and banshees took the place of our angels and saints'.[48]

---

45 Patrick J. Corish, *Maynooth College, 1795–1995* (Dublin, 1995), p. 84. **46** Emmet Larkin, *The pastoral role of the Roman Catholic Church in pre-famine Ireland, 1750–1850* (Dublin, 2006), p. 185. **47** Raymond Gillespie, 'Popular and unpopular religion: a view from early modern Ireland', in James S. Donnelly and Kirby Miller (eds), *Irish popular culture, 1650–1850* (Dublin, 1998), p. 30. **48** Quoted by Angela Bourke, 'The

The point, however, is that the felt needs of individuals, even in the spiritual realm, not only change over time but can also be manufactured. The social and demographic cataclysm of the Famine released reforming energies in Catholicism on a scale without precedent. Paul Cullen's abilities to harness these forces and lead them in a modernizing fashion transformed the face of Catholicism. The increase in the ratio of priests to people, the growth in institutions of nuns, the activity of Christian Brothers and above all the position of Maynooth as a provider of men infused in equal measure with a sense of Victorian 'respectability' and new devotional sentiments engendered in the Catholic Irish a more recognizable form of modern Catholicism – all these new apostles of respectability and ultramontane devotion were not as amenable to the old Gallican ideas of subservience to the civil authorities as had been their predecessors. Mr and Mrs Hall touring Ireland in the early 1840s could complain of the typical Maynooth products that they were 'more hostile to the British Government, than the priests of the old school who received their education in France, Italy and Spain'.[49]

By 1853 Maynooth had produced half of all the priests then working in Ireland, and some two-thirds of all current seminarians were subject to its regime.[50] The social expectations and ambitions of its students would have considerable impact on the development of Irish Catholicism over the decades from mid-century on. Of course, one of the ironies in the position of the average priest was that in the process of modernization of Irish society and the Irish church, he was placed uneasily in a position were he was expected to set new standards of behaviour. Yet often enough priests found they could best relate to their flocks only in circumstances which they were, by their profession, forced to condemn. Thus, as Theodore Hoppen comments, 'Priests, indeed, were themselves often happiest in that atmosphere of relaxed conviviality which was part and parcel of those traditional attitudes to religion they otherwise abhorred.'[51] The desire for greater social status and the fact of the general embourgeoisement of the clergy went hand in hand with Cullenite views of the role of the church in Irish society. Cullen was determined that the prevailing ethos should be recognizably Catholic in contrast to the prevailing atmosphere of a state still ruled largely in Protestant interest.

Under Cullen's direction Ireland was, in 1873, consecrated to the Sacred

baby and the bathwater: cultural loss in nineteenth century Ireland', in Tadhg Foley and Sean Ryder (eds), *Ideology and Ireland in the nineteenth-century* (Dublin, 1998), p. 85. **49** Mr & Mrs S.C. Hall, *Ireland: its scenery, character etc.*, 3 vols (London, 1842), ii, 279. **50** Patrick J. Corish, *The Irish Catholic experience: a historical survey* (Dublin, 1985), p. 172. **51** K. Theodore Hoppen, *Ireland since 1800: conflict and conformity* (London, 1989), p. 67.

Heart. This shows as one commentator has observed 'how far the idea of *Catholic* Ireland had progressed and how completely the desire of not offending Protestant sentiment had been abandoned'.[52] But such aggressiveness was not simply confined to Catholicism. Between the visits of George IV and that of Queen Victoria in 1849, all the Irish churches had moved in a more intolerant direction.[53] This can be seen not just in the activities of Henry Cooke and his declarations of pan-Protestant interest in the 1830s, or in the increasing sectarianism of Belfast from the 1820s,[54] but also in areas such as direct charitable assistance. To take but one example: during the Famine less than one third of the recipients of Church of Ireland poor relief in Dublin city were Catholics, despite the fact the Catholic population was four-fifths of the total, a disproportionate number of whom were poor.[55]

S.J. Connolly has argued that the main threat to the position of the Catholic Church in Ireland in the decades before the Famine was not in fact from social change, or Enlightenment ideas, but rather from 'developments within Protestantism'.[56] There is perhaps a tendency in some historiography to underplay the significance of the 'second reformation' and its impact on Catholic mores in the period from the 1820s to the 1860s. It was nevertheless treated with great seriousness by official Catholicism.[57] The various Protestant societies, some such as the Kildare Place Society, while doing sterling working in the field of the education of the poor, contrived to strike terror into the hearts of even the most accommodating Irish Catholic churchmen. The conversions at Dingle and Achill and those on Lord Farnham's Co. Cavan estate in the 1820s, although the best known, were by no means exceptional. While the overall numbers of conversions may have represented but a small proportion of the total Catholic population, they did occupy a symbolic importance for Catholicism. They coloured the church's attitude to other socio-political developments in the 1830s and 1840s such as the National Schools and the 'godless' Queen's colleges. These were all regarded as part of a single tapestry of developments designed to undermine and emasculate the position of the Catholic Church in Irish society.

If Catholicism was at times obsessed with the threat from Protestantism, its other great *bête noire* was social disorder. This varied between *ad hoc* violence, inspired by social grievance and directed against landlords, and

---

52 Desmond Keenan, *The Catholic Church in nineteenth-century Ireland: a sociological study* (Dublin, 1983), p. 152. Emphasis in the original.   53 Yates, *The religious condition of Ireland*, p. 297.   54 Surveyed with admirable clarity by Christine Hurst, *Religion, politics and violence in nineteenth-century Belfast: the Pound and Sandy Row* (Dublin, 2002).   55 Yates, *Religious condition of Ireland*, p. 61.   56 S.J. Connolly, *Priests and people in pre-famine Ireland, 1780–1845* (Dublin, 1982), p. 75.   57 James H. Murphy, *Ireland: a social, cultural and literary history, 1791–1891* (Dublin, 2003), p. 66.

violence with specific political intent, such as that emanating from Fenian circles. Violence potentially not only threatened the internal cohesion of Catholicism but also the loyalty of individuals to the church. This was supremely the lesson for Catholicism as a whole from the French Revolution, and it was one not lost on Irish churchmen. Once again, Bishop Patrick Plunkett of Meath identified the core of the matter for his and subsequent generations. In lambasting the national assembly of 1789, he declared that most of its members were:

> visibly under infidel influence. If our nominal *Catholics* look the same way, if the sacred rights of religion are to be sacrificed for the phantom of political liberty ... should not the ministers of religion of every rank and degree take alarm and stand upon their guard. How rapid and sudden was the transition in France, from the enthusiasm of civil liberty to the confusion and degradation of ecclesiastical licentiousness and anarchy?[58]

The problem for the church was not only a question of social instability as the inevitable corollary of violence but also the fear that such violence would bring Ireland into direct confrontation with governmental authority to the detriment of both church and people. Furthermore, the basic attitude of most churchmen was that it was the duty of individuals to support the state. To do otherwise would be to align oneself with the currents of anarchical and anti-clerical ideology as represented in the mid-century by those such as Kossuth and Mazzini. Cullen in expounding his view on these matters to Frederick Lucas MP, and editor of the Catholic newspaper *The Tablet*, would allow of only one exception to the precept of Catholic loyalty to prevailing authority and that was if government 'attacked the Church'.[59] The complication for church–state relations in Ireland since the Union was precisely the perception that certain aspects of government policy were designed to drive a wedge between the church and the Irish people and thus represented a direct attack upon the church's prerogatives. It would be impossible here to give all the details, but it is to the general outline of the problem, illustrated with some specific examples, that we must now turn our attention.

IV

At the base of the conflicts between the Catholic bishops and various British administrations in Ireland in the nineteenth century was the problem of the

58 A. Cogan, *The diocese of Meath*, iii, 270–1. **59** Edward Lucas, *The life of Frederick Lucas MP*, 2 vols (London, 1886), i, 287.

inability of the state, for the most part, to accept Catholics and Catholicism as an essential part of Irish social reality. The fundamental issue of Protestant Britain's anti-Catholicism not only made for individual disputes over issues such as that of tithes to the established church and education, but inevitably rendered the Union both unworkable and doomed to failure. The inherent contradictions upon which it was constructed led successive governments to attempt to undo its implications by modifications in its weakest link, the Church of Ireland. The whole apparatus involved in the dismantling of Anglicanism in Ireland ranging from emendation in clerical stipends, to reduction in the number of bishoprics and culminating in eventual disestablishment and disendowment, had the unintended consequence of keeping 'the Catholic Church in or near the centre of Irish politics. It had tended to entwine religion with party, to widen – if that were possible – the chasm between the sects.' The great irony of government policy taken as a whole was that 'slowly, imperceptibly, but surely it had identified Catholicism with nationality'.[60] The state under pressure from uncontrollable social realities was forced to amend its own constitution as represented by the Protestant establishment. But it was an establishment which the state in the context of the Union had erected in the first place, disregarding the main social component of Irish reality – Catholicism.

Perceived official hostility to the church lead the bishops to complain that certain aspects of government social policy rendered Irish Catholics 'the victims of the most ruthless oppression that ever disgraced the annuals of humanity'.[61] Such analysis was incomprehensible to British statesmen, who viewed their own attempts to rule justly, an at times violent and intractable country, as being marked with patience, restraint and benevolence. The prime minister, Lord Aberdeen, accused the bishops at the synod of Thurles of encouraging violence in Ireland by the ill-tempered language of their official address.

Cullen, in responding, in May 1851, refuted any such suggestion, making clear that the synod had 'exhorted the people to practise patience and resignation'. He went on to say, with what one suspects was a certain amount of tongue in cheek, that the bishops had taught the poor to 'respect the rights of property, to honour the rank and station of the great and powerful, to be obedient to those in authority, to be grateful for favours received'. He then proceeded to assure Aberdeen that 'the orators who accuse the address of leading to communism or to the violation of the rights of property can scarcely have read the passage I have just quoted'.[62] Government perception

60 Oliver MacDonagh, *Ireland after the Union* (revised edition, London, 1977), p. 23.
61 Synodal Address of Thurles, *Irish Catholic Directory* (Dublin, 1851), p. 196.
62 See Knowlton, *Popular politics*, p. 162.

of the role of the clergy in relation to disorder rarely coincided with the day-to-day reality of clerical engagement with the violent propensities of members of their flock. But the issue was by no means as straightforward as governments sometimes imagined. Not only did clerical authority have its limits, but 'pastoral concern, or as hostile critics perceived it, reluctance to lose influence over the faithful ... made [priests and bishops] shrink from total opposition to the political demands of a people suspicious of government manipulation of the clergy'.[63]

A classic illustration of this is provided by the controversy over the question of government veto in the appointment of Catholic bishops. Having at the beginning of the century agreed to both the veto and endowment, only to see the proposals withdrawn, by the 1810s when the matter was again raised the bishops had changed their minds. By then, the political management of Catholic Ireland had passed to other hands, and their lordships were compelled to follow a road which, left alone, they may have preferred not to take. The principle at issue was conceded to every government in Europe. In France, the church was virtually a prisoner of the state. Even in the greater part of Poland, Catholicism was under the control, in Catholic eyes, of a schismatic ruler in the person of the Tsar of Russia. The desires of Catholic Poland and the *real politique* of the Holy See rarely coincided. The question then in Ireland was not the issue of principle, however much the increasingly politicized hierarchy might like to portray that it was, but rather what the increasing political frustrations of the laity would permit. It was O'Connell's agitation that now caused the hierarchy to come full circle. By 1812 Catholic Ireland could have had emancipation under the terms rejected by George III in 1800. Those terms would in fact have satisfied anti-catholic opinion, and would also have been acceptable to Roman authority. By now, however, we have a situation in which churchmen were under the control of the *laity* with regard to the external operations of ecclesiastical authority. The fact that these were Catholic laity was in a sense irrelevant. The freedom of the churchmen to decide issues of procedural principle was as effectively inhibited as in the days of overt Protestant control. It was O'Connell and his circle who determined for purely secular political considerations an important matter concerning the freedom of the church to direct its own operations. In the process they also put the church in direct confrontation with government wishes. O'Connell clearly had well grounded fears about what might flow from the veto, but these touched on his own political ambitions rather than on religious considerations. As Laurence McCaffrey has succinctly put it, O'Connell feared that:

63 Donal A. Kerr, 'Government and Roman Catholics in Ireland 1850–1940', in Kerr (ed.), *Religion, state and ethnic groups* (Aldershot, 1992), p. 285.

if the British government could manipulate the appointment of
bishops the Catholic church would speak for Britishness rather than
Irishness. Nationalism would have a difficult time recruiting popular
enthusiasm against the wishes of a hostile, even a neutral Catholic
church. Consequently O'Connell decided it was better to postpone
emancipation if this meant sacrificing Ireland's most important institution to British influence.[64]

Another major field of confrontation between church and government
concerned the control over education, at both primary and tertiary levels.
Although some bishops, such as John MacHale, remained implacably hostile
to the system of national education, Rome decided that each bishop should
be free to support or reject it so far as his diocese was concerned. Various
changes to the system insisted on by both Presbyterians and Anglicans caused
further suspicion on the part of Catholic churchmen and by the late 1850s,
after nearly thirty years of its existence, the Irish bishops issued a pastoral
outlining the deficiencies of the 1831 system and demanding changes which
would yield 'a system of education exclusively for Catholics'.[65] The educational structure they envisaged would, like the national system, be financed
by the state. The bishops sent this pastoral in the shape of a memorial to the
government outlining their demands, and the chief secretary, Edward
Cardwell, replied. Cardwell made clear that the bishops' views were in some
respects 'wholly incompatible' with the foundational principles of the
national schools. What the bishops wanted, so far as government was
concerned was 'a system of sectarian education ... calculated to revive the
social divisions in Ireland, and to stimulate feelings which it is the object of
every just and liberal government to allay'.[66]

As with the queen's colleges, which had been condemned by Roman
rescripts in 1847 and 1848, the problem was one of perception. The bishops
believed education in its various guises was supremely a matter of religious
policy and thus subject to the supervision of the church; for the government
it was a question of social policy, with the addition in the Irish context of
containing competing sectarian ecclesiastical demands.[67] By contrast, some
bishops believed that government educational policy was aimed at subverting

---

64 Lawrence J. McCaffrey, 'Components of Irish nationalism' in *Perspectives on Irish
nationalism*, p. 6.   **65** *Pastoral address of the Roman Catholic archbishops and bishops*
(Dublin, 1859), p. 8.   **66** Quoted in E.R. Norman, *The Catholic Church and Ireland in
the age of rebellion, 1859–1873* (London, 1965), p. 69.   **67** Tom Inglis has, cynically,
concluded that the 1831 act was primarily intended to produce a system of social
control and to wean Catholics from treasonable sentiments. *Moral monopoly: the rise and
fall of the Catholic Church in modern Ireland*, 2nd ed. (Dublin, 1998), p. 106.

the faith of Irish Catholics, and that in particular the queen's colleges were dangerous to the faith of those who attended them. Education was not simply a political football to be kicked around by successive governments but a spiritual charisma which it was the duty of bishops as guardians of the faith to foster and protect.

In the matter of education, so far as Archbishop Cullen was concerned, the question was one of who was the arbiter of what was in the best interests of the Irish people, the queen's government or the pope's government?[68] The problem was complicated by the fact that the pope's ministers were divided among themselves, and one element in Cullen's conduct of affairs over the years of his primacy was weeding the hierarchy of its government-orientated tendencies.

Although we see in the decades from the 1830s to the 1860s some halting attempts by various governments to include more Catholics in the administration of the Protestant state, where possible, and in circumstances where it could counter or neutralize Catholic objections, government did its best to aim at non-denominationalism in public policy in Ireland. Occasionally, the state was still capable of blatant anti-Catholicism, as in the Ecclesiastical Titles Act of 1851. Even in areas where government intention was to improve the lot of Catholicism, considered as a corporate body, such as the charitable bequests legislation of 1844, the tendency was to create bodies still dominated by members of the Protestant ascendancy. Much Catholic reaction was, understandably, resentful of such posturing.

One might conclude that had the connection with Britain in the period 1801–70 been able to guarantee the fulfillment of churchmen's expectations with respect to social legislation, the Union would have had the vigorous and robust support of the Catholic Church in the shape of its hierarchy. The inability of successive governments to frame policies acceptable to and encouraging of the hierarchy's moderate 'Catholic agenda', ensured the inexorable march of Catholic aspiration in a Catholic-nationalist and anti-union direction. Of course, one can object that it would simply not have been practical politics for any government to have attempted to deliver on a programme of legislation which would have satisfied the Catholic hierarchy's aspirations. This is not the place to debate the geography of 'virtual history', but in so far as it was impossible for British statesmen, in the period surveyed in these essays, to contemplate, for example, state-endowed Catholic education at its various levels, we might here mark the parameters of the unravelling of the Union. Ruling Ireland in the interests of Ireland in the nineteenth century

---

68 Emmet Larkin, *The making of the Roman Catholic Church in Ireland, 1850–1860* (Chapel Hill, 1980), p. 38.

had to involve ruling it in the interests of the Catholic majority, without necessarily being either unfair or unjust to those who were not of the Roman faith. Not until 1868 do such considerations and their immense implications begin forcefully to make an impact upon British politicians.

For its part, in the decades after the Union, the Catholic Church harboured an abiding fear of the functioning of Protestantism in Ireland. This was not simply an aversion to the direct confrontationist and proselytizing tendencies displayed by some Protestant groups, but it also represents resistance to Protestant political ambitions. So far as Catholic Ireland was concerned Protestant dominance of the political realm was a thing of the past. Churchmen feared a return to the status quo ante of 'patriot' Ireland. This coupled with what appeared to be official government policy of secularism in social policy facilitated an alignment between church and nationalism. Such alignment brought no long term satisfaction to the church and, despite explicit efforts, restricted the comprehensive development of nationalism.

The Catholic Church and the Union

As Kevin Whelan has pointed out, the spectacle of parliamentary reform and Catholic relief in Ireland was carried out in a context where institutional Catholicism in Europe as a whole was on the wane.[1] In Grattan's splendid phrase, 'the influence of the Pope, the priest and the Pretender are at an end'. Yet, so far as Ireland was concerned the eighteenth century had seen the development of the church from a position where it had been officially persecuted to one where the external barriers to its existence and development had been removed. It did not, however, become a completely free agent able to evolve inexorably according to its own internal constitution. Nevertheless, by the end of the century it could hope to pursue its mission largely on its own terms, though still battling against the legacy that its frequently bitter experience in the eighteenth-century had bequeathed to it.

The bitterness of that experience had, of course, been vouchsafed at the hands of Irish Protestants. Even such relief as Catholics now enjoyed had been accomplished with a good deal of arm-twisting from London. Indeed, once Catholics openly and aggressively began to demand the political power they had lost as a result of the penal era, whatever sympathy they may have had in the Irish parliament quickly evaporated.[2] Furthermore, as Marianne Elliott, in echoing Lecky's famous judgment,[3] has indicated, 'England had always proved a better friend to Catholics than had their [Protestant] fellow countrymen. They had little reason to trust the Protestants, even less the Dissenters. Independence from England held no advantage for the Catholics.'[4] Equally, of course, there was little real reason to trust the English either. After all, the anti-Catholic Gordon riots of 1780 were by the century's end not yet a distant memory. On the other hand, the circumstances of the French revolution and the European wars which occurred in its wake brought the papacy and institutional Catholicism into a much closer relationship with England than, arguably, at any time since the rule of Mary Tudor in the sixteenth century. Pope Pius VI had facilitated the provision of the British fleet in the Papal States, and Sir John Hippesley MP (from 1792 to 1796 the

---

1 Kevin Whelan, *The tree of liberty* (Cork, 1996), p. 102. 2 Maureen Wall, 'John Keogh and the Roman Catholic committee' in Gerard O'Brien (ed.), *Catholic Ireland in the eighteenth-century: collected essays of Maureen Wall* (Dublin, 1989), p. 165. 3 W.E.H. Lecky, *A history of Ireland in the eighteenth century* (Dublin, 1892), iv, 462. 4 Marianne Elliott, *Wolfe Tone: prophet of Irish independence* (New Haven, 1989), p. 131.

unofficial British representative to the pope) had worked tirelessly to bring about a better understanding between the British state and the States of the Church. Thus Cardinal Berber, the papal secretary of state, could write to Hippesley in 1795 that he hoped Sir John's activities would 'knit more and more closely the ties of reciprocal interest and friendly correspondence which now unite the two said courts and the two nations, Britain and the Holy See'.[5] Hippesley had gone as far as to argue that diplomatic relations ought to be established between London and Rome,[6] a point supported by the Church of Ireland bishop of Meath.[7]

On the face of it, the proposed union between Britain and Ireland would be a means of strengthening the Catholic position in the empire as a whole, and Catholic support for the proposal would further commend that body to its English friends. When Pitt had written to Westmoreland as far back as 1792 raising the possibility of a union, he couched the proposal in the context of emancipation. But in such a way that emancipation would be politically meaningless since Catholics would be but a small minority within the United Kingdom. Westmoreland cannily replied:

> The Protestants frequently declare they will have an Union rather than give franchise to Catholics, and the Catholics that they will have an Union rather than submit to their present state of degradation. It is worth turning in your mind how the violence of both parties might be turned on this occasion to the advantage of England.[8]

In the event, there was something of a chameleon-like approach on the part of government in trying to convince the rival religious groups to accept the Union. The government had tried to make the Union appear 'all things to all men, and all creeds. For some, the Union was supported because it seemed the best mechanism for securing Catholic emancipation; for others it was welcomed as a way of closing the door on Catholics for ever.'[9]

So far as the Catholic bishops were concerned, by the end of the 1790s they were, on the whole, anxious not to be seen to obstruct government proposals. Despite vigorous episcopal attempts to reduce rebellious Catholics in 1798 to a sense of order, Dublin Castle still continued to look upon the Catholic clergy as a source of potential disruption to good order and government.

5 See, John Roche Ardill, *The closing of the Irish parliament* (Dublin, 1907), p. 22.
6 NLI MS 5027 *Hippisley correspondence*. This suggestion is made in the course of a long and undated memo addressed to the government.   7 Charles Vane, marquis of Londonderry (ed.), *Memoirs and correspondence of Viscount Castlereagh*, 4 vols (London, 1848), iii, 402–3.   8 NAI Frane MS, Westmoreland to Portland, 28 Nov. 1792.
9 Patrick M. Geoghegan, 'The Catholics and the union', in *Transactions of the Royal Historical Society*, sixth series, 10 (2000), 243–58, here 243.

Institutional Catholicism wanted and needed to demonstrate that Catholics were wholly devoted to the interests of the crown. Support for the Union became a symbol of that devotion and a mark of Catholic loyalty.

It would, however, be a mistake to think that there was uniformity of opinion on the matter even among the bishops. Archbishop Troy of Dublin could be relied upon to toe a firm government and unionist line, but other members of the hierarchy demonstrated that they were capable of more independent thinking as regards government proposals. Thus Dr John Young, the bishop of Limerick, was an early and systematic critic of the proposal, especially when it became clear that the issues of state provision and the veto would also be attached to it.[10] State financial support for the clergy he regarded as an outright bribe, and he told Archbishop Thomas Brady of Cashel that he would never accept such payment 'to acquiesce in the extinction of the independence of my country'.[11] On this point at least he had Brady's support. Brady remarked to Young that the proposed subsidy was but 'an appendage of the intended Union ... not to say a specious deceitful bait to render that business more palatable to the Catholic Body, both priests and People'.[12] This is a curiosity, since Brady was one of the signatories of the declaration of January 1799 which in principle conceded a government veto over the appointment of Catholic bishops. There it was clearly stated that 'in the appointment of the prelates of the R. C. Religion to vacant Sees within the kingdom, such interference of Government as may enable it to be satisfied of the Loyalty of the person to be appointed is just and ought to be agreed to'.[13] In government eyes, the issues of veto and provision were closely allied. Although Troy had on several occasions throughout the 1790s resisted payment of the clergy by the Irish Protestant state, by now in the context of Union he was disposed to the idea. State provision for the clergy had been championed by members of the Catholic aristocracy who were anxious to have the clergy less dependent on the 'lower orders'.[14] Clearly, this was also the view of some bishops. From a purely ecclesiastical viewpoint, however, there were complications. If the government became the paymasters of the priests, this would make them not only less beholden to their people but it would also give them a measure of independence from their bishops, and thus the nature of ecclesiastical hierarchy would be weakened.

10 Troy himself acknowledged the strength of Young's opposition. See DDA Troy papers, Troy to Young, 23 Feb. 1799. 11 Ibid. 'Copies of letters on provision and veto 1799–1801', Young to Brady, 13 Feb. 1799. 12 Ibid. Brady to Young, 19 Apr. 1799. 13 P.F. Moran, *Spicilegium ossoriense*, 3 vols (Dublin, 1884), iii, 614–15, gives the full text of the resolution and the signatures including that of Brady. 14 Charles Vane (ed.), *Memoirs and correspondence of Viscount Castlereagh, second marquess of Londonderry*, 4 vols (London, 1848–53), Cornwallis to Portland 5 Dec. 1798, ii, 36.

A further issue which troubled the conscience of some bishops was the question of discontent among the poor. Even stalwarts for Union in the hierarchy did their best to stress that social disorder among the indigent was the real threat to stability in Ireland. Bishop Francis Moylan of Cork made the point that provision for the clergy would not strengthen the influence of the priests over the very poor unless something was done for the temporal relief of those at the bottom of the social pyramid. Otherwise the result would be that

> the enemies of the poor and the enemies of the peace and good order of the country, would avail themselves of [the fact of provision and the Union] to estrange the minds of the poor people from us, by insinu-ating to them ... that we are pensioned by Government to support its measure against the people, and that we attended only to our interests without any attention to their misery and distress.[15]

As we have seen, so far as the London administration was concerned the idea of veto was clearly to be closely connected with the idea of state provision. The administration hoped for some form of government super-vision over ecclesiastical appointments such as obtained in other European countries. Such authority was normally conceded only in circumstances where the government paid the clergy. The expenditure involved was probably in excess of what the Irish executive could have met. The British government estimated that to make provision for all the priests and bishops in the country would involve an annual expenditure in excess of £235,000.[16] That the government contemplated such a massive injection of capital is clear from the survey carried out under government direction to determine the exact state of the church and needs of the Catholic clergy in the country.[17] In Archbishop Troy's opinion, a government pension for the priests had the advantage that it would enable the clergy to be free of the political influence of their people, since if they did not depend on monetary support from parishioners, they could literally afford to ignore their political opinions.

Troy, anxious as he was to accommodate government opinion, had other masters whom he had to try and satisfy. He received a letter from Cardinal Stephen Borgia, the prefect of Propaganda Fide, in June 1799 in which the cardinal said that disturbing reports had been brought to his attention to the effect that Troy had placed himself at the head of a party which was compro-mising the jurisdiction of the Holy See in Ireland.[18] Troy was forced to

15 *Castlereagh correspondence*, Moylan to Hippsley, 17 Sept. 1799, iii, 401.   16 Ibid. iv, 433.   17 Ibid., iii, 97–173, which gives a summary of the state of some of the dioceses. 18 DDA Troy papers, Borgia to Troy, 15 June 1799.

defend himself by saying that the veto proposals were a government-led initiative that underlined the fact of how deeply suspect Catholic bishops were to the government since the days of the 1798 rebellion.[19] Like all the other actors in this particular pageant, Rome was not always consistent in the matter of the veto and provision. In February, Monsignor Charles Erskine, the pope's unofficial representative to Britain, had told the archbishop of Dublin how pleased he was that the Irish bishops concurred with Lord Castlereagh's proposal to endow the clergy and that he was sure Pope Pius VI would approve whatever the Irish bishops decided.[20]

Taken as a whole, the hierarchy was inclined to the Union, not simply from self-interest in the hopes of provision, but also as a means of helping defuse the heightened sectarian tensions which had been everywhere apparent since the foundation of the Defenders and the Orange order. Undoubtedly, however, the embarrassment that the bishops experienced as a result of clerical participation in 1798 was the factor that carried the greatest weight with them as they now sought to determine how to respond to government political initiatives. Early in 1799 Troy had written to Rome that owing to the criminal actions of some priests the previous year, in supporting the United Irishmen in their rebellion, it was now only right that some demonstration of loyalty to the crown should be offered by Catholic officials in the shape of a government power of veto over the appointment of bishops and parish priests.[21]

There is perhaps a consensus among historians that the support of Catholics was not sufficient to pass the Act of Union but their opposition was enough to prevent it. Equally, as Patrick Geoghegan has argued, the government had an immense dilemma. In the context of union, if the authorities opposed concessions to Catholics, then the government would become alienated from that body, but if it supported such measures, it would remove much of the reasoning for the Union and make the measure impossible to achieve.[22] Indeed, Castlereagh told the prime minister, William Pitt, in the autumn of 1799:

> The measure could not be carried, if the Catholics were embarked in an active opposition to it, and that their resistance would be unanimous and zealous if they had reason to suppose that the sentiments of Ministers would remain unchanged with respect to their exclusion.[23]

19 Ibid., Troy to Borgia, 17 August 1799. 20 Ibid., Erskine to Troy, 24 Feb. 1799.
21 O.P. Rafferty, *Catholicism in Ulster: an interpretative history* (Dublin, 1994), p. 97.
22 Patrick M. Geoghegan, *The Irish Act of Union: a study in high politics, 1798–1801* (Dublin, 1999), p. 65.   23 *Cornwallis correspondence*, iii, 327–8.

For his part, Pitt had previously asserted in the house of commons on 31 January 1799 that emancipation could come about only if the Union was carried, but that it was nevertheless dependent upon the 'conduct and temper' of the Catholic body.[24] He was also convinced that, left to its own devices, the Irish parliament would never concede the measure. On the other hand, as the leading Catholic peer, Lord Kenmare, told Cornwallis, the lord lieutenant and commander of the army in Ireland, in 1799, a letter was circulated among Dublin Catholics assuring them that, if they petitioned against the Union, 'a motion should be made as soon as the question of the union had been disposed of in favour of Catholic emancipation'.[25] It is difficult to estimate just how sincere this proposal was. On the other side of the argument, Cornwallis had assured Pitt that such of the leading Irish Protestants who supported the Union insisted that it must be a Protestant union.[26] If Irish Protestants did not want to concede emancipation to Catholics in a united kingdom where Protestants would be in the majority, it is perhaps stretching credulity to suppose that they would be willing to concede it in a country where they were in a clear minority. Equally there was fear of the unknown across the sectarian divide as to what exactly Union would mean in political terms. On the other hand, in an Ireland which retained its own parliament, even if Catholics were emancipated, the Protestant ascendancy would continue to exercise enormous power and influence simply on the basis of its economic position and social standing. In a united kingdom, its influence would be correspondingly diluted. Of course, the more conservative elements within the ascendancy, such as Lord Clare, the Irish lord chancellor, who according to Cornwallis was 'the most right headed politician in the country' [*sic*], completely rejected the idea of Catholics sitting even in the united parliament.[27]

Although it is true at one level that Catholics were given to understand that emancipation would follow on the heels of Union, there is also evidence to suggest that some Catholics did not approve of agitation for this proposal.[28] Certainly this was a disposition shared by Lords Fingall and Kenmare in December 1798, and it represents quite a departure from their memorial to the lord lieutenant in the spring of 1797, in which they demanded complete emancipation as a consequence of their loyalty. In forwarding that petition to the home secretary, the lord lieutenant commented:

24 Brian MacDermot, *The Catholic question in Ireland and England 1798–1822: the papers of Denys Scully* (Dublin, 1988), p. 25, n. 2. 25 As Cornwallis informed Portland on 26 Jan. 1799: *Castlereagh correspondence*, iii, 52. 26 Charles Ross (ed.), *Correspondence of Charles, first marquis of Cornwallis*, 3 vols (London, 1859), Cornwallis to Pitt, 25 Sept. 1798, ii, 416. 27 Ibid. 28 Ibid., Cornwallis to Ross, 8 Dec. 1798, iii, 9.

> These persons who are principally concerned in the petition ... would
> be perfectly satisfied with the prayer of the petition being complied
> with, and they look neither to alteration in the Representation nor in
> the Establishment. They have however no influence over the active
> agitators of the Roman Catholic Committee, who look to Power and
> Authority from this concession which would not be given unless other
> changes were to follow it.[29]

The loyalty the memorialists referred to was clearly not exhibited by all their
co-religionists the following year, and this may explain why they and Troy
wanted the issue of Union to be kept quite separate from the question of
emancipation. Equally, the political ambitions of the Catholic aristocracy
varied over time.

A distinction has to be made between the expectations and ambitions of the
laity and those of the ecclesiastical authorities. At the same time it is clear that
there were varying expectations among the laity. If the Catholic aristocracy
could take a more detached view of the whole matter, the middle classes were
more concerned about their position in Irish society. Although the rhetoric of
O'Connell's position in his famous Royal Exchange speech was that, 'the
enlightened mind of the Catholics had taught them the impolity, the illiber-
ality, and the injustice of separating themselves on any occasion from the rest
of the people of Ireland',[30] the whole thrust of his life was in a sense to do
just that. One does not have to go as far as R.F. Foster in seeing O'Connell as
the 'Liberator' of Catholics rather than Irishmen,[31] but there is a sense in
which he and those who shared his economic status looked for a situation in
which Irish Protestant opinion counted for less, and their opinion correspondingly for more.

It is instructive to reflect on the fact that great indecision giving way at
times to sentiments of despair seemed to beset the deliberations of
government officials in late 1798 and early 1799, when they began to think
that Catholics would, after all, not support Union proposals. Cornwallis
wrote to Major General Ross in mid-December confessing that he had been
too sanguine about Catholic intentions.[32] By now he seemed to think that the
Catholics had become completely alienated from the British government and
its Irish policies. Cornwallis was based in Dublin, and Dublin was more
vehemently anti-Union that the rest of the country, and this was also reflected
in Catholic opinion.[33] Following yet another meeting at Lord Fingall's home

29 PRO HO 100/69 Camden to Portland, 3 April 1797, f. 176. 30 John O'Connell
(ed.), *The life and speeches of Daniel O'Connell MP*, 2 vols (Dublin, 1846), i, 25. 31 R.F.
Foster, *Modern Ireland, 1600–1972* (London, 1989), p. 317. 32 *Cornwallis correspondence*, Cornwallis to Ross, 12 Dec. 1798, iii, 16. 33 Ibid. Cornwallis to Portland, 15

in late December, Cornwallis concluded that Catholic liberal sentiment had changed to one of opposition to the measure.[34] The surprising thing is that by mid-January even the bishops seemed to give the impression that they were at best neutral on the matter. As Troy explained to Castlereagh, the Catholics had decided to regard the issue not as a matter touching the constitution of the empire but rather 'only as it might affect their own peculiar interests as a body, and on this it was judged inexpedient to publish any resolution or declaration at present'.[35] Cornwallis was inclined to believe that the Catholics had come to the conclusion that their position would be worse in a Union than in an independent Ireland. As he explained to the duke of Portland: 'the claims of the Catholics will certainly be much weakened by their incorporation into the mass of British subjects, and the English Test Laws will form a stronger barrier against their carrying the point for which they have so long contended'.[36] At the same time Portland told Kenmare that there could be no hope of Catholic emancipation unless the Union was carried. If emancipation was attempted without Union, Ireland would be deluged in blood.[37] Such scare mongering may have had some effect on Catholic thinking.

It is possible to see that both Cornwallis and Castlereagh were not above exploiting sectarian tensions to achieve the desired union of the two countries. The fear was held out to Protestants that one day Catholicism would achieve political supremacy in Ireland and that Catholics would then lord it over Protestants. To the Catholics they were prepared to say that Irish Protestants would never treat them with justice and that they would therefore be better off in a united kingdom. Bishop Moylan of Cork had written in March 1799 to the effect that it would be impossible to extinguish sectarianism in Ireland without a union with Great Britain. 'The earlier it is accomplished the better. May God give a blessing to it.'[38]

On balance, by the end of 1799 Catholic opinion had shifted once more in favour of Union. It is equally true that the enormous publicity surrounding Dublin opposition tended to distort the strength of opinion against the measure. Dublin was not the whole country. One indignant parish priest, Hugh Dowling of Tullamore, wrote to Castlereagh that he and thousands of Catholics were most angry at the rash and intemperate attitude of their Dublin brethren. In the midlands it seems Catholics were only too willing to say how much they welcomed legislative union with Great Britain.[39]

From June 1799 Castlereagh used his influence with Troy and the other

Dec. 1798, p. 19.   **34** Ibid., 2 Jan. 1799, p. 29.   **35** *Castlereagh correspondence*, ii, 61.
36 *Cornwallis correspondence*, Cornwallis to Portland, 24 Dec. 1798, ii, 29.   **37** Ardill,
Irish parliament, p. 33.   **38** *Castlereagh correspondence*, Moylan to Pelham, 9 Mar. 1799,
ii, 47.   **39** *Castlereagh correspondence*, Dowling to Castlereagh, 17 Jan. 1800, iii, 226.

bishops to get them to take a more aggressively pro-Union stance. When Isaac Corry was chosen to replace the anti-unionist Sir John Parnell, as the chancellor of the exchequer, he was returned as the member for Newry with the active support of the bishop of Dromore, Matthew Lennan. Corry was a friend of Troy, and he had written to Lennan on Corry's behalf. Lennan in response declared that 'the Catholics stuck together like a Macedonian phalanx, and with ease were able to turn the scale in favour of the Chancellor of the Exchequer'.[40]

Troy had also been active in other areas. He wrote a supporting letter to the prominent unionist Lord Glenworth demonstrating his decided opinion in favour of the measure and urging Glenworth to show it to the more 'respectable people' in Limerick.[41] Glenworth armed with Troy's approbation organized a petition in favour of union. A report, however, appeared in the *Dublin Evening Post* on 28 January 1800 saying that Limerick Catholics repudiated the petition. Troy was more particularly helpful to Castlereagh and the unionist cause in his ability to steady the nerves of wavering bishops. Archbishop Brady of Cashel, for example, was inclined to think that the bishops by interfering publicly in the issue might hinder rather than help the cause. 'I need not observe to you', Brady wrote to Troy at the beginning of July 1799,

> who know so well the dispositions of our respectable Catholics what little influence we have over them in political matters, and with what reserve and secrecy we should interfere on the present occasion, in order to ensure any degree of success to it, and to avoid censure.[42]

Brady's caution about the political influence of ecclesiastics must be offset by what we know of the state of Catholic political organization in the aftermath of the 1798 rebellion. Dáire Keogh, in an otherwise skeptical assessment of the extent of the church's political power at the end of the eighteenth century, nevertheless concedes that in the face of the backlash following on from the United Irishmen's rising, the 'leaders of the democratic majority' simply fled, leaving it to the bishops to hold back the wrath of the Protestants rulers of Catholic Ireland.[43] Indeed, as Tom Bartlett perceptively records of Troy, the archbishop was well aware that

40 Ibid., ii, 168. **41** Ibid., ii, 349. **42** Ibid., Brady to Troy, 1 July 1799, iii, 345. **43** D. Keogh, 'Catholic responses to the Act of Union' in Dáire Keogh and Kevin Whelan (eds), *Acts of union: the causes and consequences of the Act of Union* (Dublin, 2001), p. 161. See also Keogh's *'The French disease': the Catholic Church and Irish radicalism 1790–1800* (Dublin, 1993), p. 201, where he declares that 'the failure of the [1798] rebellion had established Troy at the head of the Catholic body as a whole'.

only Cornwallis stood between the Catholic Church in Ireland and the retribution of the loyalists: the current bout of chapel burning in Wexford had shown all too clearly the furious passions unleashed by the rising. Hence [Troy] took a consistent and instinctive pro-union stance. The government for its part was keen to reward him for his loyalty, but also to take advantage of it.[44]

And it was against this background that the ecclesiastical establishment had such a profound impact in determining the views of the Catholic population taken as a whole. As G.C. Bolton concluded from careful study some forty years ago, in a judgment which has withstood the test of time, 'often the local Catholics at first evinced no great enthusiasm for Union, and before they would declare themselves required the prompting of their priests and gentry [who were] themselves inclined to wait a lead from their bishops'.[45] Once again, however, the disposition of bishops was framed by a variety of factors, both internal and external to the Irish situation. Irish Protestants and French revolutionaries both shaped the thinking of their lordships, and Cornwallis had certainly taken the measure of the Catholic episcopal thinking when in July 1798 he summarized the context for Portland:

> The words Papist and Priest are forever in [Protestant] mouths, and by their un-accountable policy they would drive four-fifths of the community into irreconcilable rebellion; and in their warmth they lose sight of the real cause of the present mischief, of the deep-laid conspiracy to revolutionize Ireland on the principles of France, which was originally formed, and by wonderful assiduity brought nearly to maturity by men who had no other though of religion but to destroy it.[46]

This is an almost exact echo of Troy's sentiments as expressed in his pastoral letter of the previous year in the course of which he warned Catholics against any attempt to 'seduce you from your attachment to religion, or from that allegiance to his Majesty and duty towards Superiors of every description which Catholicism inculcates'.[47]

The lead in this had already been given by Pope Pius VI towards the beginning of the decade, in 1793. In face of the fact that several 'seditious assemblages' of lower-class Irish Catholics had been complained of to the

---

44 Thomas Bartlett, *The fall and rise of the Irish nation: the Catholic question, 1690–1830* (Dublin, 1992), p. 250.   **45** G.C. Bolton, *The passing of the Act of Union: a study in parliamentary politics* (Oxford, 1966), p. 152.   **46** Quoted in Bolton, ibid., p. 58. **47** Moran, *Spicilegium*, pp 495–6.

Holy See by the British government, the Vatican secretary of state, Cardinal de Zelanda, had circularized the Irish bishops declaring

> The Holy Father is persuaded ... the accusation can apply only to that small number of Catholics who disobeying the voice of their pastors, suffer themselves to be led astray by the democratic maxims, which are but too widely spread at the present time by the enemies of religion and of governments.[48]

It was the question of religion and of the church's freedom to propagate Catholicism which in the end determined the Irish hierarchy's attitude to the Union. Thus Plunkett in a revealing letter to Troy touching on Union, although reluctant to give an opinion on its propriety, nevertheless permitted himself to observe that as a 'separate kingdom' Ireland was never happy and contented except perhaps for the period soon after Christianity was introduced. His main point was

> Our thoughts on such occasion [the passing of the Act of Union] will not be confined to the mere temporal prosperity of Ireland; they will turn to an object of a superior order, religion and the dearest interests that depend on it. If we shall have no fear in this respect, we need not be alarmed on any other account.[49]

Furthermore one of Troy's continental Irish correspondents John Preston, a canon of Liège cathedral, made the point that one of the benefits that union might bring to Catholic Ireland was that Catholics would probably have to give up the hope of political emancipation and thus instead would 'return to a sense of their duty towards God, and of course become in every respect better subjects'.[50] An interesting comparative perspective is given by James Flynn in his study of the situation of Catholics in Ireland and Belroussia at this time. He remarks that those who sought autonomy for the church in the British and Russian empires did so because they were acting on the conviction that it was 'their religion that gave meaning to life, no matter whose government ruled their secular world'.[51]

In this light, Patrick's Geoghegan's assertion that the bishops' main objective in the face of union negotiations was to secure emancipation, is very much open to question.[52] Even his claim that Troy was perfectly well inclined

---

48 *Castlereagh correspondence*, iii, 97. **49** Moran, *Spicilegium*, iii, 603. **50** DDA Troy papers, John Preston to Troy, 28 Feb. 1799. **51** James T. Flynn, 'Contrasting similarities: Bishops Troy and Lisovskii in Ireland and Belroussia in the age of the French revolution', *Catholic Historical Review*, 87:2 (2001), 215. **52** Geoghegan,

to the Union provided the Catholic question was left open to a future date appears very doubtful.[53] So far as Troy was concerned, the issue of emancipation was irrelevant to his calculations. He wanted to fall in line with government proposals and, as we have seen, was even prepared to expose himself to the risk of Roman disapprobation. His only concern was that Catholic religious independence and the authority of the pope in strictly religious matters should not be compromised in the church's dealing with government. After all, had the intention of Troy and the other bishops been to secure emancipation as a priority, they had the perfect remedy to hand, and that was to throw in their lot with anti-union Irish Protestant opinion whose leaders, such as George Ponsonby, had explicitly promised emancipation in exchange for an anti-union declaration by the Catholic Church and people. Such a declaration would also have placed the bishops at the head of opinion emanating from the mercantile and legal classes in the Catholic community; but clearly this was a step they were unwilling to take. For the archbishop himself was, as his biograper rightly observes:

> Horrified by what he believed 'democracy' had done to the old régime and the Catholic Church in France. Troy remained not only an outsider in the lay emancipation movement of the post-Union period but by concentrating only on more narrow church interests Troy, at least unconsciously, not only worked against emancipation but also gave comfort to its enemies in and out of government.[54]

From the government vantage point there was also another danger, namely, that Catholic declarations of support were merely subterfuge. George McDonagh, a land agent on the Tisdall estate in Kells, assured Dublin Castle in January 1800 that whatever their public declarations, in private the Catholics in Meath were doing all in their power to oppose Union. The reason for this, according to McDonagh, was that Catholics still cherished the idea that some day they would be in charge of Ireland.[55] He also made the point that Meath Catholics signed petitions only at the urging of their priests, who themselves were somewhat reluctant to support the Union, 'and would not have done so only they well knew it was very much in their private interests to comply'. We can see, however, from other areas of the country

'Catholics and the union', p. 245.   **53** Ibid., p. 249. This was Castlereagh's reading of Troy's disposition. As we have seen, however, his views were more nuanced and complex than this *simpliste* analysis suggests.   **54** Vincent J. McNally, *Reform, revolution and reaction: Archbishop John Thomas Troy and the Catholic Church in Ireland, 1787–1817* (London, 1995), p. 126.   **55** NAI SOC McDonagh to Dublin Castle, 7 Jan. 1800, 1019/2.

how dangerous public political declarations by priests could be. A priest was murdered in Kildare town on Christmas day 1797 'for having exhorted his congregation to abstain from disloyalty'.[56]

McDonagh's view, however, was echoed by another Castle correspondent from Meath, George Holdcroft, also of Kells. Writing in January 1800 he informed the Irish administration that, while many signatures had been secured in favour of the Union, 'the great body of the Catholics is decidedly against'.[57] And it was precisely in Meath, that Troy had his greatest trouble in propagating the Union message. Bishop Plunkett had told Castlereagh that the Catholics of Meath were influenced too much by public opinion in Dublin and were too accustomed to listen to Meath Protestants who, like their Dublin brethren, were ardent anti-unionists. Many Catholics therefore were reluctant to declare for Union. Furthermore, Plunkett pointed out, the Meath Catholic priests found it impossible to separate themselves from the opinion of their people, on whom of course they relied for their well being.[58]

Not all Catholics were disposed to follow the Protestant lead. Bishop Caulfield told Troy at the end of July 1799 that there was a long petition circulating in Wexford favouring Union. And although Caulfield 'highly approve[d]' of the measure, he thought it better 'that the R Catholics should speak for themselves, than sign at the tail of the ascendancy without discrimination'.[59] By February 1800, on the other hand, even Plunkett had gained sufficient confidence to sign a public petition for the Union.[60] By this stage also Grattan was so thoroughly disaffected by the activity of Catholic priests and bishops in favour of Union that he could talk of them as 'a band of prostituted men engaged in the service of the government'.

This was precisely the sort of charge that the bishops wanted to avoid in relation to the possibility of state provision and why in the early days of their deliberations on the matter there was some hesitancy. There was a delicate balancing act to be maintained by the hierarchy. On the one hand, in post-rebellion Ireland the bishops could not explicitly reject the government's legitimate political intentions without attracting official opprobrium. On the other, they could not afford to completely ignore, still less alienate, the sentiments of the articulate middle classes. Equally it was also part of Troy's policy to assert the rights of the episcopacy to speak in the name of the Catholic body at a time when sections of the laity were more aggressively declaring their desire to control the Catholic community in both its political and religious aspects. Thus in a determined fashion Troy, in a pastoral letter

---

56 Bartlett, *Rise and fall*, p. 230. 57 NAI SOC, Holdcroft to Dublin Castle, 7 Jan. 1800, 1019/2. 58 *Castlereagh correspondence*, Plunkett to Castlereagh, 29 Oct. 1799, ii, 438. 59 DDA Troy papers ('green file'), Caulfield to Troy, 28 July 1799. 60 Ardill, *Irish parliament*, p. 88.

in 1798, refuted the suggestion that the bishops were the enemies of the political opinion of the Catholic faithful or that they were 'as so many mercenaries prostituting their venal pens for pensions and bribes'.[61] The archbishop of Tuam, Edward Dillon, reported to Troy in July 1799 of similar disabilities under which he laboured. His critics in the diocese described him as variously, 'an Orange bishop', 'the tool of the government', and 'well paid for my services'.[62] Yet following some reassurance from the archbishop of Armagh, Dillon authorized Troy to sign the Union petition for him.

By now, of course, not only was Pius VI dead but the Papal States were in a state of disarray, and the Roman authorities began to cast a more skeptical eye on the issue of church-state relations in Europe as a whole. Cardinal Borgia wrote a very hesitant letter to Troy outlining the difficulties he foresaw in agreeing to any arrangement that might be entered into by the Irish bishops in terms of the Union negotiations.[63] Troy, however, took the high-minded view that those governing the church from the Papal States simply did not know the difficulties under which the Irish bishops laboured. To his Roman agent, and fellow Dominican, Fr Luke Concanen, Troy wrote wondering how cautious Borgia would be 'if he were on the spot, after a fierce rebellion in which so many of our deluded people, even some priests – secular and regular – were implicated'.[64] Still smarting under the rebuke, he again complained in December that if Borgia or 'any of his colleagues were here they would find they could not without great danger to religion directly oppose the proposals of the government'.[65] Once again Troy stressed that given Catholic participation in the recent rebellion, and in particular the old chestnut of priestly collusion in the attempted revolution, some token of loyalty to the state must be offered to the government.

Indeed, the idea of loyalty to the lawfully constituted state had been the official position in Rome and Ireland through-out the 1790s. As early as 1793, Pius VI had made clear that he would use all his efforts to ensure that Catholics under British rule would always 'render themselves worthy of the protection which they now enjoy'. More especially, Pius warned the Irish bishops to confront rebelliously inclined individuals 'and warn them, by wholesome advice, against the snares laid for them by evil-designing men, whose only aim is to destroy the fundamental bases of religion and the throne'.[66] Troy himself had warned that the systematic 'opposer' of every monarchy and hierarchy would attempt the destruction of both the state and the church.[67]

61 Moran, *Spicilegium*, iii, 553. 62 Ardill, *Irish parliament*, p. 54. 63 DDA Troy papers, Borgia to Troy, 17 Nov. 1799. 64 Ibid. Troy to Concanen, 19 Oct. 1799. 65 Ibid. Troy to Concanen, 22 Dec. 1799. 66 *Castlereagh correspondence*, iii, 97. 67 Quoted in Cogan, *Diocese of Meath*, iii, 215.

Whatever reservations Cardinal Borgia had about the policy of the Irish hierarchy in 1799 they seemed to have disappeared by the following year. In July 1800 he wrote to Sir John Hippesley informing him of papal approval for the idea of state endowment for the Irish Catholic clergy.[68] By now, in an ironic twist, there had also been a change of heart in London – in the opposite direction. Troy had the unpleasant task of informing the Holy See that the government had abandoned its intention of giving the clergy a pension.[69] But we begin at this stage to see some ambiguity in Troy's attitude to the British government. At one level we can detect that Troy and his colleagues were relieved by the turn of events. They had feared that by receiving state salaries in the context of Union their independence would be compromised. They further believed that their moral teaching on the need for obedience to the state would be seen as founded purely on self-interest. It is also true that at times even Troy had wondered if the whole scheme had been thought up by the government as a means of trying to undermine the loyalty of lay Catholics to their pastors and bishops, who would be seen as paid agents of the state. This view was shared by some of the bishops amid much talk of 'Beware of Greeks bearing gifts'.[70]

There are further indications of sentiments of distrust on the part of the hierarchy when, despite the loyalty which the bishops undoubtedly displayed, they were not rewarded with the much talked-of pension. On the other hand, Troy's reservation about government intentions would become even more explicit when Cornwallis was replaced as viceroy by the earl of Hardwicke, who at times was deeply critical of Troy.[71] That this embryonic ambiguity did not grow into outright hostility to the union government was facilitated by the policy of the Holy See. On 7 August 1801 Luke Concanen forwarded to Troy a letter he had just received from Propaganda, giving the new pope's definitive judgment on the question of the provision. His Holiness, according to Propaganda, 'acknowledges the voluntary and generous liberality of the British government and is most grateful, but he would prefer the Irish Catholic clergy, whose fidelity Rome has always experienced, to follow the system hitherto observed': in other words voluntary support of the clergy by the laity. Perhaps more revealing Pius made it clear that he was

> desirous [that] the said Government be made aware that the
> Metropolitans, Bishops and all the clergy of Ireland will ever avow this
> their precise duty, always evincing by word and deed the sincerity of

68 *Castlereagh correspondence*, iii, 385.   **69** DDA Troy papers, Troy to Propaganda, 22 Dec. 1800.   **70** DDA Troy papers, 'Letters on provision', Young to Bray, 19 Dec. 1800. **71** Bartlett, *Rise and fall*, p. 276.

their invariable attachment, thankfulness and submission to the British Government.[72]

One curiosity which did emerge from the hierarchy's negotiations with the government on the issue of Union and state provision was an amendment to the catechism in Ireland at Hippesley's suggestion.[73] The aim of the new questions and answers was, in the words of Bishop Moylan, 'to impress our people with a due sense of the social and political duties of good citizens & with sentiments of loyalty and attachment to His Majesties [*sic*] person and government'.[74]

It is significant that, in some ways, the Union was a test of public opinion. Perhaps for the first time in Ireland Catholic political support was canvassed on an issue of major constitutional significance. The response was in many cases favourable and there is something monotonous in reading in the press the repeated letters of loyalty and support for the proposal which emanated from every part of Catholic Ireland. To what degree such declarations were spontaneous or heartfelt is more difficult to judge. That sectarian considerations played a part in the deliberations of some Catholics is beyond question. The Catholic community still suffered at the hands of the yeomanry and there are indications of chapel burning well into 1799.[75] In other circumstances, fear of the landlords doubtless played a part in determining the disposition to declare for or against union.[76] While it would be wrong to overestimate the strength of support of the Catholics for the legislative Union, significant numbers of priests and bishops lent their weight in favour of the Union, and at least the government thought this was both important and helpful in determining the response of lay Catholics.

Pitt, for one, could see that having the Catholics support the measure would make for a period of more tranquil social stability in Ireland. His main concern, however, was not with the relative freedoms of the Catholics but rather with the security of the realm and all other issues must be subservient to that paramount consideration. There is a sense in which this was also true for the bishops and the leading Catholic aristocrats. For the latter, concerned as they were for their titles and social standing, emancipation would bring no observable benefits. For the majority of the bishops, their support for Union was a demonstration of their loyalty and a guarantee that they had definitively separated the Catholic community from the scourge of the United Irishmen's violence and rhetoric, overlaid as this was with French revolutionary

---

72 DDA Troy papers (green file), Propaganda to Concanen, 7 Aug. 1801. 73 *Castlereagh correspondence*, iii, 134–5. 74 NLI MS 5027 Hippesley papers, Moylan to Hippisley, 1 Mar. 1800. 75 See for example Moran, *Spicilegium*, p. 577, Caulfield to Troy, 1 June 1799. 76 Bolton, *Irish act of union*, pp 133 and 152.

sentiment. This was the whole thrust of high ecclesiastical policy throughout the 1790s, not only in Ireland but throughout Europe. Association with radicalism had virtually destroyed the church in France, and had brought the pope to a position where he was a puppet of Napoleon. In such circumstances, the Irish church had to show itself firmly on the side of the British government in protecting Ireland from French ideas and revolutionary change. The government had determined that the only way to achieve this was by Union, and no other policy could have commended itself to the Catholic hierarchy taken as a whole.

The issues of endowment and veto were, to some extent, tangential to this central ecclesio-political reality. So for that matter was emancipation. The idea of emancipation based on democratic accountability was quite foreign to the church's view of how society ought to work. Its significance in the Irish context, as we have seen, was as a social ambition for the parvenu middle classes. As R.B. McDowell observed, 'What can be safely said is that the early months of 1792 saw the emergence of the Catholic middle classes, the urban businessmen and the respectable farmers, as an unmistakable and potent force in Irish public life.'[77] Even so by the end of the decade, their hour had not yet come, in terms of the shaping of Ireland's political destiny. For the bishops Catholic emancipation, as an instrument in the democratic process and as a constitutional foundation in the new state, could have no allurement, conditioned as they were by the highest authority in the church to regard democracy and the political rights of peoples as a dangerous element in French revolutionary thinking. Emancipation could have at most a psychological attractiveness, in that Catholics would be able to take high office in the United Kingdom and this would enable the bishops to bask in the reflected glory of members of their flock making headway in the political sphere. But in and of itself, emancipation at that stage would do nothing to further the intrinsic interests of Catholicism in Ireland. A more pressing problem was that of sectarianism and revenge attacks by Orangemen on Catholic property and churches. Bishop Caulfield had written to Troy in anxious and pleading tones towards the end of 1799: 'If the Union is not passed and something done Wexford will be destroyed.'[78] The bishops' anxiety was already at fever pitch in view of the fact that the Irish house of lords had earlier in the year rejected the bill giving the annual subvention to St Patrick's College, Maynooth.

Doubtless for some elements in the Irish Catholic body, emancipation was an important issue. Those Catholics of O'Connell's social standing looked for a situation in which their ambitions for political power could be realized,

77 R.B. McDowell, *Ireland in the age of imperialism and revolution, 1760–1801* (Oxford, 1979), p. 397.   78 DDA Troy papers, Caulfield to Troy, 10 Nov. 1799.

despite their protests that their desire was simply to align themselves with the rest of the political opinion in the country. Perhaps there was something disingenuous on O'Connell's part when he asserted that the dilemma facing the Catholic body was either to be 'reduced to the necessity of ... submitting to the disagreeable imputation of approving a measure as detestable to them, as it was ruinous to the country; or once again, and he trusted for the last time, of coming forward as a distinct body'.[79]

More immediately, it was the fear of violence from the peasant classes that captured episcopal attention. There was a great gap between the rulers and the ruled, between those at the top of the social ladder and those at the bottom. But it is perhaps stretching the point, as in the case of Kevin Whelan, to think that the institutional church had so separated itself from its people that the episcopacy simply echoed the gentry's disengagement from the peasantry.[80] It is, however, within such categories, as much as considerations of charity, that we must set Moylan's repeated calls on government that something be done for the poor, an issue in which he had support from other members of the hierarchy including Bishop Caulfield. As late as December 1800 Moylan had pleaded with the government via Hippesley to put the bishops in a position 'to help our poor more than we can do at present'. He added that he was sure 'it is in the interests of His Majesty's Government to support us in these sentiments'.[81] The poor, after all, had least to lose and therefore were potentially the most reckless in any social upheaval. It was this and the continual experience of sectarian backlash that prompted the majority of bishops to take the attitude of subordination to government wishes.

The government's agenda therefore with regard to the veto and provision was a side show, but one which they were happy to pursue for two reasons. One such reason was undoubtedly the question of control over the Catholic Church, which had long been a feature of political administrative policy in Ireland at least from the time of the 1704 registration act. The other was the rationale of giving the clergy a measure of independence from the Catholic community. This was especially important precisely because of the transformation taking place in the social expectations of Catholics, which had been brought about by the relief acts. While the government could be certain that ecclesiastical leaders could resist the undifferentiated and largely unarticulated expectations of the peasantry, the same could not be said of the influence of the professional classes over the clergy. And it was, after all, these classes in Dublin and elsewhere who were most resistant to episcopal dictat in

79 O'Connell, *Life and speeches*, pp 21–2.   80 Whelan, *The tree of liberty*, pp 94–5.
81 NLI MS 5027 Moylan to Hippesley, 6 Dec. 1800.

the matter of the Union. This was the class to fear so far as its influence on ecclesiastical opinion was concerned and state provision would help distance the clergy from this more educated, articulate and less compliant membership of the Catholic body.

Famously, Pitt, Cornwallis, Castlereagh and Edward Cooke, the Irish under secretary, all resigned from government when emancipation was not carried in the aftermath of Union, because they believed that Britain had broken faith with the Catholics over the issue. On the other hand, there is no evidence from bishops' correspondence to show that they saw the matter in the same terms. Of course, even for them emancipation would have been as so much icing on the cake, but they had neither sought it nor expected it. Their interests lay in other than ephemeral democratic directions.

It was clearly the belief in some sections of the British political establishment that Catholic support for the Union would have to be bought. Thus the cabinet in November 1799 had informed Castlereagh that so far as it was concerned 'his Excellency need not hesitate in calling forth Catholic support in whatever degree he found it practicable to obtain it'.[82] Nevertheless, no official compact was entered into, although Cornwallis did imply that emancipation would follow soon after Union. This assurance might have been necessary in the case of certain political elements within the Catholic body but not so far as the bishops were concerned, and they were in a position, for the most part, to at least impose their view of things on the lower clergy and on those inclined to take clerical direction in political matters.

Of course, it was in the long run a miscalculation of the first order, in itself a result of sectarian prejudice, not to grant emancipation as a consequence of Union. Catholics over the long term had no incentive to abide by a policy which brought them no tangible benefits, and which in some ways left Ireland at an economic disadvantage and thus was a disadvantage to Catholics as to everyone else. By the time emancipation was granted, the political climate had changed to the extent that the constitutional union itself would become the problem rather than merely Catholic engagement in the benefits of the political nation. In this the bishops were as blinkered as the British establishment. They neither looked for emancipation nor initially regretted its absence. But they too had miscalculated. In their case, unlike that of the British state, such was the prestige of their religious position that little permanent damage was done to their abilities to shape the political orientation of their flock. Troy's basic instinct, however, that the role of bishops must be played out other than in the political arena might have gone far in reconciling the competing influences in Irish, and indeed in British, society.

---

82 Geoghegan, 'Catholics and the union', p. 255.

2

Catholic and Protestant relations in Derry in the episcopacy of Charles O'Donnell

In reconstructing any aspect of the history of the Derry diocese, the historian is hampered by the fact that no Catholic archives are preserved in Derry before 1939. Moreover, the normally fruitful mine of information for Irish Catholic activity, the archives of the congregation of Propaganda fide, is virtually bereft of reference for Derry in the period of O'Donnell's episcopacy 1798–1823.[1] Such information as can be had must be gleaned from other sources. Nonetheless the task of delineating the details of the relationship between Catholics and Protestants at this critical period is an important one since in some ways it provides a paradigm for our under-standing of later nineteenth-century developments.

Despite the fact of the incursions at Maghera, the hanging of rebels in Derry city, and the assistance the Derry insurgents gave to their Antrim comrades, Derry, on the whole, escaped from the worst of the ravages of the 1798 rebellion. Although Catholics were numerous, they did not seem to pose a political threat to constitutional stability. The higher clergy in particular were anxious to avoid any implication in politics. Thus Richard Reilly, archbishop of Armagh, wrote to the Revd Henry Conwell, parish priest of Dungannon: 'Mention nothing to me in your letters of the politics of the times. Tho' we are far from meddling in politics ourselves it is still dangerous to report the conduct or sentiments of others as regards to such topics.'[2] In setting the tone in his diocese for a differential attitude to the political *status quo*, Charles O'Donnell was well equipped both temperamentally and by training. He was a man of continental education, a doctor of the Sorbonne, and had liberal tastes. The leadership he gave to the Catholic community was such as to encourage loyalty to the institutions of government, and respect for those Christians separated from the Catholic body by considerations of religious conviction. In such circumstances one would expect that relations between the communities would therefore be fairly cordial. On the whole, this proved not always to be the case.

If O'Donnell's leadership predisposed an environment which encouraged

1 O'Donnell did write at least one *relatio status* on the diocese, which was presented at Propaganda by the agent of the Irish bishops at Rome in the spring of 1816. It is not, however, especially revealing. DDA Troy papers AB2/28/1, Agentii to Troy, 20 Dec. 1815.   2 AAA Reilly papers, Reilly to Conwell, 13 Sept. 1797.

friendly relations between Catholics and Protestants in Derry during his reign as bishop, he was merely inheriting a situation bequeathed to him by his predecessor, and uncle, Philip McDevitt.[3] Towering over both was of course the patrician and avuncular figure of Frederick Hervey, earl of Bristol, and Anglican bishop of Derry, 1768–1803. Indeed, there is some suggestion that McDevitt owed his position as Catholic bishop to Bristol's influence. [4] Catholic polemicists have not always been kind to Hervey. Cardinal Moran, for example, maintained that from Hervey's private correspondence one could see that he had 'an intense hatred of the Catholics of Ireland, and that he hoped by friendly dealings with them to weaken their affections for Rome …'[5]

Such invective notwithstanding, we know that Bristol had contributed to the building of the Long Tower church, the first purpose-built Catholic place of worship in the city since the reformation. Such was his sway that he persuaded the local corporation to also provide financial assistance. This was but one of several occasions when Protestants contributed funds for the Long Tower church, and by 1819 the London Irish Society had granted ten pounds to help repair the building.[6] In fact, Bristol contributed to and facilitated Catholics projects throughout Derry on a number of occasions. Having built the temple at Downhill in 1788, he allowed mass to be said in it each week for his Catholic servants and paid the officiating priest one guinea a month for his exertions.[7] This is not the only occasion when Protestants contributed to the stipends of Catholic priests. A town meeting at Coleraine in May 1792 voted an annual grant to the local Catholic curate of £20.[8] More surprisingly, that anti-nationalist zealot, the Revd Henry Cooke, himself a native of Maghera, told a house of lords committee in 1825 that Catholic clerical income was considerably increased when Protestants attended Catholics funerals since they contributed more than Catholics to the collections customary on these

3 Such nepotism was not uncommon in Ulster Catholicism in the eighteenth and nineteenth centuries. O'Donnell in his turn tried to have his nephew Daniel O'Colgan appointed as coadjutor with right of succession in 1817; only his death from cholera prevented O'Colgan inheriting the bishopric. W. Doherty (ed.), *Derry Columbkille* (Dublin, 1899), p. 121; B.J. Canning, *By Columba's footsteps trod* (Derry, 1984), p. 21. 4 We are told that McDevitt was promoted to the bishopric 'through the interest of Bishop Hervey, earl of Bristol, who had formed an intimacy with him on the continent'. Thomas Colby, *Ordnance Survey memoirs of Londonderry* (Dublin, 1837), p. 70. 5 P.F. Moran, *The Catholics of Ireland under the penal laws of the eighteenth century* (Dublin, 1900), p. 199. 6 Ibid. In 1824 the Society donated £30 for the Catholic school in Derry, two year later it gave a further £20 with an additional £10 annual grant thereafter. Cf. R. Smith, *The Irish Society, 1613–1963* (London, 1966), p. 78. 7 A. Day and P. McWilliams (eds), *Ordnance Survey memoirs of Ireland: parishes of county Londonderry*, xi (Belfast and Dublin, 1991), pp 53 and 61. 8 John Brady, *Catholics and Catholicism in the eighteenth-century press* (Maynooth, 1965), p. 283.

occasions.[9] Bristol's generous example was also clearly matched in many instances by Protestants of all denominations throughout O'Donnell's episcopacy. The Catholic chapels in the parishes of Balteagh, Ballyscullion, Dungiven and Maghera, to mention but a few, were all built with Protestant and Presbyterian help. At the same time such testimonies of ecumenical harmony have to be set alongside the burning of Catholic chapels at Killeman in 1807[10] and Tamalaght O'Crilly near Kilrea in 1810. On that occasion, however, £120 of the cost of repair was levied on the county by the Derry assizes the following year.[11]

There is no question but that O'Donnell was wedded to the idea of support for the government in the vicissitudes of the political, and increasingly, sectarian strife that afflicted Ireland in the closing years of the eighteenth century. Such problems as did arise were to continue into the new century, but by that time Catholic demands for political equality had, under the leadership of Daniel O'Connell, helped to exacerbate an already delicate situation, and were to serve to increase Protestant hostility to and suspicion of Catholic intentions.

William Knox, the Church of Ireland bishop of Derry from 1803 until 1831, testified before the parliamentary committee on the state of Ireland in 1825 that the Protestants of Derry were universally hostile to the idea of removing the civil disabilities of Catholics.[12] Knox himself was strongly in favour of Catholic emancipation,[13] but this was by that stage becoming a minority view in Protestant ecclesiastical and political circles. Soon after the turn of the century, the English chief justice, Lord Ellenborough, lamented the 'dangerous organization of the R.C. church in Ireland', and pledged himself to resist any further concessions to Catholics.[14] In fact, however, it is clear that the Catholic Church in Ireland was acting as a check on the more violent and extreme proclivities of its politically active members.

As was so often the case, the nature of the relationship between Catholics and Protestants was determined by events elsewhere. Following the French revolution, the Holy See sought to have closer links with Great Britain, and

9 *Minutes of evidence taken before the select committee of the House of Lords appointed to inquire into the state of Ireland*, HC 1825 (181, 521), ix, p. 213.   10 AAA, Reilly papers, Reilly to Conwell, 5 Mar. 1807. Although in Co. Derry, Killeman is in the Armagh diocese.   11 Day and McWilliams, *Ordnance survey memoirs Londonderry*, xv (Belfast, 1992), p. 106.   12 Ibid., p. 283.   13 Edward Maturin, *Brief memoirs of all the bishops of Derry since the reformation with a brief sketch of the history of the see* (Derry, 1867), p. 65.   14 PRONI Redesdale papers T.3030/10/5/C.23. Ellenborough to Lord Redesdale, 2 Oct. 1803. Some two decades later Redesdale was to tell the newly appointed lord lieutenant, Lord Wellesley, that there could be no peace in Ireland until 'the Catholics shall have no hope and the Protestants no fear'. Ibid. Redesdale to Wellesley, 8 Dec. 1821.

therefore the behaviour of Irish Catholics became an important factor in papal calculations in its dealing with the London government.[15] There was also a genuine fear among the Irish Catholic bishops that if the domestic political situation was not carefully handled they might suffer the same fate as their French colleagues. This fear was increased, given Napoleon's treatment of Pope Pius VII. The loyalty of the Catholic bishops to the institutions of the British state has to be seen in this context, as indeed it was by contemporaries. Thus Charles Broderick, Church of Ireland archbishop of Cashel, wrote to Lord Redesdale that it was precisely because of such considerations that the Catholic bishops were sincere in their endeavours to prevent their flocks from countenancing a French invasion.[16] To this end the prefect of Propaganda Fide, Cardinal Antonelli, wrote to the Irish bishops in 1795, on behalf of the pope, praising them for their loyalty to King George III, and warning them to expel from their flocks those tinged with the spirit of republicanism.[17] Such sentiments were not lost on the Irish bishops who, in the face of the 1798 rebellion, issued a declaration chastising the 'deluded people now in rebellion against his Majesty's government', and expressing their horror that, in addition to the crime of treason, some of the insurgents had given 'their designs a colour of zeal for the religion they professed.'[18] O'Donnell was among the prelates who signed this declaration. His name was also among the list of subscribers to the pamphlet *Youth Instructed* by the Augustinian friar William Gahan, published on the eve of the 1798 rebellion and which sought to undermine the 'idle speculations, wild ideas and conjectures' of Tom Paine, and revolutionary ideas generally.[19]

By the mid-1790s Catholics in Derry had already shown that they were anxious to dissociate themselves from revolutionary ideas. The parish priest and parishioners of Ballinderry published a declaration in January 1798, recognizing that some Catholics had been seduced from their duty of allegiance by 'the wicked designs and diabolical practices' of the United Irishmen. Protesting their own determination of 'supporting our gracious sovereign King George' and opposing his enemies, they also made clear that their motivation in declaring their loyalty was to show that the 'most perfect good understanding has ever subsisted between us and our Protestant brethren'.[20] This was followed by similar declarations from priests and congregations in the parishes of Kildress in March and Omagh in June.[21]

15 P. O'Donoghue, 'The Holy See and Ireland 1780–1803', *Archivium Hibernicum*, 34 (1976–7), 100. 16 PRONI Redesdale papers T.3030/11/20/x21, Broderick to Redesdale, 3 Sept. 1803. 17 DDA Troy papers AB2/116/6 (64), Antonelli to Irish bishops, 7 Feb. 1795. 18 DDA, Troy papers AB2/116/7 (102). 19 D. Keogh, *'The French disease': the Catholic Church and Irish radicalism, 1790–1800* (Dublin, 1993), p. 162. 20 *Londonderry Journal*, 16 Jan. 1798. 21 The diocese of Derry in addition to

Finally, and perhaps ironically, on 12 July 'the Catholics of Ulster' as a whole issued a loyal declaration and regretted that a single priest in the diocese of Derry had helped the rebels.[22]

A little while before this, and perhaps somewhat belatedly, O'Donnell issued a pastoral letter to be read at all masses in the diocese on Sunday 1 July. He reminded Catholics of the absolute precept of scripture to 'respect, obey, and support the sovereign power'. He then outlined all the benefits of freedom of religion which Catholics enjoyed under George III. In addition he adverted to the fact that the government had provided Maynooth College for clerical education, and he reminded his flock that it was now possible for Catholics to buy property and to hold military and civil office under the crown. Most significantly of all, O'Donnell asserted that it was because Protestants 'of every description' had contributed 'with a most bountiful and liberal hand' that many Catholics now enjoyed chapels for divine worship.[23] At the same time he refuted the idea that priests were to have pensions from the government. Such a suggestion was put about by people acting 'out of self-interest' whose object was to undermine the influence of the clergy with their people.

If by such protestations of loyalty Catholics sought to ensure harmonious relations with Protestants, the technique did not always work.[24] The previous autumn Sir George Hill, MP and sometime mayor of Derry, assured the Dublin authorities that 'we have nothing to dread from the Catholics' of Derry, 'since the spirit of this county might at any moment it became necessary be roused against [them]'.[25] An anonymous correspondent put it to the readers of the *Londonderry Journal* that Catholics had joined in the rebellion as part of a campaign to achieve emancipation, under the direction of the priests, and it was precisely because of such clerical influence that Catholic emancipation must never be granted.[26]

If Presbyterian political power was the bugbear of government concern in 1798, never forgetting that official Presbyterian opinion was against the

the whole of the county includes approximately half of Tyrone, about one-sixth of Donegal and has a small toe-hold in Antrim.   **22** Keogh, '*French disease*', p. 189. On the other hand the *Londonderry Journal* of 12 June 1798 records that a priest trying to escape from the rebels in Maghera was taken by them and was compelled to fall into their ranks. These were not the only Ulster priests involved in United Irish activity. **23** *Londonderry Journal*, 10 July 1798.   **24** James MacCaffery remarks that even the most submissive of the Irish clergy were still regarded with grave distrust. *History of the Catholic Church in the nineteenth-century*, 2 vols (Dublin, 1909), ii, 143.   **25** NAI Rebellion papers, 620/32/139, Hill to E. Cooke, 23 Sept. 1797. This is in contrast to his fears of a Presbyterian insurrection that year. Hill to Pelham, 20 Mar. 1797, Rebellion papers, 620/29/96. See also Revd Isaac Ashe to Sackville Hamilton, 27 Jan. 1796, ibid., 620/23/14. I owe this point to Dr Ian McBride of King's College London. **26** *Londonderry Journal*, 14 Aug. 1798.

United Irishmen,[27] the focus soon changed to the threat from the Catholics. Whatever community of interest that may have existed between Catholics and radial Presbyterians in Derry soon dissipated as sectarian and official hostility grew. Brigadier General G.V. Hart reported to Dublin in 1803 that Presbyterians in Derry were now 'outdoing one another in expressions of loyalty', and that the reason for this was the fear of growing Catholic power.[28] Such sentiments were echoed at the same time by Robert Fowler, writing from Strabane to say that Catholics in Derry and Donegal had been buying fire-arms and were determined 'shortly to try their strength'. Consequently the Presbyterians were 'undoubtedly completely disunited from the Catholic body'.[29] One factor in the growing fear of Catholics was the rapid increase in the size of the Catholic community. By 1808 there were 3,500 Catholics in Derry city, out of a total population of 10,000, an enormous number given that up to a generation or so earlier Catholics had been forbidden to live in the city.[30] It has been suggested that fear of Catholic political and economic recovery had long been a uniting bond between Anglicans and Presbyterians in Ulster.[31]

All this is in marked contrast to Presbyterian–Catholic relations in the previous decade when they had united to wage 'guerrilla war', even if such an alliance had already collapsed by the outbreak of rebellion.[32] By that time defenderism had made its appearance in Derry bringing in its wake increasing sectarian tensions.[33] Equally the defenders helped, temporarily, to swell the ranks of the United Irishmen in the county, alarming the government and causing it to have west and central Co. Derry proclaimed. It is also clear that there was less Catholic involvement in the United Irish movement in Co. Derry than in other areas of Ulster.[34] If in Derry, as in so much of Ulster, United Irish activity did not serve to unite Presbyterian and Catholics to the extent that has been generally thought,[35] we can also see that further alien-ation between the communities came about as the result of the activities of

---

27 The Derry presbytery of the church reported to the Synod of Ulster in August 1798 that the Revd Robert Steel, who had been found guilty of treason, was removed from the list of the presbytery's ministers, and that two probationary ministers had been similarly dealt with. *Records of the General Synod of Ulster*, iii, 1778–1820 (Belfast, 1898), p. 205.   **28** NAI SOC 1025/34, Hart to Sir Edward Littlehales, 29 Aug. 1803.   **29** NAI SOC 1025/73, Fowler to —, 13 Aug. 1803.   **30** E. Wakefield, *An account of Ireland, statistical and political*, 2 vols (London, 1812), ii, 616.   **31** S. Clark and J.S. Donnelly Jr (eds), *Irish peasants: violence and political unrest, 1780–1914* (Manchester, 1983), p. 143.   **32** D. Murphy, 'Parliamentary politics and society in mid-Ulster, 1790–1837', in *Derriana: the journal of the Derry Diocesan Historical Society* (1979), 92.   **33** NAI Rebellion papers 620/31/171, R. Lowry to T. Pelham, 29 June 1797.   **34** Nancy J. Curtin, *The United Irishmen: popular politics in Ulster and Dublin, 1791–1798* (Oxford, 1994), pp 69 and 73.   **35** Hereward Senior, *Orangemen in Ireland and Britain, 1795–1836* (London, 1966), p. 22.

two radically opposed sectarian groups, the Ribbonmen and the Orange order.

Sir George Hill reported to Dublin in 1796 that there were no Orangemen in Co. Derry.[36] The following year he stated that he had been asked if he would countenance or 'at least wink at the introduction of the *Orange business* into this neighbourhood'.[37] His own disposition was to resist it, but he was willing to take guidance on the matter from Dublin Castle. His general attitude is perhaps indicative of the initial disdain for the order found in all the ranks of the upper classes. At the same time he was willing, in case of necessity, to make use of the order to help curtail Catholic political activity.

Some years later Hill assured the Dublin government that there were few Orangemen 'in this part of the north'. Nonetheless, Protestant feeling was quite strong, and such sentiments 'properly regulated it is not either my intention or wish to abate'.[38] Equally we can see that the Orange phenomenon had begun to colour the relations between the communities. Increasingly clear indications of this appeared in the celebrations to mark the siege of Derry in August and December each year. At the same time there is evidence that Catholics and Protestants both customarily participated in such commemorations. The Catholic veneration of the memory of William of Orange was not peculiar to Derry Catholics. Well into the 1820s Catholic emancipationists frequently referred to James II as a bigot and a tyrant, and expressed gratitude for William's defeat of James. It is difficult to know if this was a mere ploy to show that Catholics were loyal to the Act of Settlement and could thus be given political rights, or if it was a sincere sentiment.

It is also apparent that by the early years of the nineteenth-century events such as the Siege of Derry commemorations had acquired a much more marked sectarian edge, and the yeomanry had begun to wear Orange lilies when participating in the festivities which only served to further alienate them from the Catholic community.[39] At the same time we have evidence from Maghera that both communities equally took part in Orange and Green celebrations. Shamrock was worn by all on St Patrick's Day, and 'the juice of the barley' consumed; similarly all donned Orange lilies on 12 July.[40]

36 NAI, Rebellion papers 620/23/6, Hill to Cooke, 6 May 1796.   37 Ibid. 23 Sept. 1797 (italics in original).   38 NAI SOC papers 1573/36, Hill to Littlehales, 13 Dec. 1813.   39 One 'old Derryman' attested in 1811 that he could not remember orange being worn as an emblem before the foundation of the yeomanry. But he also remembered that yeoman officers forbade the wearing of orange as 'tending to denote a party distinction, and not to celebrate a glorious event in the history of our city': *Londonderry Journal*, 28 Oct. 1811. We can also see from that year that 'orange' had become a derogatory term. The Catholic priest Cornelius O'Mullan denounced the Derry corporation as 'orange' in the course of a speech in Dungiven in November 1813: *Londonderry Journal*, 9 Nov. 1813.   40 J. Graham, *A statistical account of the parish of Maghera in*

Hill's assertion about the absence of Orange influence in Derry at this period must be treated with some circumspection. After all, even in the famous 'battle of the Diamond' the defenders were reinforced with supporters from south Derry.[41] The columns of the *Londonderry Journal* also reveal that by 1798 Orangeism had become an issue in Catholic–Protestant relations. In the parish of Cumber in November that year Catholics had attacked and maltreated a number of Protestants on 'account of their being Orangemen'.[42] The *Journal* in reporting this incident was anxious to stress that Catholics as such had nothing to fear from the Orange order, but on the contrary they too 'are equally the objects of its protection, with all his majesty's loyal subjects'. Here then was the nub: only in so far as Catholics sided with rebellion were they seen as enemies. But as time went on it became increasingly difficult for Protestants to discriminate between 'loyal' and 'disloyal' Catholics.

Captain Sir William Smith informed Major General Fryers of the bitter relations that existed between the 'Orangemen and ribbandmen' in the Lough Swilly area in December 1813.[43] Such tensions were by no means novel. The defenders for example flocked to the United Irishmen a decade earlier largely because of the growth of the 'nascent Orange movement among Protestants'.[44]

It would be easy to exaggerate the importance of Orangeism as a staging post in the deterioration of the relationship between the communities. The order was perhaps more of a symptom than the cause of hostilities. Henry Cooke in his evidence before the house of lords committee in 1825 conceded that the Orange order had some deleterious effect on the minds of Catholics. Nevertheless he observed that 'those past quarrels may be traced, especially in the county Derry, to a much earlier date'.[45] The fact, however, remains that Catholic experience of the order in Derry became increasingly identified with militant Protestantism and anti-Catholicism.

The marked appearance of defenderism in mid-Ulster for the first time in the winter of 1797–8 marks something of a turning point in violent confrontation between Catholics and Protestants in Derry. There is, however, little evidence from the county that defenderism and ribbonism were symptomatic of any deep hatred for Protestants or the English, or that Pastorini's prophecies had the kind of influence on ribbon activity in Derry, that they

the diocese of Derry (Dublin, 1813), p. 18. **41** Jim Smyth, *The men of no property* (Dublin, 1992), p. 111. **42** *Londonderry Journal*, 27 Nov. 1798. **43** NAI SOC 1537/37 Smith to Fryers. Fryers forwarded this letter to Dublin Castle on 17 December and confirmed that 'great discontents and animosities are still existing in Londonderry'. **44** A.T.Q. Stewart, *The narrow ground: aspects of Ulster 1609–1969* (London, 1977), p. 103. **45** *Minutes of evidence on the state of Ireland, HC 1825* (181), ix, 212.

were to have had elsewhere in Ireland.[46] Having said that, Protestant fears of physical violence from Catholics became associated with organized attacks from ribbon bands, much in the same way as Catholics feared organized Protestant violence. One factor in ribbon popularity among Catholics was undoubtedly fear of the yeomanry, which in Derry, as in much of Ulster, was a completely Protestant force. Hence General Charles Egerton, commander of the army in Ulster, testified that his Catholic orderly of twenty-three years, who had been honourably discharged from the army, could not get a position with the yeomanry in Kilrea because of his religion.[47]

Violence, or fear of it, was, of itself, not necessarily the cause of alienation between the communities. Segregation, and hence physical division, in Derry city was the result of historical factors, and of the fact that when Catholics began to migrate to the suburbs from Inishowen they settled willy nilly in the Bogside area. Bishop Knox was also convinced that in general there was little contact between Catholics and Protestants. The communities tended to live separately, and even the clergy had little opportunity for meeting one another.[48] Long mutual estrangement in many areas of the county served to reinforce stereotypes, especially at times of heightened friction such as the Emmet rebellion of 1803, though it must be said that the county was relatively free from actual violence at that time.

It would be inaccurate to suggest that such hostility as did exist between Catholics and Protestants arose simply because of political considerations. Presbyterians and Catholics both had resentments against the established church, but this did not prevent displays of enmity towards each other,[49] and Methodists in the Dungiven areas in particular met with 'violent opposition from the Roman Catholic priests, who denounce them and execrate them without mercy'.[50] Independent observers were keen to suggest that Catholic peasants in the north of Ireland were generally less bigoted than their co-religionists in the rest of the country.[51] Not all observers were equally sanguine, and when John Slade, secretary of the Irish Society from 1789 to 1831, made his tour of the society's Londonderry holdings in 1802, he emphasized the 'duty and necessity of completely planting the Protestant religion in the north of Ireland'.[52]

Nonetheless, the question of political power was uppermost in both Catholic and Protestant thinking when either group was dealing with the

46 James S. Donnelly Jr, 'Pastorini and Captain Rock: millenarianism and sectarianism in the Rockite movement 1821–4', in Clark and Donnelly, *Irish peasants*, p. 104. 47 *Minutes of evidence* ... (1825), p. 222.   48 Ibid., p. 281.   49 Murphy, 'Parliamentary politics', pp 18–26.   50 William Shaw Mason, *A statistical account or parochial survey of Ireland*, 3 vols (Dublin, 1814–19), i, 333.   51 Wakefield, *Account of Ireland*, ii, 732. 52 John Slade, *Narrative of a journey to the north of Ireland in 1802* (London, 1803), p. 135.

other in the early years of the nineteenth century. Whatever Irish Catholics might feel about the need for further political gains, the view from Rome was very different. Writing to the Irish bishops in 1806, the Congregatio de Propaganda Fide warned that it might be best to shelve the idea of emancipation. Stressing the religious freedoms Catholics actually enjoyed, it argued that 'one violent step now could ruin all'.[53] From the following year Derry began to experience something of the O'Connellite agitations against the proposed veto over the appointment of Catholic bishops, and the campaign for Catholic emancipation, which undoubtedly contributed in large measure to the deterioration in relations between the communities.[54] The Vatican's sentiments were clearly in tune with Bishop O'Donnell's thinking as was to become clear in a celebrated dispute over agitation for Catholic political rights. In Derry city, this agitation was led by one of the most fractious Catholic priests in the diocese, Cornelius O'Mullan.

Conventionally, Ulster Catholics have been regarded as holding aloof from the political pretensions of the rest Catholic Ireland in the period under discussion.[55] At the same time the growing sectarian bitterness as witnessed by the yeomen disputes in 1811 and 1812[56] and the infamous Maghera riot of 1813, followed by rioting in Dungiven and Colraine in the following months, served not only to increase tensions but also to stir up enthusiasm for O'Connellite rhetorical excess.

Fr Cornelius O'Mullan the administrator of the Catholic chapel in Derry city, was in the forefront of political excitement in the county and was believed by the authorities to have extensive contacts with ribbon societies in mid and west Ulster.[57] O'Mullan had also been involved in attempts to set up a Catholic school in Derry against the expressed wish of Bishop O'Donnell, who preferred what one might call the system of 'integrated education' then operating in Derry.[58] O'Mullan was therefore at the centre of political and religious turmoil, which was to see him suspended from his priestly duties and imprisoned for a month, having been indicted for riot and assault.

A violent altercation occurred at the chapel in Derry on Thursday 4

53 DDA Troy papers AB/28/1, Propaganda to Troy, 9 Aug. 1806. **54** Dermot Murphy, *Derry, Donegal and modern Ulster, 1790–1921* (Derry, 1981), p. 41. **55** Kevin Whelan, 'The regional impact of Irish Catholicism 1700–1850', in W. J. Smith and K. Whelan (eds), *Common grounds: essays on the historical geography of Ireland* (Cork, 1988), p. 264. **56** *Londonderry Journal*, 17 Sept. 1811, 17 Nov. 1812 and 29 Sept. 1812. **57** This association continued long after O'Mullan had ceased to live in Derry. NAI SOC 1831/22, Revd G.V. Sampson to Dublin Castle, 13 Jan. 1817. Sampson enclosed testimony from a ribbon informant and added that the priest was 'a mischievous propagandist'. **58** The evidence for this emerged at O'Mullan's trial: *Londonderry Journal* 5 Feb. 1814. O'Mullan actually wrote to the Church of Ireland bishop, William Knox, asking for money for the school. Knox, on this occasion, refused to help.

November 1813, following a meeting concerned with the Derry representation to the Catholic board in Dublin. Among the resolutions passed on that
occasion was one to the effect that Catholics could not get justice from jury
trials, and another stated that Irish Catholics should seek the assistance of the
'Allied Powers' for the redress of their grievances.[59] O'Mullan in the course
of his speech cast aspersions on Bishop O'Donnell and referred to the Revd
Daniel Colgan as 'an Orange priest, the hireling of an Orange corporation'.[60]
By this time O'Mullan had quite a history of causing disturbances for the
ecclesiastical and civil authorities in Derry. With Sir George Hill, who
presided as chief magistrate at his trial, he had previously had a long 'paper
war'.[61] O'Mullan had also been responsible for unpleasantness at a siege
commemoration banquet by refusing to drink the loyal toast.[62] As a result of
the November riot, O'Donnell suspended the turbulent priest. O'Mullan's
supporters were determined to have their revenge and attacked the bishop in
the Long Tower chapel on 28 November. O'Donnell then, melodramatically,
claimed that O'Mullan's supporters were determined to murder him, and
asked the authorities for protection.[63]

Although O'Mullan was accused by Sir George Hill of having a violent
attitude both to Protestants and to Catholics who opposed him,[64] his defence
counsel, Nicholas O'Gorman,[65] was able to show that he had in fact lived on
good terms with his Protestant neighbours 'and all classes of his countrymen'
in Derry for upwards of nine years.[66] He was, however, found guilty of
causing disorder and there attached to him a reputation for divisiveness and
for having soured community relations in Derry. Despite the fact that he lost
the case, O'Gorman was carried in triumphal procession through Derry, and
this occasioned several violent incidents.[67] In this instance, the magistrates
could not prosecute the offenders against public order owing to the intimidation of witnesses. By this time the Catholics in Derry were deeply divided

---

59 *Dublin Evening Post*, 29 Jan. 1814.   **60** Ibid. Colgan as we have seen was the
bishop's nephew. This incident may well be the origin of the bishop's nickname 'Orange
Charlie': Colby, *Ordnance survey memoirs*, p. 70.   **61** *Dublin Evening Post*, 11 Jan. 1814.
62 Ibid., 5 Feb. 1814.   **63** NAI SOC 1537/35, George Hill to William Gregory, 4 Dec.
1813.   **64** John Hempton, *The history of Derry* (Londonderry, 1861), pp 141–2.
65 O'Gorman was one of O'Connell's chief lieutenants, and it is a mark of the close
relationship between O'Mullan and the Catholic board that O'Gorman was sent by the
board to defend him. Cf. Maurice R. O'Connell, *The correspondence of Daniel O'Connell*,
ii (Shannon, 1972), p. 33, n.2. O'Mullan went as a chaplain with the Irish expedition to
Venezuela in 1820. However, he soon quarrelled with its leader John Devereaux who,
upon O'Mullan's death in November 1821, wrote of him that he had 'a turbulent
restless disposition of mind that did not know well what to be at to gain some
distinction or notoriety in life …' Ibid., p. 339.   **66** *Dublin Evening Post*, 17 Feb. 1814.
67 PRONI Hill papers, D642/A/ 14/6, Hill to Peel, 14 Jan. 1814.

between what Hill described as 'the subjects of the Roman Catholic board [and] ... The Roman Catholics who resist their authority'.[68]

Hill was nevertheless determined to press his advantage, however slight, over Catholic political pretensions. He organized a meeting in Derry of 'freemen and freeholders' to discuss the agitated state of the county. The meeting addressed a memorial to the prince regent, calling for the abolition of the Catholic board. The memorial was signed by, among others, Bishop Charles O'Donnell.[69] The chief secretary, Robert Peel, was furious that the prince had been approached directly, since such royal interference was 'impossible except on advice from the Irish government'.[70]

It is tempting to see the O'Mullan fiasco as something of a watershed in Catholic agitation for political rights at this period. From 1815 until the O'Connellite movement took off in earnest in Derry in the episcopacy of Bishop James MacLaughlin, an ardent supporter of O'Connell,[71] Catholic energies were channeled into ribbonism. O'Donnell became increasingly disillusioned with public life and asked Rome for an assistant bishop to help him in the administration of diocesan affairs. He maintained, however, a great antipathy to lawlessness and gave information to the authorities which on at least one occasion led to the arrest of a prominent ribbonman, John Gaynor.[72]

In the decade before O'Donnell's death, Derry at times seemed gripped in a frenzy of inter-communal violence. Peel, writing to the prime minister, Lord Liverpool, adverted to the growing animosity between Protestants and Catholics in the north of Ireland as a whole, and spoke of a 'natural predilection for outrage and lawlessness which I believe nothing can control'.[73] The economic depression which afflicted Derry in the years 1815–17 was seen by some officials as a reason for the upsurge in violence in the county.[74] Increasingly, Protestant farmers and 'industrious labourers' were used to suppress Catholic trouble, at a time when disaffection had spread to Catholic soldiers stationed in Derry.[75] Many incidents were nakedly sectarian, and the concomitant violence often mindless. In March 1820 two Protestant brothers were attacked as they tended their fields near Limavady, one of whom was 'most inhumanly beaten until the assailants considered him dead'.[76] An Orangeman named Downie who, 'having rendered himself

68 NAI SOC 1565/56, Hill to Peel, 10 Jan. 1814. 69 *Dublin Evening Post*, 17 Feb. 1814. 70 PRONI Hill papers, D642/A/14/13, Peel to Hill, 21 Mar. 1814. 71 By 1821 of all the Ulster bishops only O'Donnell and Dr Patrick Curtis of Armagh opposed O'Connell. 72 NAI SOC 2360/1, Hill to Dublin Castle, 12 Jan. 1822. 73 BL Add. MS 38,195, Peel to Liverpool, 15 Oct. 1813, f. 9. 74 Thus for example, NAI SOC 1831/24, Derry Brigade Militia Major S. Carter to Colonel Carey, military secretary, Dublin Castle, 23 Jan. 1817 and again 28 Jan. 1817. 75 NAI SOC 1831/28, Revd GV Sampson to William Gregory, 5 Feb. 1817. 76 NAI SOC 2187/41, Revd E. Thackeray to George Hill, 12 Mar. 1820.

conspicuous' in a riot with Catholics disappeared and Catholics took revenge on his brother by destroying his potatoes, and when he bought a gun to protect himself, they 'beat and cut him dreadfully'.[77]

Full-scale riots were reported in a number of instances in the 1820s. The most serious of these was undoubtedly at Maghera on 12 June 1823 in which nine people lost their lives and between sixty and seventy were injured.[78] That Catholics were responsible for most of this violence is beyond question; the difficulty is in determining its cause. It is perhaps possible to trace its foundation to frustration at the lack of political progress and even on occasion to provocation. The Derry magistrates, however, writing of the Dungiven riot in August 1823 said that there had been no Orange parade, 'nor any manifestation of Protestant feeling' in that town for a decade.[79]

Hatred of Protestantism by Catholics cannot be ruled out as a simple cause: after all some of the shouts at the beginning of the Maghera riots were to the effect that 'now is the time to destroy all Protestants'. On the other hand, Major William Webb reported in August 1822 that even Presbyterians in Derry appeared, yet again, to be disaffected with the established church and had committed a number of outrages.[80] Earlier that year Sir George Hill had reported that there had been renewed and sustained efforts to unite Presbyterians and Catholics 'upon the former United Irish principle' but that these attempts were proving unsuccessful.[81] An important element in Catholic antipathy to Protestants was fear of the militia. Hill himself admitted that the Derry corps of five hundred was exclusively Protestant, although he assured the Dublin authorities that they had kept their promise to refrain from playing party tunes or wearing party emblems. A different account, however, of the Derry militia was given by the provost of Strabane, Sir George Burgoyne. He claimed that the militia had 'the reputation of party', and its use as an impartial enforcer of the law was therefore limited.[82]

By the time of O'Donnell's death in July 1823, Derry Catholics and Protestants were as divided as they had been at anytime in his episcopacy. The inter-communal riots at Maghera and Magherafelt in June that year were among the worst incidents of violence the county had seen since 1813 and arguably since 1798. For all that O'Donnell's funeral was quite an ecumenical affair. The clergy of the Church of Ireland, including the dean of Derry, were

---

77 NAI SOC 2520/47, Lt J. Marshall to Dublin Castle, 6 Aug. 1823.   **78** NAI SOC 2520/38, Revd James Knox and Ensign James Elliot to Dublin Castle, respectively 15 Jun. and 13 Jun. 1823. In a second letter the same day Elliot revealed that the Catholics started the riot and 'have of course suffered the most'.   **79** NAI SOC 2520/45, Derry magistrates to marquis of Wellesley, 15 Aug. 1823.   **80** NAI SOC 2360/26, Webb to Revd Andrew Hamilton.   **81** NAI SOC 2360/7 Hill to William Gregory, 27 Jan. 1822.   **82** NAI SOC 2360/28, Burgoyne to William Gregory, 6 May 1822.

there in force as were the 'dissenting ministers' of the neighbourhood. The mayor and corporation also took part, and the funeral knell was solemnly tolled from the Protestant cathedral for the whole morning of the funeral. Press reports were anxious to underline the fact that at the chapel 'the numerous Protestants who were present were treated with the most marked politeness, and accommodated with seats to the exclusion of the Roman Catholics'.[83]

Despite such good manners, the 'spirit of contention' which De Latocnaye had noticed on his visit to Derry so many years before, was still very much a reality.[84] The picture was, however, not entirely bleak. There was still considerable contact between Catholics and Protestants. Large numbers of children were educated together, although O'Donnell's death marked a point after which Catholics increasingly conducted their own exclusive schools.[85] In some parts of the county there was also quite a degree of intermarriage.[86]

One factor, however, which caused Catholic antipathies, at least towards the established Church, was the fact that Church of Ireland rectors were regularly called upon to functions as magistrates. Given that the forces they had at their disposal were often the local militia, who, as we have seen, too frequently had the reputation of being anti-Catholic, it became increasingly difficult in Catholic eyes to separate out the sacred duty of the Protestant ministers from their secular law-enforcing activities, tinged as these were with a certain prejudice against Catholics. At times, the pastors were seen merely as instruments of the Protestant state directed against Catholics, despite many examples of friendliness and generosity.[87]

From the Protestant viewpoint, 'the great influence the Roman Catholic clergy possess over the peasantry of Ireland'[88] long remained a matter of both admiration and consternation. There was a lingering fear that such influence might be turned from religious and moral suasion, to become active in the political sphere. This was the main factor governing Catholic-Protestant relations at that stage of the nineteenth century: the rise of Catholic political power. Protestant anxiety was well expressed by G.V. Sampson, himself a clergyman of the Church of Ireland and a magistrate, when he observed:

> If to the Catholic the power was for a day entrusted, that very day must fiat a sequence of calamity ... To the acts of political humiliation; and

83 *Londonderry Journal*, 27 July 1823 and *Strabane Morning Post*, 29 July 1823. 84 Chevalier De Latocnaye, *A Frenchman's walk through Ireland 1797–8* (Belfast, 1917), p. 202. 85 B. Bonner, *Derry: an outline history of the diocese* (Dublin, 1982) p. 258. 86 Ibid., p. 247. 87 One of the first people injured at the Maghera riot was the Church of Ireland curate John Collhurst who was deputizing for his absent rector, Revd James Knox, the local magistrate. NAI SOC 2520/37, Knox to Dublin Castle, 15 June 1823. 88 Graham, *Statistical account of Maghera*, p. 20.

under the bloody feet of contending chieftains would be trampled down, perhaps forever, all hope of popular privilege – all chance of social improvement.[89]

89 G.V. Sampson, *A memoir of the chart and survey of the county of Londonderry, Ireland* (London, 1814), p. 96. This contrasts with his pro-Catholic pamphlet published anonymously two decades earlier: *Remarks on the state of the Catholic question in Ireland . . .* (Belfast, 1793).

3

Nicholas Wiseman, ecclesiastical politics and Anglo-Irish relations in the mid-nineteenth century

English Catholicism in the middle decades of the nineteenth century was an extremely complex phenomenon. In the years after 1829 English Catholics were determined to take their rightful place in society. No longer could they be regarded as politically inferior to the Protestant fellow countrymen. Now at last they were in a position to lay to rest the age-old charge that adherence to papism was evidence of disloyalty to the crown. Into this ideal picture of the union between solid English virtues and the Roman obedience there intruded two factors designed to precipitate a shattering of the new-found confidence of the Catholic aristocracy and middle classes. The converts by their academic standing exposed the lack of real educational attainments on the part of the majority of hereditary Catholics.[1] They were regarded with suspicion by the old Catholics, and seemed to possess a 'cockiness' about their Catholicism which was anti-pathetical to the 'timid retirement of the hereditary Catholics'.[2] Their brand of Catholicism had none of the inhibitions of a bygone age. They were not afraid to make a scene or wash their religious laundry in public.

The rapid expansion of the Irish element in English Catholicism brought untold problems to a church striving to make its way in genteel Victorian society. The injection of membership from Ireland also brought opportunities. Now, for the first time since the seventeenth century, there was an occasion for a rapid expansion of English Catholicism. This required flexibility and a bold deployment of resources if the immigrant Irish were to remain within the church. The intriguing and perplexing element in all this, so far as the hereditary Catholics were concerned, was that as time went on the religious aims of the converts seemed to unite with the spiritual needs of the Irish poor.

The impact of Irish Catholicism on the English was enormous. The church's hold on the Irish population both fascinated and repelled English Protestants, and helped to contribute to anti-Catholicism in Britain as a

---

1 Wilfred Ward, *The life and times of Cardinal Wiseman*, 2 vols (London, 1897), ii, 224 where Ward draws attention to an article in *The Rambler*, November 1848 in which 'the educational shortcomings of the old Catholics were alluded to in plain language'.
2 Bernard Ward, *The sequel to Catholic emancipation, 1830–1850*, 2 vols (London, 1915), ii, 31.

whole. The pastoral problems of the Irish in urban centres in England demanded attention and resources which the emergent English church could ill afford. To say the least, the conditions of the Irish in Britain, in both pre- and post-famine days, were appalling. The squalor was overwhelming. If they had work at all, it was in the worst occupations, where they were overworked and poorly paid, many of them being carried off to an early grave. Denis Gwynn has noted that 'Our people through neglect, disorderly habits and most of all through drink were in a state of the deepest poverty and degra-dation.'[3] This of course did not account for all Irish immigrant experience, but certainly the great majority lived under very difficult conditions.

At a political level, Irish and English Catholics had different hopes and expectations. By the 1840s, when O'Connell's repeal movement was gaining ground, the 'hereditary' Catholics looked with alarm at their co-religionists on the neighbouring isle. They feared that in any adverse encounter with the British government Catholicism as a whole would suffer. This hostility to Irish Catholic political radicalism was shared also by the converts. Irish Catholicism, of course, was not an undifferentiated mass. There were clear political divisions within the church community. The leading lights of Irish Catholicism in the 1840s, archbishops William Crolly of Armagh and Daniel Murray of Dublin, were securely in the pro-British 'Castle Catholic' camp. Their religious and political objectives were firmly opposed by some of their episcopal brethren, led by that 'lion of the West', John MacHale, archbishop of Tuam.

In England, the man appointed to provide the leadership in the amalgam of competing political and religious ideologies that made up mid-nineteenth-century Catholicism was Nicholas Wiseman. The violent events surrounding the restoration of the hierarchy by Pius IX in 1850 came as a severe blow to those who believed that English Catholicism had come of age by the early decades of Victoria's reign. The vehement anti-Catholic bigotry displayed up and down the country, in response to the 'papal aggression', shocked the authorities in England and Rome. Most surprised of all was the newly appointed cardinal archbishop of Westminster. The 'aggression' was, ironi-cally, partly the result of Wiseman's own ill-considered remarks about 'ruling' parts of London and the southeast of England.[4] Queen Victoria interpreted Wiseman's words as 'a direct infringement of my prerogatives'.[5]

3 Denis Gwynn, 'The Irish immigration', in George A. Beck (ed.), *The English Catholics, 1850–1950* (London, 1956), pp 265–90, here p. 268.   4 *Out of the Flaminian Gate of Rome.* The infamous line read, 'at present and till such time as the Holy See shall think fit otherwise to provide, we govern the counties of Middlesex, Hertford, and Essex as ordinary thereof …': Ward, *Sequel*, i, 542.   5 Stanley Weintraub, *Victoria* (New York, 1987), p. 213.

Although Wiseman was clearly the dominant figure in the Catholic England of his day, opinion is divided as to his suitability for the task of governing the church in his adopted land. Born in Spain of Irish parents, his mother, after her husband's early death, took up temporary residence in Ireland, and it was in Waterford that Wiseman first learned English.[6] Although thoroughly English in sympathies and habits, Wiseman was, in some respects, an odd choice to head the church in England. His main qualification for the post was that he had been completely 'Romanized'. He had lived in Rome as a student and then as rector of the English College from 1818 until 1840. Perhaps more than any other individual Wiseman helped to inculcate an ultramontane spirit in the English scene.

John Bossy is convinced that the choice of Wiseman as a bishop and subsequently as a cardinal was 'a break in continuity', with what had previously obtained in the English church. In his view, Wiseman was not well attuned to the spirit and ethos that had marked English Catholicism in its struggle for survival from the reformation to emancipation. 'Wiseman', he writes, 'was of course not a man who had centuries of English Catholicism in his bones'.[7] This is perhaps to state the obvious. It is nevertheless indicative of a residual resentment at the prospect of individuals of foreign ancestry being given authority in the English Catholic community.[8] What is clear is that Wiseman distrusted the cisalpine tendencies of many of his predecessors and contempories. Equally, his wide learning and experience enabled him to appreciate the concerns of the church and the world beyond the narrow parameters of the Catholic community of nineteenth-century England. Edward Norman has observed that 'the details of Wiseman's early life indicate the extent to which he stood by background outside the old Catholic English world to which he was later called'.[9]

Even this is by no means certain. Wiseman as a political Tory was socially acceptable among the English Catholic aristocracy. His establishment tastes reflected their own, notwithstanding the rather complex nature of some of

6 Wiseman never considered himself anything other than an English Catholic. In his open letter to Lord Shrewsbury in 1841 he declared, 'Let us English Catholics mourn over our coldness in ... zeal. Let us English clergy lament our deficiencies ...' etc. Peadar MacSuibhne was quite wrong to assert that Wiseman might be claimed as the first Irish cardinal: *Paul Cullen and his contempories with their letters.* 5 vols (Naas, 1961–77), i, 161. It is a claim Wiseman would have refuted.   7 John Bossy, *The English Catholic community, 1581–1850* (London, 1975), p. 387.   8 Michael Trappes-Lomax would write to Bishop Amigo of Southwark in a dispute over Ireland in 1920 that Amigo's foreign extraction was 'an insult to English Catholics while that you should set yourself up as their representative or as a critic of their representatives is nothing short of an impertinence'. Cf. Michael Clifton, *Amigo: friend of the poor* (London, 1987), p. 81.   9 Edward Norman, *The English Catholic Church in the nineteenth century* (Oxford, 1984), p. 113.

his friendships with Old Catholic families. He could also appeal to the inflated sense of superiority which, as a nation, the English at times displayed. In a widely reported sermon at St John's church in Salford in 1850 Wiseman could say, 'there is no doubt, my brethren, that never in the history of nations, was any people advanced beyond ours at the present time, in all that constitutes social and intellectual greatness'.[10] Such sentiments were not calculated to endear him to the Irish. There is, in fact, evidence to suggest that Wiseman was particularly distrusted by the Irish bishops.[11] But what of Wiseman himself: did his cast of mind and sympathies lead him to certain anti-Irish sentiments in the conduct of the affairs of the English church?

Superficially, the evidence might lead one to conclude that Wiseman was as sympathetic to the Irish as he could possibly be. He made two visits to Ireland. In 1841 he preached at the opening of St Andrew's church in Dublin and he also visited Maynooth. There he met John William Russell. The famous Dr Russell was to be an important friend and collaborator of Wiseman for the rest of his life. At one point in their friendship Wiseman appealed to Russell for help in finding Irish priests for the Westminster diocese: 'I am in great want of 3 or 4 good priests. Have you any of that character not immediately wanted by their bishop, who could be even lent for two or three years, if not given? I will take your word for their suitableness.'[12] Wiseman's second visit to Ireland in August and September 1858 was marked by a triumphal progress through the country. The visit was accompanied by a generous and spontaneous outpouring of religious fervour and emotion at the presence on Irish soil of a cardinal of the Roman Church.

It is clear that from some of the Irish Wiseman evoked a great deal of affection and respect. This is certainly true in the case of the 'Liberator', Daniel O'Connell. We have the testimony of Canon Bernard Smith that when O'Connell visited Oscott College, the centre of Wiseman's operations in the early 1840s, it brought out the Irish side of the future cardinal's character, 'as he and O'Connell walked about the college arm-in-arm, telling good stories to one another and laughing heartily'.[13] This would seem to indicate an affection for the Irish on Wiseman's part that was also reciprocated. The picture is, however, complicated by contrary indications. Paul Cullen, despite the warm reception he accorded Wiseman on his 1858 tour, disliked and distrusted him.[14] One source of Cullen's *animus* was Wiseman's

---

10 Ibid.   11 This in part, as we shall see, was as a result of his association with the earl of Shrewsbury who was regarded as 'the enemy of Irish Catholics': Ward, *Sequel*, ii, 14.   12 AAW Wiseman papers, Wiseman to Russell, 19 Mar. 1858.   13 Ward, *Sequel*, i, 350.   14 Cullen regarded Wiseman as being 'very hostile to Irishmen'. AICR, Kirby papers, Cullen to Tobias Kirby, 25 Aug. 1842. Ambrose Macaulay, *Dr Russell of Maynooth* (London, 1983), p. 295, rejects the charge.

conduct concerning the Catholic university in Dublin. Newman had unadvisedly proposed Wiseman as chancellor, and this was a snub to him that was not lost on Cullen, or on the other Irish bishops. This, though, tells us more about Newman's lack of sensitivity to the Irish situation than about Wiseman's. The *débâcle* surrounding Newman's bishopric was an instance which demonstrated the archbishop of Westminster's inability to appreciate the complexities of Irish ecclesiastical politics.[15]

Mention has been made of Wiseman's friendship with Russell. This, however, can scarcely be taken as indicative of a temperamental attachment to the Irish. In many respects Russell was a most unrepresentative Irish priest, rather after the manner of Troy, Murray and Crolly, than MacHale or indeed Cullen. Even Russell's sympathetic biographer indicates Russell's extensive friendship with the Anglo-Irish upper classes and comments that this was 'unusual in nineteenth-century Ireland'.[16] After his visit of 1858 Wiseman continued to maintain views on Ireland and the Irish which strike the modern reader as distinctly odd. In a lecture about his tour to Ireland, delivered in London before an enthusiastic audience in November 1858, Wiseman gave his assessment of the post-famine state of the country. He was well aware of the history of British injustice in Ireland. For hundreds of years, he declared, the country had been subjected to 'every form of oppression and wretchedness', but now all that had passed.[17] He saw the famine in the contorted commonplace and English terms of the nineteenth-century mind, as a 'visitation of God'. In the face of this 'visitation of mercy and justice' the Irish 'murmured not'. Wiseman commends them for their forbearance. Then surprisingly he goes on to outline what he saw as the benefit of the famine. This was: emigration. Before the great hunger, the people were too stubbornly attached to the land, 'there was a want of energy and enterprise'. Instead there was 'that clinging to the soil, to the love of their afflictions ... which prevented ... many who could not find employment at home from finding it elsewhere'.[18] Not only did the famine produce a diversification in agriculture but it reduced the population, in the cardinal's view, to a 'just proportion'. Wiseman's analysis has a peculiarly Malthusian ring and can scarcely have been guaranteed to enhance his reputation with his Irish religious contemporaries. It is, however, in the more directly political field that Wiseman's assessment of the role of Irish Catholicism and its impact on England is worked out. It is to this aspect of his thought that we must now turn.

15 Newman was convinced that it was Cullen who had prevented him from being made a bishop. Henry Tristram, *John Henry Newman: autobiographical writings* (London, 1956), p. 319.   **16** Macaulay, *Russell*, p. 295.   **17** N.P.S. Wiseman, *Impressions of a recent visit to Ireland* (London, 1859), p. 8.   **18** Ibid., p. 9.

In part, the fragmentation of religious unity between Catholics in England and Ireland can be explained by the difference in attitude to the Oxford Movement. Wiseman and his circle had hoped to secure O'Connell's support for the converts. Conversely O'Connell's political principles were unacceptable to many of the 'high and dry' Tories among the Oxford men. E.S. Purcell in his biography of Ambrose Phillips de Lisle comments that 'Irishmen in England under O'Connell's sway, bishops and priests alike, were as loud-tongued as Protestants and Dissenters in denouncing and ridiculing the Oxford Movement'.[19]All this placed Wiseman in an invidious position. Not only were English Catholics opposed to the converts on religious grounds, but Irish Catholics distrusted them on political grounds. There were exceptions to this in Ireland. Churchmen such as Murray and Russell, who favoured the Union and opposed O'Connell, were well disposed to the converts. Indeed, Newman records of Dr Russell that he 'had, perhaps, more to do with my conversion than anyone else'.[20]

Wiseman, by the mid-1840s, had long been associated with O'Connell. They had collaborated in the founding of the *Dublin Review* in the late 1830s. The future cardinal had made it clear, however, that the *Review* was intended as a forum for sound Catholic teaching and not as a platform for O'Connell's political opinions. 'I have avoided in any way', he wrote to Frederick Lucas, 'taking part in the political questions of the day, especially such as divide Catholics, to the great detriment of a better cause.'[21] In saying this Wiseman was somewhat disingenuous. In fact he held strong political views and was not averse to taking sides in political contests. He disliked the notion of repeal of the union between Britain and Ireland. 'I can see', he wrote, 'no Catholicity in the repeal movement; I fear it is thoroughly of this world ...'[22] He was more concerned to avoid public division in the emerging Catholic body than he was with the intrinsic justice of righting Irish grievances. This is why the 'Irish party' in London so distrusted him when he moved there as coadjutor to the vicar apostolic.[23] They also feared that he might try to have some direct influence in Irish affairs. In Catholic circles he publicly rejected such a suggestion. There is, however, some evidence from his letters that he was quite prepared to intervene when necessary in party political matters.

His Anglo-Irish Catholic correspondent, Lady Bellew, put it to him that he had political ambitions for his associates. 'Is it true', she wrote, 'that you are anxious to get Mr Bowyer into Parliament and that he has an idea of

19 E.S. Purcell, *Life and letters of Ambrose Phillips de Lisle*, 2 vols (London, 1900), i, 293.   20 J.H. Newman, *Apologia pro vita sua* (revised edition, London, 1865), p. 194. 21 Ward, *Sequel*, ii, 44.   22 Ward, *Wiseman*, i, 419.   23 Richard J. Schiefen, *Nicholas Wiseman and the transformation of English Catholicism* (Shepherdstown, PA, 1984), p. 163.

Dundalk? If so, I think he would easily get in – if you take him in hand in any way.'[24] It was this sort of intrigue on Wiseman's part that so infuriated Irish churchmen in their dealing with English Catholics in general. Wiseman's correspondence with Russell of Maynooth also reveals very wide political interests. In 1841 he assured Russell that the 'real' Oxford men had resolved to stop attacking O'Connell, an expedient that he obviously favoured. Even here, however, Wiseman's motives were mixed. Quite a number of the students at Oscott College in Birmingham were Irish, and Wiseman feared that too much public criticism of O'Connell by the Oxford converts, and the circle associated with Wiseman personally, would have an adverse effect on the numbers of Irish parents sending their sons for schooling to the college. Indeed in a letter to the Earl of Shrewsbury he makes this point quite explicitly.

> [I]f O'Connell were to put a ban upon the College it would be ruined. We are therefore obliged to *manager* so as not to make him our enemy. Dr Walsh feels this most sensibly, and is perhaps more anxious than myself that we should stay clear of all political partisanship. And this will perhaps best explain much of my mode of proceeding.[25]

Against the charge that he favoured Tory candidates in Ireland Wiseman wrote an impassioned letter to Russell in May 1859:

> I never sent Mr Middleton to Drogheda. I did not see him before he went. I never wrote to him – I did not answer the letter he sent me. I never recommended, encouraged or spoke in his favour. In a word I had no more to do with him than any Orange candidate.

All the indications are that Wiseman was in fact involved in considerable political activity. This notwithstanding, he protested to Shrewsbury that he had no intention to 'burn my fingers' with Irish affairs.[26]

In working to ensure that Catholicism was placed on a sure footing, it was inevitable that Wiseman would seek the advice and assistance of prominent lay Catholics. One of his difficulties was that these were divided among themselves, as we would expect, in their political aspirations. It was therefore unavoidable that Wiseman would be drawn into these divisions. Too often the public perception was that he sided with the more conservative element,

---

24 AAW Wiseman papers W3/3 Bellew to Wiseman, Holy Thursday 1851. Sir George Bowyer, a Catholic convert, was Liberal MP for Dundalk 1852–68 and for Wexford 1874–80. 25 UCA Wiseman papers 856, Wiseman to Shrewsbury, 12 Sept 1842. 26 Ibid. 906, Wiseman to Shrewsbury, 2 Nov. 1847.

which tended to be hostile to Ireland, and thus Wiseman himself earned a reputation of being opposed to the Irish.

We have already seen something of the close personal friendship between Wiseman and O'Connell. In many respects O'Connell's leadership enabled successful political agitation to occur in circumstances that otherwise would probably have led to violence. Occasionally, of course, O'Connell's frustration at the lack of political progress led to ill-tempered outbursts in which he flirted with the possibility of violence in order to achieve his main political aim, repeal of the Union. In his famous 'Mallow defiance', for example, he declared: 'I think I perceive a fixed disposition on the part of some of our Saxon traducers to put us to the test. Gentlemen, you may soon have the alternative to live as slaves or die as freemen.'[27] Despite what Wiseman regarded as his rebarbative political views, O'Connell's influence remained important for the stability of the English Catholic community. At the same time he made his opposition to O'Connell's political ambitions all too clear. In a letter to the earl of Shrewsbury he claimed that he had outdone that noble lord in his opposition to the repeal movement. 'Repeal, universal suffrage, democracy etc., I have all along hated and detested them and do so as yet.'[28] Although, as we have seen, he resisted any attempt to introduce O'Connellite politics in the *Dublin Review*, this was not always possible to achieve. In 1844 we find him writing to Shrewsbury about an article in the review which had appeared in support of O'Connell.

> Your Lordship is of course aware that the article on O'Connell in the last review is of Irish authorship – the production of a very enthusiastic admirer of O'Connell's thought, though he does not go to all his lengths. In the state in which the *Review* was at that moment, we could not have well prevented the expression of such feelings.[29]

Here Wiseman indicates the expediency of keeping the good will of O'Connell's party to ensure the success of English Catholic interests.

For their part, O'Connell and Shrewsbury had long been at loggerheads in their respective political opinions. Although Shrewsbury acknowledged the great debt English Catholicism owed to O'Connell arising from emancipation, he was nevertheless vehemently opposed to O'Connell's political campaign of the 1830s and 1840s. Shrewsbury's supercilious public letter of 1841, *On the present posture of affairs*, accused O'Connell's methods of being anti-religious. He argued that while it was true to some extent that Irish Catholics were persecuted, nonetheless, 'we have often seen a little

27 Denis Gwynn, *Daniel O'Connell* (Cork, 1947), p. 232.   28 UCA Wiseman papers 856, Wiseman to Shrewsbury, feast of St Stanislaus 1842.   29 Ibid., 853 Sept. 1844.

opposition, even a little persecution, become highly advantageous to those who are the objects of it'.[30] Shrewsbury also rejected what he called the 'principles of equality' since once such notions take hold, 'the crown rolls in the dust ... (and) the mitre is trodden under foot'.[31]

O'Connell in responding to Shrewsbury, accused him of trying to encourage English Catholics to abandon the Whigs in favour of the Tories. Furthermore, in O'Connell's view history showed that the social and political programme of English Catholics as a whole was fundamentally anti-Irish. 'You, my lord', he wrote, 'know as well as I do, that the English Catholics have in their day of power been as oppressive and as contemptuous of the Irish as the English Protestants have been since.' Some English Catholics still had 'as bitter a hostility as ever to the Irish'.[32] One great bone of contention between both men was the involvement of priests in politics, a subject with which Wiseman was also concerned. O'Connell castigated Shrewsbury's position on the matter. There were no such complaints, he argued, when Irish priests were prominent in agitating for Catholic emancipation, a measure which benefited English Catholics: 'The Irish priesthood was then struggling to free you from political degradation.' Shrewsbury had then praised them for their efforts, but now he vilified them because they were struggling for the good of Ireland.

Another of Shrewsbury's adversaries on Irish matters was Frederick Lucas, the prominent Catholic journalist, and subsequently MP for Kilkenny. Indeed, up to the time of his death in 1853 Lucas was something of a gadfly in English Catholic circles. Having been initially against repeal he became an enthusiastic convert to the cause, declaring that the English government of Ireland was illegal. As the 1840s progressed, he became a very vocal critic in his opposition to British government policy in Ireland. Nor did he reserve his vituperation for government alone. Lucas severely criticized English Catholics for their lack of understanding of the Irish situation, and for, as he saw it, selling out the interests of religion for social and political gain. He famously attacked Shrewsbury in 1842 because Shrewsbury had set up a rival newspaper to *The Tablet*, which occasioned Wiseman to withdraw his support of Lucas's paper. Lucas was a relentless campaigner for justice and spared no

---

30 *A second letter to Ambrose Phillips de Lisle from the earl of Shrewsbury on the present posture of affairs* (London, 1841), p. 22. 31 Wiseman in an open letter to Shrewsbury touched on a similar theme when he mentioned the coolness and distance between the poor and the aristocracy, 'which was unknown in Catholic times – [but] which the modern frenzies of Chartism and Socialism are doing their utmost to arouse into hatred and enmity': N.P.S. Wiseman, *A letter on Catholic unity addressed to the Rt Hon. the Earl of Shrewsbury* (London, 1841), p. 7. 32 Daniel O'Connell, *Observations on the corn laws* (Dublin, 1842), p. 47.

one in his protests on behalf of the oppressed. In a typical piece of invective he once declared

> The English of the upper and middle classes are Pharisees to the very marrow of their bones. With full bellies, roofs wind and water tight, warm hearts, soft beds and a balance with the bankers, enough (as they think) to ensure them against Providence itself, they sit arrogantly on the cries of the starving, naked, broken-hearted men.[33]

Such hyperbole made enemies for Lucas in Britain and Ireland among Catholics and Protestants alike. Neither Shrewsbury nor Wiseman had much respect for Lucas or his paper. So great did Wiseman's hostility become that he had a notice printed in the *Roman Gazette*, publicly disavowing his connection with Lucas's paper.[34] By July 1849 Wiseman could tell Shrewsbury, 'I am sure of this: that I have so clearly and to no small cost separated myself from *The Tablet* by public avowals that nobody can or does consider me of the same views, nor as a favourite with it.' In a somewhat vindictive mood Wiseman rather hoped that Lucas' moving the newspaper to Dublin that year would be his undoing. He argued, revealingly, that while the Irish were quite happy to have an Englishman in England fighting their cause, they would react unfavourably to Lucas attempting the same thing in Ireland. '[T]hey will not feel the necessity of a stranger coming to their help in their own country, where they know themselves to be quite able to help themselves.'[35]

From the other side of the political spectrum Wiseman took much comfort from his friendship with another of Shrewsbury's associates Ambrose Phillips de Lisle. De Lisle had converted to Catholicism while an undergraduate at Cambridge. Like many of his generation and class he saw the role of the church in Ireland as an agent of law and order, and he became increasingly alarmed by O'Connell's activities. In March 1842 he had written to Shrewsbury that O'Connell's 'mission for good' was at an end; 'the most we can hope for is to counteract and nullify his evil machinations'.[36] De Lisle's political outlook was quintessentially conservative to the extent that in 1869 he would oppose Gladstone's policy of disestablishment of the Church of Ireland. He had also raised with Shrewsbury the possibility of founding a Catholic political party or at least a union of Catholic and Tory interest. In

---

33 Edward Lucas, *The life of Frederick Lucas MP*, 2 vols (London, 1886), i, 292.
34 The announcement was placed in the *Gazette* by Cardinal Bofindi. The choice of Rome for this disavowal was in the hopes of undermining Lucas's creditability with the Roman authorities. See UCA Wiseman papers 495, Wiseman to Shrewsbury.   35 Ibid., 954a, 21 July 1849.   36 Purcell, *de Lisle*, i, 293.

the early 1840s he recognized the overwhelming preponderance of O'Connell's influence: 'if we could once gain O'Connell then all would be well ... That he is in the main truly zealous for the Catholic cause I believe, but his mind is quite poisoned by the leaven of Whig principles, which he imbibed in early life.'[37] At the same time he encouraged Shrewsbury to denounce O'Connell, as this found support among the Oxford men. Further, he regarded the repeal agitation as not only 'anti-papal' but 'anti-Christian'. 'Its object is to divide..., to *atheize* (if I may use such a word) the State, not to guarantee the independence of the Church, ... it is an attempt to act out on a great scale the impious theory of Lamennais'.[38]

This, then, was the background to Wiseman's operations as a bishop. While personally friendly with members of all parties, he allowed his political and religious policies to be influenced by those on the right of English society. That this should be so is hardly surprising. What is interesting is that, despite his clear alignments, he liked to give the impression that he was politically neutral. It could be argued that such a course was necessitated by his friend-ships with men like Shrewsbury and de Lisle, who were after all great benefactors of the church in their day. Equally one might suggest that Wiseman was handicapped by an obsessive need to make the church a respectable institution in English society. Before the restoration of the hierarchy, and to some extent even after the events of 1850, Wiseman cherished an ambition that the Catholic Church might bring substantial influence to bear on the political and social life of Britain. This too was a factor in determining his conduct of ecclesiastical affairs.

There are two incidents of major importance which help to shed light on Wiseman's political and religious policies and it is worth examining them in some detail. The earl of Shrewsbury had a much publicized dispute with Dr John MacHale, the archbishop of Tuam, concerning clerically-inspired violence. The traditional view is that Wiseman held aloof from the contest. But is that really the case? Wiseman's part in the events surrounding the attempt to establish diplomatic relations between the United Kingdom and the Papal States presents several curiosities which help to substantiate the view that he was unsympathetic to Irish susceptibilities. It is to these events that we must now turn our attention.

It had long been a charge against the Irish Catholic clergy that they inter-fered too much in politics. By the mid-1840s, with the famine and growing restlessness in Ireland, political agitation became increasingly violent, culmi-nating in the futile rebellion of 1848. One of the problems English Catholics faced was to convince their fellow countrymen that Catholicism *per se* was not

37 Ibid., ii, 304.   38 Ibid., 327.

inimical to law and order in Ireland. This is the basic point put to Archbishop
MacHale by, another of Wiseman's associates, the earl of Arundel and Surrey
in an exchange of letters which appeared in the pages of the *Morning
Chronicle*. The suggestion was that priests denounced landlords from the altar
and these denunciations so inflamed ordinary Irish Catholics that the
landlords thus vilified, were subsequently murdered. 'These', wrote Arundel,
'are the melancholy accusations to which I am unable to reply.'[39] In his
response MacHale rightly pointed out that it was the clergy who held Irish
society together at a time of social disintegration. This fact was at least
implicitly recognized by some members of Wiseman's circle. Thus Aubrey de
Vere wrote to de Lisle:

> [I]n Ireland, the Catholic Church is the only power capable of resisting
> Revolutionary ideas: yet hostility to the cause of the Catholic religion
> on the part of the Government would eventually render it impossible
> for the Catholic party to aid, as they would wish to aid, the party of
> order.[40]

In the autumn of 1847 Major Denis Mahon, an evicting landlord of
Strokestown, Co. Roscommon, was shot dead. Lord John Russell, the prime
minister, wrote an 'open letter' to the Irish clergy criticizing them for inciting
people to violence. Archbishop MacHale replied to Russell in vigorous terms
rebutting the accusation. Lord Farnham, an Irish Protestant, spoke in the
house of lords in early December and accused the parish priest of
Strokestown, Michael McDermott, of having instigated Mahon's murder.
The earl of Shrewsbury, in a fit of pique, wrote to Dr George Browne, the
bishop of Elphin and McDermott's hapless episcopal superior, demanding an
investigation into the allegations. The bishop began an inquiry but before the
results were made known Shrewsbury launched a public attack on the Irish
hierarchy. Moreover, he criticized MacHale's letter to Russell saying that it
was 'unjustly accusatory of the government, imputing blame when praise was
due, and yet stronger still, apologetic for crime.'[41] To add insult to injury he
referred to the famine in words which implied that its severity and length was
a judgment of God on the Irish for their ingratitude for all that had been done
for them. It is perhaps worth giving at some length the details of his diatribe.

> If that effort [on the part of the government to relieve the famine] were
> not altogether successful, if it fell short of the necessitation of the case,
> the defect at least was not in the intention, but may, with far more

39 Ward, *Sequel*, ii, 136.   40 Purcell, *de Lisle*, ii, 130–1.   41 Ward, *Sequel*, ii, 141–2.

justice and propriety, I venture to submit, be imputed to the unerring though inscrutable designs of God who so blurred the eyes of our rulers that *His* visitation might not be averted by any human ingenuity; and I would even suggest it as a subject for reflection whether that visitation were not aggravated ... because my Lord, sufficient expression of gratitude has been withheld from the Government and the people of England, for the generous sacrifices which in their charity, as in their duty, they were pleased to make last year ...[42]

MacHale in a spirited reply suggested that Shrewsbury had written his letter at the behest of the government. He was also of the opinion that his noble opponent was more interested in the 'sacred rights of property', than in the starving mass of Irish peasants, which continued to suffer at the hands of unscrupulous landlords. And while concerned to deny the charge of incitement to violence against the landlords, MacHale made it clear that if more help were not forthcoming from the government to ameliorate the effects of starvation, then 'the preachings of a St Paul could not persuade thousands to lie down and die'.[43] In the same letter, in a blistering attack upon Shrewsbury's integrity, MacHale remarked, 'the reader has no doubt already learned to appreciate the value of your hypocritical pity' for the conditions of the Irish poor.[44]

One must guard against the temptation to view the conflict involving MacHale, Arundel and Shrewsbury as simply occasioned by McMahon's death. There was throughout the period of the 1840s and 1850s growing resentment of the radical wing of Irish Catholicism on the part of the English Catholic aristocracy. The MacHale and Cullen faction, odd bedfellows in this regard, were seen as the 'enemies' of English Catholic values. According to Wiseman, it was the MacHale party which gave the impression at Rome of England 'as a tyrant, and [they themselves] as the great ... supporters of religion in England'. Rather ominously in the view of the date when this letter was written to Shrewsbury (November 1847), Wiseman adds: 'I should not, of course, like what I have written to get out, but it may guide your lordship in anything you have to write.'[45]

Shrewsbury in replying to MacHale in January 1848 accused him of direct interference in political activity, in a manner which was incompatible with his office as a bishop. He emphasized the fact that MacHale and his supporters had done much damage to the cause of Catholicism in England and condescendingly added,

42 Ibid., p. 143 (italics in original). 43 Bernard O'Reilly, *Life of John MacHale, archbishop of Tuam*, 2 vols (New York and Cincinnati, 1890), ii, 77. 44 Ibid., p. 80. 45 UCA, Wiseman papers, 906.

Had you received my letter according to the design with which it was written, you [would] have gone far to redeem the character of the Irish Church in the opinion of the English people; but you have chosen otherwise and have only made bad worse.[46]

Inevitably Frederick Lucas was also drawn into this controversy. In an editorial in *The Tablet* on New Year's Day 1848 he remarked that

The stories of priestly instigation to murders are a collection of the grossest, foulest and most unfounded falsehoods, manufactured on system and poured like leprous distilment into the ears of dozing John Bull, for a purpose as wicked as that of the adulterous beast, from whose crimes this illustration is taken.[47]

Lucas issued a barrage of complaints against Shrewsbury's attitude towards MacHale and the Irish clergy. By this time the Catholic community as a whole in England was in a state of ferment. A conference of priests at Newcastle-upon-Tyne resolved that it deeply regretted that the earl of Shrewsbury

should have joined the enemies of the Catholic faith, in preferring charges, so monstrous and so utterly groundless, against the Catholic clergy of Ireland – more especially in the instance of the Very Rev. Mr McDermott – and is astonished, that his lordship should have so outstepped his province as to become the spiritual censor and adviser of his Grace the Archbishop of Tuam.[48]

Although Wiseman made no public pronouncements about this particular incident he kept up his frequent correspondence with Shrewsbury during the altercation. He informed the earl that he had arranged for him to see Monsignor Bedini in London. Archbishop Bedini, then on his way to Rome, having been the papal nuncio in Brazil, had the ear of several important officials at the papal court, and in addition was a 'great friend of Cardinal Alteiris'. 'I told him', Wiseman remarked, 'your lordship would probably wish to speak to him on Ireland, and he already in two days knew all about the MacHale business.'[49] To be fair to Wiseman he made it clear that he was not going to involve himself directly in the MacHale–Shrewsbury dispute. He yet again declared that he had no intention of getting mixed up with Irish politics

46 *Reply to Archbishop MacHale's letter to the earl of Shrewsbury* (London, 1848), p. 3. This printed letter was not in fact sold on the open market 'in consideration of the excited state of public affairs in Ireland'.   47 *The Tablet*, 1 Jan. 1848.   48 *The Tablet*, 8 Jan. 1848.   49 UCA Wiseman papers 912, Wiseman to Shrewsbury, 2 Feb. 1848.

and was therefore grateful to Arundel and Shrewsbury for not having consulted him before they wrote their respective letters.[50] At the same time he listened to the invective that came from Shrewsbury's pen against all who opposed him. Lucas was 'really just what Lord Clarendon described MacHale, an *unredeemable ruffian*'. Like Wiseman, Shrewsbury consistently condemned *The Tablet* which 'published those silly and absurd resolutions of the Irish clergy – those unmeaning protests of some few of the English clergy against my letters'.[51]

Given the public nature and the evident bitterness on both sides of this particular dispute, it is hardly surprising that sooner or later Rome should become involved. A letter was sent from Propaganda to Archbishop Daniel Murray of Dublin asking for information about Lord Shrewsbury's allegations. The letter was 'leaked' and appeared in the Dublin press, causing a sensation of hostility at what was seen as English Catholic interference in Irish ecclesiastical and political affairs. Already in the previous February, Cullen, then rector of the Irish College in Rome and agent for the Irish bishops in their dealings with the papal authorities, informed MacHale that the Catholic primate, William Crolly, had written to Rome concerning the dispute. Crolly had taken the attitude that the charges of the clergy inciting murder were untrue. At the same time he observed that the other accusations, of the use of churches for political meetings, and the harangues delivered by priests against individuals were '*nimis verae*' (that is, only too true). Cullen warned MacHale that it was presumed that Murray would write in a similar vein and that MacHale should do all in his power to prevent this. 'But it would not be right', he added, 'to prevent priests from advocating the rights of the poor, and pointing out to the rich the duties of their station.'[52]

Wiseman's determination not to enter into the details of this particular dispute was more than simply a desire to steer clear of Irish politics. He had almost simultaneously been involved in the delicate process of trying to negotiate the possibility of diplomatic relations between Britain and the Holy See. It was this fact more than anything else that made Wiseman suspect in the eyes of the Irish hierarchy and which caused him to tread softly on the ground of the famine dispute.

In July 1847 Wiseman arrived in Rome with a brief from the vicars apostolic to plead for the restoration of the Catholic hierarchy in England and Wales. Pope Pius IX discussed his own political difficulties with Wiseman, particularly the presence of Austrian troops in the Papal States. He sent Wiseman back to England with the request to inquire as to the possibility of establishing diplomatic relations between London and Rome. The pope

50 Ibid., 918, 18 Mar. 1848. **51** Ibid., 915, 11 Mar. 1848. **52** Bernard O'Reilly, *MacHale*, ii, 114.

hoped that such relations would strengthen his hand in trying to secure the withdrawal of Austria from his domains.

When Wiseman arrived in London on 11 September, he went straight to the foreign office, where he explained the pope's predicament. He then set about producing a long memorandum for Lord Palmerston, the foreign secretary. The government had, in fact, already decided to send Lord Minto on a mission to Italy, as ambassador at large to the various governments there. The purpose of Minto's mission was to consolidate Britain's influence in the Italian peninsula. As a result of Wiseman's discussions it was decided to add the Papal States to Minto's itinerary, with the instruction to discuss with the pope the details of a possible exchange of ambassadors. Wiseman relished the turn of events. He wrote to Shrewsbury, '[Lord Palmerston] sent for me the other day, and told me that [my] letter entirely guided the government in sending Lord Minto to Rome; and that I might take to myself the entire credit of all that her Majesty's government had done.'[53] Minto's mission had to take account of the realities of the relations which then obtained between England and the Papal States. In his letter of appointment Palmerston advised Minto that

> Her Majesty cannot properly be advised to accredit you in any official capacity to the Court of Rome. At Rome therefore you will not be Minister Plenipotentiary, but rather as a member of H. M. Government fully-informed of the views and sentiments and opinions of that Government and entirely possessing the confidence of you sovereign and of your colleagues.[54]

Later Minto was told that he was the 'authentic organ of the British government at Rome'.[55] Events in Italy had moved very quickly, and the Austrians agreed in December 1847 to withdraw from Ferrara, and to abide by the protocols of the Congress of Vienna. The immediate assistance of Britain was no longer necessary, and consequently the need for diplomatic relations less urgent. Nonetheless, the London government had its own reasons for seeking closer co-operation with the papal court: Ireland.

All parties to the issue of diplomatic links between the United Kingdom and the Papal States were well aware of the repercussions such relations would have in Ireland. Wiseman had emphasized with Palmerston that this was indeed an important aspect of the case. The pope had, for example, issued, on 23 October 1847, a rescript against an important aspect of the government's Irish policy, the queen's colleges. In conversation with Lord

53 UCA Wiseman papers 506, Wiseman to Shrewsbury, undated but probably October 1847. 54 PRO FO 44, 29. 55 Ibid., 44, 30.

Greville, Wiseman had stressed that the condemnation of the queen's colleges by Pius IX had been the result of there being no British ambassador in Rome to put the government's view on the matter. 'Irish ecclesiastical affairs are managed by MacHale through Franzoni, Head of Propaganda, who has the Pope's ear.' Wiseman furthered advised that Minto should communicate with Monsignor Ventura, 'who is deeply interested in Irish affairs, and anxious for [a] British connexion'.[56] Meanwhile, in several dispatches from Rome Minto recorded his dealing with the pope on Irish affairs. Initially at least he was inclined to be cautious. He wrote to Palmerston, 'whatever the Irish clergy's political activity I cannot honestly advise his Holiness to interfere by any act of his authority'. The reason he gives for this is oddly that 'the Irish priesthood affected a good deal of independence and a somewhat limited allegiance to the Holy See'.[57] This did not prevent Minto making numerous accusations about the extent of clerical involvement in political violence, as his foreign office dispatches show. When the pope wanted to know the extent of priestly violence, Minto was, to begin with, somewhat coy, and in his first exchange was content to observe that 'the practice is unfortunately too extremely prominent to admit of any attempt to enumerate the cases of daily occurrence'.[58] He subsequently gave quite extensive details from information supplied by Lord Clarendon, the lord lieutenant of Ireland, and this intelligence made a great impact on the Holy See.

A rearguard action was now fought in Rome to counter any influence that Minto might exercise on Irish affairs. Cullen, writing to MacHale, reported that Minto had only limited success with Pius. He was, however, of the opinion that if English law was modified then a permanent British representative could be expected at Rome and this would have disastrous consequences for Irish affairs.[59] Subsequently Cullen warned MacHale against 'English lies and English interference'. Meanwhile Minto was finding it difficult to make headway in getting the pope to issue a specific condemnation of individual priests for their part in violent activity. This was despite 'our British friends and the ambassador [Minto] ... working heaven and earth against us: calumnies are not spared'.[60] Nonetheless the pope did issue a general injunction to the Irish bishops in March 1848 urging peace in Ireland,

---

56 Lytton Strachey and Roger Fulford (eds), *The Greville memoirs, 1814–1860*, 5 vols (London, 1938), v, 470. The entry is dated 7 Dec. 1847. On 15 December, Greville records that he called on Russell (the prime minister and Minto's father-in-law) and told him what Wiseman had said. Russell informed Gerville that he had ordered a parliamentary bill to be drawn up to facilitate the exchange of ambassadors. **57** PRO FO 44, 227, 19 Dec. 1847. **58** Ibid., 44, 234, 30 Dec. 1847. **59** MacSuibhne, *Paul Cullen*, iv, 307. **60** Ibid., p. 310.

without dwelling on the purported misdeeds of the clergy. Cullen now actually became quite excited about what appeared to be a British diplomatic flop. Shrewsbury informed Wiseman in March 1848 that one of his contacts had been stopped in a Roman street by Cullen, and the Irishman could not contain his ebullience. "'Now," he said "we shall see a different language to Ireland. Now we shall see England on her knees and Lord John [Russell] and all our calumniators begging pardon ... Now I trust the day is come for England to be *crushed*" and a good deal more of the same.'[61]

A flurry of diplomatic activity ensued. The majority of Irish bishops feared that in fact Minto's mission would ultimately succeed and that papal policy in Ireland would be reversed as a result of British diplomatic posturing. MacHale and William O'Hagan, the bishop of Ardagh and Clonmacnoise, arrived in Rome in April 1848 to appeal to the pope not to be swayed by the British arguments and in particular not to change his mind about the queen's colleges.[62]

Russell in the meanwhile pressed ahead with the enabling legislation. The diplomatic relations bill was introduced in the house of commons in January and given its second reading on 17 February 1848. As soon as the text became available Wiseman sent a copy to Rome. There it appears to have been favourably received. The Vatican secretary of state wrote to Wiseman on 22 February stating that,

> in accordance with the desire expressed by your Lordship to Mgr Santucci ... in your welcome letter of the 7inst., I immediately placed before His Holiness the Bill, enclosed in the letter. *How agreeable an impression it has produced on the mind of His Holiness, you may yourself easily imagine.*[63]

Opposition to the proposal was now stirring both inside and outside parliament. The opposition peers Aberdeen and Stanley pointed out that had there been diplomatic relations in 1845, Rome would undoubtedly have objected to the queen's college act. The government would have construed this as interference in the internal affairs of the United Kingdom and been forced to recall the British ambassador from Rome in protest. By contrast, Lord Beaumont, a Catholic, argued that a representative was needed at Rome to put the government case in the face of disinformation circulated by Irish Catholics. The opposition to the diplomatic bill forced from Lord Lansdowne

61 UCA Wiseman papers 549, Shrewsbury to Wiseman, 25 Mar. 1848 (italics in original).   62 Bernard O'Reilly, *MacHale*, ii, 158.   63 N.P.S. Wiseman, *Words of peace and justice addressed to the Catholic clergy and laity of the London district on the subject of diplomatic relations with the Holy See* (London, 1848), p. 6 (italics in original).

the admission that the government hoped that in the light of formal relations with the Papal States Rome would use 'its peculiar influence in certain parts of Her Majesty's domains'. Lord Stanley seized on this statement and took it to be an admission that the government had abrogated its responsibilities in Ireland and hoped to rule that nation through Roman influence. On this point Lucas accused Lord John Russell of saying,

> we have tried to govern Ireland by coercion, and have failed; we have tried to govern it by means of conciliation and have failed also. No other means are now open to us except those which we are resolved on using, to govern Ireland through Rome.[64]

Catholic opinion outside parliament hardened into opposition to the measure. Two of the English vicars apostolic, Bishops Briggs and Ullathorne, joined the majority of their Irish colleagues in expressing reservations about the wisdom of the proposal. Lucas organized a mass protest against the bill in March 1848 and was instrumental in drawing up a memorial for the pope spelling out in no uncertain terms that the bill was really intended as yet another attempt by the government to coerce Ireland. This so infuriated and embarrassed Wiseman that he issued an open letter, to which reference has already been made, denouncing those laymen who opposed diplomatic relations. In addition he protested about the methods they used to get support for their position. He sarcastically denounced Lucas and his supporters who obviously thought British 'diplomatic wiles too subtle for the Apostolic See'. Wiseman also cast aspersions on the social standing of those who had signed Lucas' memorial for the pope. He drew attention to the fact that the names of Howard, Arundel's family name, and Talbot, Shrewsbury's family name, did not appear among the memorialists, and their absence would be noted in Europe, since theirs were 'names associated with the glories of the English Catholic past'.[65] Wiseman warned the laity in a hilarious turn of phrase not to interfere in the affairs of the church. He also reminded them that the pope had the right to enter into diplomatic relations with whom so ever he chose. As a *coup de grace*, he declared that, 'if the original bill could be carried, it would be our duty as Catholics to aid its adoption, to the utmost, as a measure of justice and reparation to the Holy See'.[66]

At the beginning of March 1848 Shrewsbury had already entered the fray with his own pamphlet in favour of diplomatic relations. Unlike Wiseman he did at least attempt to tackle the issue of Ireland in a straightforward way. Adverting to Minto's mission he asserted that Minto had been misrepre-

64 Edward Lucas, *Frederick Lucas*, i, 300.　**65** Wiseman, *Words of peace and justice*, p. 13.　**66** Ibid., p. 10.

sented and was 'believed to be one of the great conspirators against the lives, the liberties and the religion of the Irish people'.[67] Shrewsbury's solution to the Irish problem at that stage was to recognize Catholicism as the religion of its people and treat the Catholic Church as the established church in the country. Diplomatic relations were a step along that road, and by April he was writing to Wiseman that 'diplomatic relations with Rome becomes every day a matter of greater importance'.[68]

Wiseman could not have been unaware of the impact of his public stance on Irish Catholics in general and on the clergy in particular. The picture was complicated for him by the assurances he received from both Crolly and Murray as to their good will towards him. Murray wrote to him in March, 'as to Lucas's attempt to deprive your lordship of the confidence and regard of the Irish clergy, I thank God it has been an utter failure.'[69] On the other hand he knew, since Ullathorne had told him, that the Irish in Rome were all against him.[70] At the same time Ullathorne praised Wiseman's stand against lay interference in an ecclesiastical matter. In his reply Wiseman remarked, 'I can assure your lordship that the expressions of indignation at the lay dictation in ecclesiastical affairs are very strong on all sides.'[71] Needless to say, the condemnation of lay interference referred only the meddling in ecclesiastical matters of those who took the opposing view to Wiseman's. And lest he be misled as to the true feeling of the Irish about the whole issue, Lady Bellew was to inform him that she had never heard anything as violent as the manner in which all the clergy in Ireland (Murray excepted), had spoken about the possibility of a nuncio in London.[72]

The diplomatic relations bill passed all stages in parliament and was given the royal assent in August 1848. It was never acted upon. Two amendments had been introduced at the committee stage in the lords which ensured, from Rome's viewpoint, that it would be a dead letter. The act withheld from the pope the title of 'Sovereign Pontiff', and it stipulated that the papal nuncio could not be a cleric. If Wiseman was disappointed with this turn of events, he betrayed little hint of it. In fact, rather boastfully he wrote to Shrewsbury in November 1848 that as far as the affairs of Ireland were concerned 'we have not had a single Catholic political speech since last spring: and I think I shall be able to give you many interesting accounts of progress in many ways'.[73] Quite what the progress might be Wiseman gives no hint.

As we have seen, Wiseman was peculiarly insensitive to the effect that his

67 John Talbot, *Diplomatic relation with Rome: a letter to the earl of Arundel and Surrey* (London, 1848), p. 19. **68** UCA Wiseman papers 921, Shrewsbury to Wiseman, 13 April 1848. **69** UCA Wiseman papers 530, Murray to Wiseman, 20 March 1848. **70** Ward, *Sequel*, ii, 221. **71** Ibid., p. 201. **72** AAW Wiseman papers, Bellew to Wiseman, 1 Nov. 1848. **73** UCA Wiseman papers 936, Wiseman to Shrewsbury,

actions had on Irish public opinion. Although Lucas' stance is perhaps to be regarded as but one extreme, in the matter of diplomatic relations and the resentment about accusations of clerical inspired violence, he does seem to have captured much more accurately the mood of the country than Wiseman did. It remains nonetheless true that Wiseman's position was not necessarily inspired by antipathy to the Irish as such, but rather by the need to secure the position of English Catholics in their own country. That his views might have adverse repercussions in Ireland seems not to have particularly disturbed him. He certainly distanced himself from the leading lights of Irish radicalism, but this of itself need not indicate anything other than the fact that he was a cautious English churchman.

It would not be an exaggeration to say that Wiseman's standing among the bulk of Irish opinion formers never really recovered from the *débâcle* of 1847–8. Although he was well received during his visit of 1858, the affection shown him was more with regard to his office than his person. Dr Patrick Moran writing to his uncle, Archbishop Paul Cullen, of Wiseman's visit to Rome in 1853 said that,

> [Wiseman] has occasionally made flattering allusion to Ireland; I suppose he is anxious to conciliate the wild Irish ... He is the centre of all the English and *some others* here ... The Irish generally keep aloof from him ... he had the opportunity of insinuating some things here which are very injurious to the good cause of Ireland.[74]

This perhaps reflects the continuing distrust that he engendered in most of the emerging leadership in the Irish Church of the 1850s. When the older generation of 'Castle bishops' began to die Wiseman's reputation among Irish churchmen began also to dwindle. Cullen remained deeply suspicious. Writing to Monsignor Barnabò at Propaganda in 1854 he asserted that Wiseman was not well informed on Irish affairs and that many Catholics looked on him with fear, 'or at least suspicion'. Cullen even excused himself from going to Wiseman's funeral on the flimsy pretext that he 'had a cold'.[75]

Wiseman was very obviously a product of that tendency in English Catholicism which regarded Englishness as perhaps a more important virtue than Catholicity. At the same time the difficulties under which he laboured made it virtually impossible for him to give imaginative leadership to the church which the circumstances of mid-nineteenth-century England required. That said, any given approach was bound to give rise to opposition. After all, Wiseman's successor, Henry Edward Manning, in demonstrating

November 1848. **74** MacSuibhne, *Cullen*, ii, 159. **75** Ibid., v, 20.

his sympathies for the poor and the Irish alienated many among the ranks of the English Catholic upper and middle classes. Wiseman perhaps over-estimated the ability of the English nation to cast aside 300 years of anti-Catholic and anti-Irish prejudice. He clearly believed that England as a whole might well return to the fold of Peter, and this hope, unrealizable as it must have seemed to many of his contempories, determined his strategy in managing church affairs. He thought that English political antipathy to Ireland represented the greatest block to making Catholicism acceptable to the average mid-century Englishman. On the other hand, a mere display of antipathy to Irish radicalism on his part was unlikely to neutralize the anti-Catholicism that was all too pervasive in Victorian England.

It has been suggested, by the most impeccable of sources, that snobbery was one of the main constraints under which English Catholicism laboured.[76] By the early decades of the mid-nineteenth century, the English church saw itself as a genteel and persecuted minority, loyal and faithful to England, but also to its own somewhat eccentric religious traditions. It was not a church of the masses and, moreover, had no wish to be. Wiseman, although to some extent a product of this general cultural ethos, was nonetheless too pastorally inclined to ignore either the plight of the converts or the presence of the Irish in English congregations. At the same time, like the hereditary Catholics, he accepted the fact that Irish Catholicism was alien to the experience of most of the English Catholic community, and he was therefore concerned to concen-trate his efforts elsewhere. The Irish in the English church were to be tolerated more than integrated into the life of the church.[77] His ultramontane instincts facilitated an appeal to religious devotion which met the religious and spiritual needs of the Irish within the English church. As for the political muscle of Catholic Ireland, his attitude was that it needed to be harnessed for the advancement of Catholicism as a whole and not in the parochial interest of emerging Irish nationalism. The advancement of Catholicism had different objectives in Ireland and England. In the ensuing struggle between competing interests, not unnaturally given his temperament and the sense of inferiority of English Catholicism as a whole, Wiseman's sympathies lay with England rather than Ireland.

---

76 Christopher Hollis, *The monstrous regiment* (London, 1929), p. 66.   77 As one prominent historian of the period has commented, Wiseman was forced to follow a policy of 'conciliation and consolidation'. Any social radicalism on his part would have alienated the hereditary Catholics: V.A. McClelland, *Cardinal Manning: his public life and influence, 1865–1892* (London, 1962), p. 6.

4

Carleton's ecclesiastical context: the Ulster Catholic experience

The intention here is not so much to examine minutely William Carleton's own writing on Ulster Catholicism, although reference will be made from time to time to relevant sections of his work, but rather to give some idea of the general circumstances of Catholicism in Ulster in the first half of the nineteenth century. In doing so I shall focus on three aspects in particular. The first concerns the conditions within which Catholics practised their faith. Where was the focus of faith for Catholics, what did they actually believe, what were their day-to-day concerns, and how did the Church respond to those concerns? Secondly, I shall examine the area of Catholic–Protestant relations: the positive and negative aspects of how the two communities dealt with one another. Thirdly, I want to look at the question of Catholic ecclesiastical leadership, to say something of the nature of clerical life and the quality of the leadership that priests and bishops offered the Catholic community from the foundation of the Royal College of St Patrick at Maynooth in 1795, until the synod of Thurles in 1850.

The circumstances of Ulster Catholicism in the early to mid-nineteenth century cannot be described as particularly propitious. The north was slow to recover from the effects of penal legislation. Church accommodation was not nearly sufficient to meet the needs of the people, and religious instruction and catechesis were at an especially low ebb.[1] Historians are divided on whether or not the north was worse off than the rest of the country in the popular perception of the nature of Catholicism. What is certainly clear is that many Catholics were almost entirely ignorant of the content of the Christian faith and practised, indeed if they practised at all, what amounted to little more than a folk religion.[2] Well into the century, we have reports from various priests that while people had 'a great faith' and 'deep feelings of piety', they

1 See Oliver P. Rafferty, *Catholicism in Ulster, 1603–1983: an interpretative history* (Dublin, 1994), pp 98ff.   2 Brendan Bradshaw has convincingly argued that the most important element of the Catholic Church's survival in Ireland in the aftermath of the reformation was not so much the practice of Catholicism as such, but rather the creedal or confessional aspect of group identity. Catholicism was a collective self-identity for the community. Bradshaw's 'The English Reformation and identity formation in Wales and Ireland', in Brendan Bradshaw and Peter Roberts (eds), *British consciousness and identity formation: the making of Britain, 1533–1707* (Cambridge, 1998), pp 44–7.

were nonetheless ignorant of such basic tenets of Christianity as the doctrines of the Trinity and the Incarnation.[3] Ten years later one exasperated missioner declared that 'the people of Ulster seem never to have heard of the act of contrition nor [know] how to say the *Confiteor*'.

Superstitions were rife even at times among those aspiring for the priesthood. Carleton records the story of one such would-be Melchizedek in *The Station*. There Briney tells his father Phaddy that when he is a priest he will 'translate all the Protestants into asses and then we'll get our hands *red* of them altogether'. To which Phaddy replies, 'Well, that flogs for cuteness, and it's a wondher the clergy doesn't do it, and them has the power, for t'would give us pace entirely.'[4] Such notions of the magical power of the Catholic clergy were at times shared equally by Protestant peasants and made the priest feared by that stratum of society in both communions. This is a point which is often forgotten. We are accustomed to think of the superstitious Catholics and overlook the fact that Protestants too were steeped in superstitions of one sort or another.

William Shaw Mason in his *Parochial Survey of Ireland* records that in the parish of Hollywood Co. Down, superstitions among Protestants were 'not without a considerable hold over their minds, the beliefs in witches and fairies is as firm as any article of the creed'.[5] Similarly the *Ordnance Survey Memoirs* for Co. Down, 1832–4 and 1837, record of the parish of Blairs (partly in Antrim and partly in Down) that in both Catholic and Protestant communities 'the greater number believe in fairies, elves and the visitation of departed spirits, … another absurdity is the bewitching or overlooking of cattle'.[6]

Two other examples will not only further illustrate the tale of Protestant superstitions but also give some indication of general Protestant mores in early nineteenth-century Ulster. The parish of Longfield West in Co. Tyrone lies south-west of Drumquin, not far from Omagh. The 1834 *Ordnance Survey Memoirs* record that 'the people of this parish are very civil and obliging, whereas if you proceed four miles northward you will meet with a very uncouth race. The former are mostly Catholics, the latter Presbyterians. The former are, however, very dishonest and insincere, the latter on the contrary are mostly upright men.' But, and here's the rub, 'both parties are

3 AAA Dixon papers, Revd James Dixon to Archbishop Dixon, 26 Feb. 1856.
4 William Carlton, *Traits and stories of the Irish peasantry* (definitive edition, Dublin, 1842–4, reprinted Gerard's Cross, 1990), p. 132.   5 William Shaw Mason, *A statistical account or parochial survey of Ireland*, 3 vols (Dublin, 1814–19), ii, 87.   6 Angelique Day and Patrick McWilliams (eds), *Ordnance Survey memoirs of Ireland, parishes of Co. Down (1833–8)*, 4 vols (Belfast, 1990), iii, 32.

very superstitious'.[7] The neighbouring parish of Longfield East was mostly Protestant. 'The inhabitants' we are told were

> generally poor, but a few possess independence. They are in a lamentable state of ignorance respecting religion. No parish has been more neglected by its ministers. Until lately part of the church has been used as a barn, and divine service very irregularly performed. The Presbyterians are little better taught than those of the Established Church. The Protestant places of worship and the bible are much neglected.[8]

One regrets that David Hempton and Myrtle Hill in their otherwise commendable study, *Evangelical Protestantism in Ulster Society, 1740–1890*, make no allusion to the unorthodox flaws in Protestant practice and belief.[9] When they do mention superstition, it is always Catholic superstition and thus they help to perpetuate the caricature that Protestantism is a system of rational Christian belief and Catholicism one of superstition. It is also important to bear in mind that the 'second reformation' also acted as a means of reforming Irish Anglicanism and Presbyterianism from the 1820s on, as did the Ulster revival in the late 1850s. But even here the revival did not take place in an environment free from the superstitions of its devotees.[10]

For its part, even before the famine Ulster Catholicism had entered into a phase of internal reform. Although in the 1830s and 1840s we find occasional references to open air masses in counties Antrim, Tyrone and Derry, such instances are increasingly rare. By 1864, the diocese of Clogher had 82 chapels, yet this was only four more than it had in 1844, thirty years earlier there were 32. Although the statutes of the ecclesiastical province of Armagh in 1834 made the holding of station mass and confession compulsory, it is also clear that the reform-minded clergy found such practices increasingly distasteful. Thus Patrick Moran, the future cardinal archbishop of Sydney, writing to his uncle Paul Cullen in Rome in 1842, observed:

> The holding of stations for mass and confession in private houses is the very worst system … The young clergyman is brought into contact with his female penitents. The result is that confessions are often

---

7 Day and Williams (eds), *Ordnance Survey memoirs of Ireland, parishes of Co. Tyrone (1825, 1833–5, 1840)*, 2 vols (Belfast, 1993), i, 129. 8 Day and McWilliams, *Ordnance Survey memoirs … Tyrone*, i, 31. 9 David Hempton and Myrtle Hill, *Evangelical Protestantism in Ulster society, 1740–1890* (London, 1992). 10 See David W. Miller, 'Did Ulster Presbyterians have a devotional revolution', in James H. Murphy (ed.), *Evangelicals and Catholics in nineteenth-century Ireland* (Dublin, 2005), p. 52.

invalid or sacrilegious. It is almost impossible that the poor country
people ... could disclose their sins, struggling with their natural reluctance to avow their guilt.[11]

Another element in the falling-off of interest in stations was the fact that as
the century progressed Catholicism became an increasingly urban
phenomenon and access to chapels became easier.

Although Catholics were in general poor, in more prosperous circumstances, as for example in the 'linen triangle' where they managed to acquire
some wealth, their social habits and expectations varied little from those of
their Protestant neighbours. Mother Emmanuel of the Convent of Mercy in
Newry, the sister of Lord Russell of Killowen, recalled for Russell's
biographer that on Sundays after dinner 'each one of us read a chapter of the
bible aloud while Mamma and Dada listened respectfully'.[12] But even for
those lower down the social scale the clergy tried to instill a sense of order and
decorum. Diocesan regulations often advert to the need to protect the
sabbath, and Mason's *Parochial Survey* and the *Ordnance Survey Memoirs*
record many instances of the fact that 'crowded meetings for the purpose of
amusement do not take place as formerly, such meetings being opposed by the
Roman Catholic clergy'.[13]

On the point of bible reading, the Russell example is not exceptional.
Lower-class Catholics were often taught to read the bible, in some instances
of course by Protestants. Carleton himself testified to the fact that his father
knew almost the whole bible by heart, and this conforms to a pattern from the
early years of the century whereby Catholic bishops were much concerned to
have the bible printed and distributed. In 1840 Michael Blake, the bishop of
Dromore, issued the Douay New Testament and in the preface indicated that
among his pastoral duties that of nourishing his flock 'with the *pure* word of
divine revelation, I consider the most important'.[14] Three years later William
Crolly, archbishop of Armagh and former bishop of Down and Connor,
claimed to have distributed more copies of the Old and New Testaments than
anyone else in Ireland.[15] Indeed, between 1817 and 1852, 308,600 copies of
the Douay version of the bible or the New Testament had been circulated in
the dioceses of Dromore and Down and Connor. At the very least this should

11 Quoted in Robert Lee Wolff, *William Carleton, Irish peasant novelist: a preface to his
fiction* (New York and London, 1980), p. 38.   12 R. Barry O'Brien, *The life of Lord
Russell of Killowen* (London, 1901), p. 23.   13 Day and McWilliams, *Ordnance Survey
memoirs ... Down*, iii, 30.   14 *The Douay New Testament* (Belfast, 1840), p. iii. The
publisher for this edition was a Newry Protestant Robert Greer who managed to sell
4,000 copies of the book within a few months.   15 Ambrose Macaulay, *William Crolly,
archbishop of Armagh, 1835–49* (Dublin, 1994), p. 101.

make us cautious about asserting that nineteenth-century Ulster Catholics were unfamiliar with biblical Christianity.

Other aspects of Catholic life seem equally at odds with an ultramontane perspective. Catholic places of worship in the early to mid-century were, in many instances, unrecognizable as the Catholic chapels of subsequent generations. They were for the most part unadorned, being simply whitewashed; the blessed sacrament was not reserved, they were opened only on Sunday for services; and icons or religious images were few or non-existent.[16] Furthermore, the clergy did not always wear recognizably clerical garb, and were addressed by the civil titles of 'Sir', 'Mister' or 'Doctor'.

Many of the features of what we take to be traditional Irish Catholicism are relatively late imports from continental Europe. Devotion to the Sacred Heart, Stations of the Cross, the Forty Hours devotion, sodalities and confraternities of various descriptions, parish missions – these are all associated with reform and in particular with reform-minded individuals such as Cardinal Paul Cullen. What Carleton portrays for us in his stories and novels is a picture of a Catholicism which, even in his own lifetime, was passing away. Furthermore, we witness in the lives of his characters a resistance to reform and indeed modernity.[17] The peasants clung to their old ways in defiance of their priests. To take but one example: the *Downpatrick Recorder*, itself an organ of conservative and Orange opinion, reported in June 1862 that crowds of people had gathered on mid-summer's eve at Struel well near Downpatrick, for what the newspaper described as 'degrading and immoral practices'. On that occasion, two priests from Downpatrick went out to the well to urge the people to return to their homes. Some did as they were instructed but, we are informed, 'most refused to budge, and many were heard to speak in bitter terms of the interference of the priests, which they seem to regard in something of the light of an outrage on religion'.[18]

Ironically, Carleton as a reformer of Catholicism, if indeed that was his intention, and a traducer of the priests, played into the hands of the clericalization of Irish Catholic life. The point of much of the Catholicism of the Irish peasantry, before the 'devotional revolution', is that it was relatively free from clerical control. The visits to holy wells, pilgrimages to places such as Lough Derg, or the recitation of the rosary and other prayers, were undertaken without the need for clerical supervision. The individual therefore had

16 Paddy Killen (ed.), *St Macartan's Church Loughlinisland bicentenary, 1789–1989* (Belfast, 1989), pp 30–1. **17** Such resistance was a feature of Irish life throughout the century. Ironically, by the 1890s it was the Anglo-Irish in the shape of those such as Douglas Hyde who led the resistance to the modernization of Ireland. Joseph Lee, *The modernisation of Irish society, 1848–1918* (Dublin, 1992), pp 137–41. **18** *Downpatrick Recorder*, 28 June 1862.

a greater say in his or her own spiritual life than would be the case later in the century. In other words, individuals took responsibility for themselves before God without the mediation of the priest: in many ways a very Protestant notion. In a sense this is what Carleton failed to see and so in his recording of the grosser sides of popular piety he was, in fact, giving support to clerical reformers. He was therefore, in his own way, a bit like Cardinal Cullen, who worked for the abolition of abuses, and wanted all religious activity to be more rationally based, and subjected to greater clerical control.

Even in its ultramontane expression popular piety could rouse the suspicions of high-placed ecclesiastics. Bishop Blake of Dromore in criticizing the writings of St Alphonsus Liguori, especially tomes such as *The Glories of Mary*, objected that 'fanatics will avail themselves of his works … to represent the Catholic Church as an encourager of the most shameful corruption of morals and the rankest superstitions'.[19] This was a common fear among ecclesiastics in the years before the famine: that Protestants systematically mis-represented Catholicism for propaganda purposes. Indeed, Archbishop Reilly of Armagh complained in 1812 that Protestants put great effort into trying to show that 'the religion of Catholics is hateful to God and the bane of society'.[20]

This conveniently leads us into a consideration of what we might describe as the totality of relations between Catholics and Protestants in Ulster in the period under discussion. For his part Carleton, even in his most Protestant days, was inclined to be sympathetic to the circumstances in which Ulster Catholics found themselves. In the preface to the *Traits and Stories of the Irish Peasantry*, dated 1 March 1830, he noted that

> The English reader, perhaps, may be skeptical as to the deep hatred which prevails among Roman Catholics in the North of Ireland, against those who differ from them in party and religious principles, but when he reflects that they were driven before the face of the Scotch invader, and divested by the settlement of Ulster of their pleasant vales, forced to quench their fires on their father's hearths, and retire to the mountain ranges of Tyrone, Donegal and Derry, perhaps he will grant, after all, that the feeling is natural to a people treated as they have been.[21]

One could dismiss this as a typical piece of Carleton rhetoric, but on the other hand it does give some insight into the perceptions of Ulster Catholic peasants about their circumstances.[22] Equally, one could perhaps, if we

19 AICR Cullen papers, Blake to Cullen, 27 Jan. 1842.   20 ADDC MacMullen papers, Reilly to MacMullen, 8 Dec. 1812.   21 William Carleton, *Traits and stories of the Irish peasantry*, 2 vols (Dublin, 1830), i, pp xxiv–v.   22 Such sentiments also help

exclude from consideration Belfast and Newry, draw a distinction between Catholic experience east and west of the Bann. The clear minority status of Catholics in most of Antrim and Down meant that they posed relatively little threat to the majority Protestant community. In these circumstances their treatment by Protestants was not necessarily unkind. In areas such as Fermanagh and Tyrone, where the communities were more evenly balanced numerically, there tended to be greater tensions and more possibility that such tensions would be expressed in sectarian violence.

Undoubtedly one factor in hostility between the two communities from the beginning of the nineteenth century was the activity of the Orange order. The riots in Downpatrick in June 1802 or in Belfast in December 1813 may not have been connected with Orangeism, but these were probably the exceptions in the violent disturbances in the first half of the century. In Derry, the December Orange demonstrations were often accompanied by violence. In Ederney, Co. Fermanagh, in 1824, Orangemen attacked a peaceful St Patrick's day parade, as a result of which several Catholics were shot and wounded; even the parish priest was attacked and injured. Violence flared again in mid-Ulster in 1829 and 1830. Pitched battles were waged in and around Stewartstown, Co. Tyrone, in July 1829, to be matched in the following summer by equally bitter rioting at the Maghera Orange demonstration. In general then, Orange parades were often accompanied by aggressive sectarian attacks launched by one community or the other. In Armagh in 1845, Archbishop Crolly pleaded with the authorities to have the traditional Orange march re-routed or at least kept from the centre of the town. His pleas fell on deaf ears, and in the riot which followed the demonstration one Catholic was murdered.[23]

If this incident has an all-too-contemporary ring, so does the description Carleton gives of a raid by the yeomen on his home when he was about ten years old. They arrived at two or three in the morning, accusing his father of being a 'rebellious old dog', and searched the house because they believed there was a gun hidden there. The only 'weapon' was a tin gun which a Protestant friend, Sam Nelson, had given Carleton. Carleton remarks:

> My readers will be surprised to learn that one of Sam Nelson's brothers was among this scroundrelly gang, and never once interfered on our behalf. No man knew better than he that this midnight and

to explain David Krause's judgment that Carleton was 'unable to forget his overpowering religious and racial memory'. See 'Carleton, Catholicism and the comic novel', *Irish University Review*, 24: 2 (1994), 217.   **23** The full story of this particular incident can be followed in R. Ó Muiri, 'Orangemen, Repealers and the shooting of John Boyle in Armagh, 12 July 1845', in *Seanchas Ard Mhacha* 11: 2 (1985), 435–529.

drunken visit was a mere pretence, deliberately founded upon the history of the tin gun which his brother Sam had given me and my brother John. My readers may form an opinion of the state of society, when they hear that there was not an individual present that night in this gross and lawless outrage with whom we were not acquainted, nor a man among them who did not know everyone of us intimately.[24]

The notion that Catholics could not, at least in Ulster, receive justice or fair play from the hands of the officials of the state, became a fairly consistent trope throughout the nineteenth century and beyond. It is also important to keep in mind, in discussing at least the early decades of the century, that many Catholics – and particularly the clergy – were at pains to profess and demonstrate their loyalty to the state. The point then is that even in a stable constitutional situation, Ulster Catholics felt themselves to be victims of state oppression – not on account of their political opinions, but by virtue of their religious affiliation. This lack of evenhandedness on the part of state officials can be illustrated time and again, from the relatively trivial example in July 1809, when magistrates acquitted three Protestants of having stolen vestments from the Catholic church in Enniskillen despite the fact that they had been caught red-handed, to the notorious Dolly's Brae affair in 1849. It is perhaps worth mentioning that, in Fermanagh, even by 1880 there was only a single Catholic magistrate in the whole county out of a total of seventy-two.

The Dolly's Brae incident near Castlewellan, Co. Down, became something of a *cause célèbre* in the relations between the two communities in Ulster. An attack by Orangemen left several Catholics dead (the estimation of the number who died varies), and much Catholic property was destroyed. For their part, the magistrates not only failed to keep order, but they actually sided with the perpetrators of the crimes. Such was their alignment with lawlessness that they refused even to take evidence against the ringleaders of the atrocities. An independent official inquiry castigated the magistrates for their open sectarianism.[25] On this occasion, however, central government acted decisively. The magistrates, who included Lord Roden, were dismissed and parliament passed the Party Processions Act (1849), which forbade Orange and political demonstrations. The law was widely disregarded, especially by Orangemen, and was finally repealed in 1872. The significant thing for the Ulster Catholic experience in this instance was the fact that central government acted to curb the more egregious facets of local Protestant and Orange hostility. When these constraints were removed after

24 David J. Donoghue (ed.), *The life of William Carleton*, 2 vols (London, 1896), i, 32.
25 *Papers relating to an investigation held at Castlewellan into the occurrences at Dolly's Brae, on 12 July 1848*, HC 1850 [1143], p. li.

partition, the Catholic community would draw on its folk memory to convince itself that it could never expect justice from its native Protestant neighbours.

It would be misleading to neglect the fact that Protestants perceived Catholicism to be not just a religious threat but also a political danger. The more immediate problems were represented by the movement for Catholic emancipation up to 1829 and then by O'Connell's agitation for repeal of the Union. The difficulty in both cases, so far as Protestants were concerned, was the extent of clerical involvement in direct political agitation, and therefore the specifically political ambitions of the Catholic Church in Ireland. It might seem strange that on this very point Irish Protestants should have an ally in the court of Rome. On a number of occasions up to 1850 various popes had written to the Irish clergy reminding them of the need to steer clear of politics and to concentrate on their pastoral duties.[26] For the most part, the bishops, at least the Ulstermen among them, were careful to observe these stipulations. The most notorious offender against these injunctions was, however, once again Bishop Michael Blake of Dromore, who was an ardent champion of O'Connell. The bishops, under pressure from Rome, had agreed in 1839 not to allow church buildings to be used for political meetings. In 1840, Blake hosted a demonstration in the grounds of his own church in Newry to collect the tribute to O'Connell, on the pretext that he was honouring O'Connell's contribution to Catholicism and not his politics.[27]

Archbishop William Crolly of Armagh, by contrast, had forbidden the collection of the O'Connell rent at chapels in his diocese. He alone of all the Ulster bishops was against repeal. There can be no doubt that the repeal agitation help further to alienate Ulster Protestants from their Catholic neighbours. On the other hand, it must be said that there was no inevitability in the alliance between radical politics and Ulster Catholicism. On St Patrick's day 1874, Bishop Patrick Dorrian of Down and Connor declared that he would not like to see home rule if he thought it would lead to religious bitterness or decline in trade or agricultural production.[28]

Radical politics however, had their limits, and the priests acted as agents of order in their attempt to curb the violence of such clandestine groups as the ribbonmen. The evidence for this is widespread, in both official condemnations of ribbonism by bishops, and from correspondence between individual priests and bishops. Furthermore we can often enough see that ribbonism was strongest in areas were the church was relatively weak.

26 K.B. Nolan, 'The Catholic clergy and Irish politics in the 1830s and 1840s', in J.G. Barry (ed.), *Historical studies IX* (Belfast, 1974), p. 120. **27** John F. Broderick, *The Holy See and the Irish movement for the repeal of the Union with England, 1829–1847* (Rome, 1951), pp 61–2. **28** Ambrose Macaulay, *Patrick Dorrian, bishop of Down and Connor, 1865–85* (Dublin, 1987), p. 228.

Protestants, however, often thought that the Catholic clergy acquiesced in the ribbonmen's lawlessness, and this further contributed to a souring of relations between the communities. On the other hand, one has to be careful not to generalise too much even on political questions. After all, the Presbytery of Bangor, representing the Presbyterian Church in north Down, voted in favour of Catholic emancipation in 1827 (even if it did change its mind in 1829), and as Finlay Holmes points out, when Henry Cooke proclaimed the banns of marriage between the Presbyterians and the Church of Ireland at Hillsborough in 1834, he knew that he was not speaking for all Presbyterians in forming a pan-Protestant alliance against Catholic social and political pretensions.[29]

Equally it is true to say that in general terms the church's political ambitions were quite circumscribed, and in many respects it was willing to live within the bounds of what was politically possible. Thus if the church could obtain all it most cherished: Protestant disestablishment, denominational education, the suppression of disorder, and agrarian reform from a heretical government in London – so much the better. If that proved impossible and the only means of securing the church's interests lay in some measure of limited self-rule, then that must be sought. The primary loyalty was to the church, and the concern of ecclesiastical authority was to secure the most favourable conditions possible within which to conduct the church's work. That work was directed to the spiritual needs of Catholics and, to that extent, its political purposes were neutral. Protestants, however, were correct in discerning that one of the features of ultramontane Catholicism was the desire to control political activity, however directed. Many elements in Irish Catholicism resisted such encroachments, but not on such a scale as to reassure Protestants of Catholic benevolence, should Catholics ever gain the upper hand socially or politically.

Relations between Catholics and Protestants, despite what we have seen, could be very harmonious at times. Henry Cooke, of all people, testified before the select committee into the state of Ireland in 1825 that Orangemen and Catholics in Co. Down were on the friendliest of terms.[30] In 1866, when the retired Catholic bishop of Down and Connor, Dr Cornelius Denvir, died, Cooke was among a number of Presbyterian and Anglican clergy who attended his funeral. The sympathy which pervaded some Presbyterian and Catholic circles in the run up to the 1798 Rising, survived well into the nineteenth century.

In his report on the state of the church in the diocese of Clogher in 1804,

29 Finlay Holmes, *Our Presbyterian heritage* (Belfast, 1985), p. 106. **30** *Report from the Select Committee on the State of Ireland*, Parliamentary Papers (1825), viii, p. 363.

during the Napoleonic wars, Bishop James Murphy informed the authorities in Rome that he had recently built a number of chapels, and he continued:

> We have at present six more nearly finished, and if God in his mercy is pleased to grant this Empire an honourable peace shortly, I hope with his assistance and that of our Protestant neighbours, for indeed they have been kind to us on these occasions, we shall get chapels round all the diocese in a few years.[31]

This is a fairly consistent theme in Ulster Catholicism for most of the century. Given the relative poverty of the community, the Catholic Church was dependent on the generosity of wealthy Protestants for the growth of Catholic infrastructure.

There are very many examples that one can draw on. To take a few at random: by 1837 the Catholic parish of St Tiernagh, Roslea, in East Clones could boast of the first purpose-built bell tower in the Clogher diocese in 300 years. The cost was £600 and we are informed that 'Protestant labour and Protestant money greatly contributed to the work'. Richard Armstrong, a Protestant of Ballygawley, Co. Tyrone, bequeathed £25 in 1838 for the relief of the poor in the parish of Errigle Kieran. This was matched the following year by the generosity of Sir Arthur Brooke, who donated a site for a Catholic chapel in Brookeborough, Co. Fermanagh. The Catholic priest Patrick Curran obtained a grant of land from Lord Castlereagh in 1811, on which to build the first Catholic church in Newtownards, Co. Down. Castlereagh's family, the Londonderry's, maintained some patronage in Catholic affairs in northeast Down well into the nineteenth century.

One ironic feature of Catholic–Protestant relations is the fact that individuals could simultaneously be charitable yet hostile. Thus, for example, the Church of Ireland rector of Killanny, Co. Monaghan, contributed, in 1817, £100 to the Catholic poor of his parish, despite being the author of several anti-Catholic tracts. In areas such as the Glens of Antrim, relations were fairly good. Here, intermarriage was a factor that tended to promote cross-community harmony. The yeomanry too, surprisingly, contained both Catholics and Protestants. As was so often the case in such circumstances, much depended on the outlook of the local priest and minister. The Church of Ireland curate in the parish of Ardclinis, which included such areas as Glenarm and Cusendall, testified in 1819 that in his parish 'little or no bigotry prevails, and it must excite very pleasing sentiments that the Catholic

31 Seosamh Ó Dufaigh, 'James Murphy, bishop of Clogher, 1801–24', *Clogher Record* 4: 3 (1968), 460.

clergyman, the Revd Daniel McDonnell, does everything in his power to promote a good understanding among the inhabitants of the parish'.[32]

On the vexed question of schooling, several of the Ulster bishops were committed to the principle of mixed education. When the parliamentary commission of inquiry into education visited Belfast in 1825, Bishop Crolly was called on to testify before it. The commission put to Crolly that it believed him to be 'favourable to the system of united education, as tending to extinguish party animosities and generating party feeling'. In his reply to this point, the bishop observed that, 'I think [mixed education] must be an effectual means of suppressing the spirit of party, particularly if proper precautions were taken to prevent undue influence or predominant power on one side or the other.'[33]

Crolly was, in some respects, himself a product of 'mixed education', having attended the classical school in Downpatrick conducted by the Presbyterian clergyman James Neilson. Indeed, Neilson's school was something of a training ground for future Catholic bishops of Down and Connor, since Crolly's two immediate successors, Cornelius Denvir and Patrick Dorrian, both received their early education there. Similarly Edward Kernan, the bishop of Clogher 1824–44, attended the Protestant Portora Royal School in Enniskillen. Portora continued to educate both Catholics and Protestants together until 1891, when the then Catholic bishop, Anthony Donnelly, asked for a share of the school's endowment to set up his own college in Monaghan, and surprisingly enough, it was given to him.

From the 1830s, however, the education issue, initially at the primary and subsequently at the queen's college level, served to stiffen Catholic antagonism not just to the state but also to Protestantism. The concessions given to Presbyterians in the first decade of the operation of the national schools system caused Catholics to have serious doubts about the advisability of Catholic children attending such schools. The opposition to the queen's colleges became, in some respects, a more directly political affair. Daniel O'Connell opposed the colleges since he saw them as a plank in the government's attempts to kill off the repeal agitation by granting concessions to Irish Catholics. O'Connell's supporters were, however, divided on the matter. The Young Ireland group was enthusiastic, not only because the colleges would give the opportunity for a more widely educated laity, but also because they would promote harmony between Catholics and Protestants. Such talk smacked of indifferentism to the minds of some bishops, but not, however, to those such as Crolly and Denvir who were tolerably disposed to

---

32 Mason, *Parochial survey*, iii, 27–8.   33 *Appendix to the fourth report of the commissioners of Irish education inquiry*, HC, 1826–7 (509), xiii, p. 357.

the institutions. Indeed, Crolly hoped that the northern college might be located at the heart of his diocese in Armagh.

Of a more pressing nature was the so-called 'second reformation', which provoked opposition from all sections of Catholic opinion. Relations between the two communities became increasingly strained as aggressive Protestant proselytizing was promoted in many parts of the country. In Derry, the street preachers of this new reformation caused a riot late in 1826, whilst in Downpatrick, when the preachers first made their appearance, the parish priest warned his flock that Satan himself had appeared among them. In many towns throughout Ulster, Catholic priests and Protestants ministers challenged one another to debate the central issues of the reformation and the differences generally between Catholicism and Protestantism. As so often, such debates were acrimonious and the overall result was simply an increase in tension.

The lasting problem was that good relations having been soured as a result of these experiences in the 1820s, it was to prove difficult to repair the damage to inter-faith harmony. We have, however, quite an amount of evidence to show that friendly contacts between the two religious communities did indeed survive the second reformation. Much depended on the quality of ecclesiastical leadership, and it is to this aspect of Carleton's social and religious context that we must now turn our attention.

Thanks to the labours of André Boué and his discovery of Carleton's memo to Peel of 3 November 1826, we have some idea of what Carleton thought of the Catholic clergy and how he viewed the leadership they gave to the Catholic community.[34] At a political level he was deeply suspicious of priestly activity. He believed that many of the candidates for the priesthood before going to Maynooth had connection with what he terms 'flagitious combinations', in other words secret revolutionary societies of one sort or another, and that after ordination they continued to symathize with and tolerate such organizations. Carleton saw this as a 'terrible exposure of the settled and systematic disaffection of the Irish Roman Catholic Church'. He went on to say that the priests are to be feared because of their habitual hypocrisy, and because of the undying fire that burns within them, 'black, malignant and designing, systematically treacherous and false, and inherently inimical to Protestants'. Robert Wolff says of the memo that Carleton 'repays all the snubs, real or imaginary, ever inflicted on him by the Catholic clergy'.[35] How accurate is Carleton's characterization of the clergy both in the memo and in his imaginative writings? Is his picture of the disloyal, greedy, drunken and ill-educated priest of early to mid nineteenth-century Ireland true?

34 Wolff, *Carleton*, p. 19.   35 Ibid., p. 22.

In the rebellion year of 1798, of the 69 seminarians at Maynooth we find that 59 swore on oath that they had never been United Irishmen. Eight others swore that they had flirted with radicalism before entering the college, but had thought better of it and took the oath of allegiance (which remained a requirement for all seminarians, as well as for professors and domestic staff at the college until the late 1860s). Two others refused to answer any questions about their political affiliations. They, along with their repentant United Irish colleagues, were promptly expelled.[36]

In 1826, however, the Revd John Cousins, a former Catholic priest, now a clergyman of the established church, testified before the commission of inquiry on Maynooth that on entering the college most students had no political views, but rather were politicized by the few radicals among the student body. He further pointed to what he saw as an ideological gap between the trustees and the professors on one side, and the students on the other.[37] Further confirmation of Carleton's views can be had in the late 1840s when the lord lieutenant, Lord Clarendon, warned John MacHale, the archbishop of Tuam, that 'the exercise of spiritual authority is doubted, and the press asserts and the public believes that the Catholic clergy are the irresponsible promoters of disaffection and disorder'.[38]

On the other hand, we do have to remember that the political atmosphere of the early Maynooth years was dominated by the French émigré clergy. They brought with them sentiments of loyalty to the monarchy and ideas that were completely opposed to any form of radicalism or republicanism. Archbishop Murray of Dublin, one of the trustees of Maynooth, believed that the palpable lesson of the French revolution was that throne and altar stood or fell together.[39] Whether or not this atmosphere of loyal devotion had much of an impact on students remains an open question. James Doyle, Catholic bishop of Kildare and Leighlin, observed in his *Conciliation in Ireland*, published in 1824, that in ruling Ireland

> the minister of England cannot look to the exertions of the Catholic priesthood: they have been ill treated, and they may yield for a moment to the influence of nature. This clergy with few exceptions, are from the ranks of the people, they inherit their feelings … they have imbibed the doctrines of Locke … and they know more the principles of the constitution than they do of passive obedience.[40]

36 Patrick J. Corish, *Maynooth College, 1795–1995* (Dublin, 1995), p. 19.   37 *Eighth report of Commissioners of Irish Education*, HC 1826–7 (89) xiii, p. 182.   38 BLO Clarendon papers, Irish deposit box 50, Clarendon to MacHale, 5 Dec. 1847.   39 Ibid., Murray to Clarendon, 25 Jan. 1849.   40 W.J. Fitzpatrick, *The life, times and correspondence of the Rt Rev. Dr Doyle*, 2 vols (Dublin, 1861), i, 339.

These suggestions were immediately refuted by a group of Maynooth professors who protested their own loyalty and insisted that they inculcated in their students only ideas of steadfastness to the constituted authorities.[41]

Further evidence of the loyalty of the clergy can be found in the conduct of Patrick MacArtan, the parish priest of Loughlinisland, Co. Down, who testified against Thomas Russell for the latter's part in the Emmet rebellion of 1803.[42] In addition, MacArtan addressed a letter to the local landlord, Matthew Forde, which was signed by 1,320 of his parishioners, declaring the intention of Catholics in the area to 'defend the present order of things as by law established'.[43] For this proof of their loyalty the Catholics asked only 'the protection of the laws, and the confidence of our Protestant brethren'. All of this despite the fact that MacArtan's church had been burnt on several occasion and that he had been personally manhandled by Orangemen.

Ulster churchmen could at times carry their desire to express loyalty to the crown to extraordinary lengths. When Queen Victoria and her husband visited Ireland in the famine year of 1849, four of the five Ulster bishops (the archbishopric of Armagh was vacant at the time) signed the loyal address to be presented to the couple. Their signatures were secured even before Archbishop Murray of Dublin had inserted into the address, at the insistence of some bishops elsewhere in the country, 'a slight allusion to the sufferings of the poor, in a way, however, which could not possibly give offence'.[44]

Is Carleton's characterization of the clergy as highly politicized, drunken, money grabbing and greedy for the things of this world correct? The statutes in force in the diocese of Clogher between 1789 and 1822 specifically state that 'no one on account of failing to pay the stipend [of the priest] should be refused the sacraments at Easter'. This point was reiterated by the National Synod of Thurles in 1850 and tends to suggest that that priests were over-anxious to ensure that their parishioners pay them their dues. The Clogher statutes also add: 'wishing that it may be impressed, not on tablets of stone but on the fleshy tablets of the heart ... that you abstain from drunkenness and intoxication', adding that a priest who gets drunk will be punished with suspension. Such injunctions were common, but they were not always heeded. Even the aged bishop of Raphoe, Patrick MacGettigan, could in his declining years be seen drunk in public. Playing cards (often for money) and drinking could be tolerated up to a point; harder to stomach were the sexual misdeeds of the clergy and there were some spectacular lapses from that most difficult of virtues, chastity.

41 Corish, *Maynooth College*, p. 62. **42** *Belfast Newsletter*, 25 Nov. 1803. **43** James O'Laverty, *An historical account of the diocese of Down and Connor, ancient and modern*, 3 vols (Dublin, 1878–84), i, 100. **44** BLO Clarendon papers, Irish deposit box 50, Murphy to Clarendon, 25 Jan 1849.

   This is to indicate the worst aspects of clerical misbehaviour, and it is far
from being the whole picture. Even quite hostile commentators of the period
have quite complimentary things to say of Catholic priests. Henry Inglis, in
his *Ireland 1834* found that very many of the Maynooth-trained priests,
whatever their lack of educational accomplishments, were nonetheless 'charitable and heedful of the poor; and ... grudged no privations in the exercise
of their religious duties', an example he thought which might serve as a
model for the clergy of the established church. We can also see a slow but
gradual improvement in the educational standards of the Maynooth students.
From the turn of the century, the college began to offer a better education,
despite the fact that in not a few instances it had to deal with relatively poor
abilities in its students. A number of observers, however, continued to
contrast the Maynooth product unfavourably with the continentally trained
priests. Inglis again testifies that

> I found the old foreign educated priest, a gentleman, a man of frank
> easy deportment, and generally good information; but by no means so
> good a Catholic as his brother from Maynooth: he I found either a
> coarse vulgar-minded man, or a stiff, close conceited man; but in every
> instance Popish to the back bone: learned I dare say in theology, but
> profoundly ignorant of that which liberalizes the mind: a hot zealot in
> religion; and fully impressed with, or professing to be impressed with
> a sense of his consequence and influence.[45]

To say the least not a flattering picture.
   Patrick Corish in his history of the college, is inclined to think that
Maynooth students of the nineteenth century came from better-off
backgrounds than their eighteenth-century equivalents, and thus had more
access to a good general education.[46] The Church of Ireland rector of
Donaghmore, Co. Down, could in the late 1860s say of Fr Felix McLaughlin,
the local parish priest, that he was a 'most kind, good-natured priest of the
old school', his Maynooth education notwithstanding.[47] Furthermore Dr
Denvir, in his report to Rome on the state of the diocese of Down and
Connor in 1845, declared that the reason Catholicism had made such
progress in Ulster was precisely the influence of the Maynooth-trained
priests.
   It is important, then, not to labour under the misapprehension that the
Ulster clergy were ill-educated, or that the bishops were not selective in those

45 Henry David Inglis, *Ireland 1834*, 2 vols (London, 1835), i, 340. **46** Corish,
Maynooth College, p. 40. **47** J. Davidson Cowan, *An ancient Irish parish past and
present, being the parish of Donaghmore County Down* (London, 1914), p. 348.

whom they promoted to the priesthood. Archbishop Thomas Kelly of Armagh in writing to Paul Cullen, then rector of the Irish College Rome, said that he was distressed to hear Cullen's report of the stupidity of some of the students from Armagh. He told Cullen that if the candidates were 'merely competent' it would be better if they were ordained for an Italian diocese where 'they could be employed with some advantage to themselves and religion than in a country where heresy is to be combated with all the zeal that our resources can furnish'.[48]

In general, one has to conclude that ecclesiastical leadership, at least at the episcopal level, was of a fairly high order. Some of the most accomplished and ecumenical figures in the Ulster episcopacy such as Crolly and Denvir were, moreover, products of Maynooth. In the lower ranks of the clergy, without wishing to ignore the obvious educational and personal failings of some individuals, it must be observed that there is nothing to suggest other than that most priests were serious and devout individuals. Indeed, it was their concerted application to their duties which helped transform the face of Ulster Catholicism so that by the end of the century it is clearly a different phenomenon from that which Carleton wrote about in the 1820s and 1830s.

Carleton had a grudge against Maynooth, for various personal reasons, and it is not without significance to observe that some of this prejudice about the college was shared by Cardinal Cullen. When Cullen became archbishop of Dublin, he set about building his own seminary, precisely because he believed that priests produced by Maynooth were too sympathetic to radical political ideas. Of course he also thought that the place was filled with Gallicanism, and so the students were as disloyal to Rome as they were to the British crown.

In conclusion it must be emphasized that nineteenth-century reform of Catholicism in Ulster was, as in the rest of Ireland, a process that was already underway by the time Paul Cullen arrived in Ireland as archbishop of Armagh in 1850. The reform, especially under the impetus given it by Cullen's presence, involved the gradual abolition of stations, restrictions on wakes, assertions of orthodox Christianity over superstitions, emphasis on temperance over drunkenness and the reform of culture and morals. In many ways we witness a sweeping away of an Irish outlook and way of life to be replaced with a genteel moralism. So much had the 'civilizing' agenda of English liberal thought permeated Ireland's ecclesiastical ruling class, that we see the church interpreting its role in terms of, and measuring itself against, the mores of English civil society. The church then, far more effectively than the state ever could, laboured to reduce Irish society to a gradual sense of

48 AICR Cullen papers, Kelly to Cullen, 2 Oct. 1834.

manners and order. What we see at work in nineteenth-century Ireland is the last round in the struggle between a modern Catholic way of life and a traditional Gaelic view of how Catholic life should be lived.

Carleton was, in some ways, an unwitting tool in that process. By exposing so effectively the shortcomings of the Irish Catholic peasant's outlook on life and religion, he played into the hands of the reformers and strengthened their resolve to show that Carleton merely parodied what he knew of Irish peasant Catholicism. Carleton, in recording, also sat in judgment on a way of life, as indeed did other reformers of Irish religious and cultural life, reform-minded priests and bishops. This is precisely the irony: Carleton, as a convert from Catholicism, put himself in alliance with ultramontane Catholicism in the struggle for modernity over traditionalism.

It must be a matter of regret that nineteenth-century Ireland did not produce a Protestant Carleton: one who would have portrayed insights into the thoughts and feelings, patterns of behaviour, and even superstitions of the Ulster Protestant peasant. Equally, perhaps, such a picture would not have differed so very markedly in its underlying features from the one that Carleton paints of the Catholic peasantry.

5

Disraeli, Catholics and Ireland

Disraeli could write to his secretary, Montagu Corry, in October 1866, 'My Roman Catholic policy as distinguished from my Irish policy has always been shaped with reference to the English Roman Catholics, a most powerful body, and naturally Tories.'[1] That Disraeli should make a distinction between Catholic Ireland and Roman Catholics in England might, on the face of it, seem an obvious thing to do. It is probably true that at a political level, after emancipation English and Irish Catholics went their separate ways with relation to their respective social and political expectations. On the other hand, both in the late 1850s and early 1860s Disraeli, whatever his leader Lord Derby might think, did give some consideration to the possibility of winning over Irish Catholics to the Tory cause.

In 1861 Disraeli told Lord Stanley that his aim for twenty years had been a union between the Conservative Party and Irish Catholics.[2] In a speech at Wycombe in December 1834, when Disraeli was still feverishly trying to get into parliament, he held out the possibility of concessions to Irish Catholic sentiment on the grounds that Ireland being 'agricultural, aristocratic and religious' might naturally be Tory with 'a little careful handling'.[3] However, as unlikely as this might at first seem we must not neglect the fact that Disraeli did support some causes dear to the heart of Catholic Ireland. By the late 1850s he was a resolute opponent of Italian nationalism and therefore a defender of the Papal States and the temporal power of the pope. At the 1859 general election he urged the appointment of more Catholics to the Dublin administration. In 1864 Disraeli refused to meet Garibaldi in London at a time when the grandees of the Liberal Party were falling over themselves to consort with the great Italian revolutionary hero. Such was Disraeli's popularity in certain Irish Catholic circles that in July 1864 he secured the support of twenty Irish Catholic MPs in a vote of no confidence in Palmerston's Liberal government.

There was a variety of reasons why Catholics should support Disraeli. In principle, at least, he was in favour of denominational education, paid for by the state; furthermore he had long advocated compensation for tenant improvement, taxes on absentee landlords and government support for

1 BLO Disraeli papers B/XX/D/22, Disraeli to Corry, 16 Oct. 1866.   2 Paul Smith, *Disraeli* (Cambridge, 1996), p. 118.   3 The speech is reproduced in full in William Hutcheon (ed.), *Whigs and Whiggism* (London, 1913), pp 23–40.

railway development in Ireland. All these policies were designed to appeal to the Irish Catholic voter. But in what sense could a Catholic–Tory alliance be 'practical politics'; was such a notion merely 'a piece of Disraeli escapism'? Dermot Quinn has observed that, 'Disraeli ... talked about a catholic alliance, publicly and privately, without infusing the words with political meaning. Indeed to *dream* of such an alliance was to admit of its impracticality.'[4] One does not have to be quite so cynical to appreciate the incongruity of the proposition; nevertheless the idea of a Tory–Catholic rapprochement was to persist well into the 1870s, long past a time when it could have been feasible.

As late as May 1878 Isaac Butt observed that, 'a very general feeling is pervading the Roman Catholic body that their true and natural alliance is with the Conservative Party'.[5] The *Freeman's Journal* of the previous March was perhaps more accurate in its reflection that:

> the phenomenon of the Irish Catholic Conservative which was heretofore possible, and which would, if the government had settled the education question, have been so common as to cease to be exceptional, is now an impossibility.[6]

But why should this have been the case? Why should there have been the possibility of general Catholic support for the Tories and why should this have centred around Disraeli's view and ambitions? To attempt to answer these questions it is necessary to look at Disraeli's two careers as a writer and as a politician.

Even before he entered parliament, Disraeli had embroiled himself in Irish affairs. In the election of 1834, when he was standing as an independent, he had advocated the abolition of Church of Ireland tithes from Catholics.[7] This was part and parcel of a radical phase that Disraeli had been going through since the late 1820s, which even saw him giving support to the Chartists.[8] His radicalism, however, was not getting him elected to parliament and, like many people in such circumstances; he began to change his tune. Adopted as the Tory candidate for the Taunton bye-election in 1835, he took the opportunity to criticize Daniel O'Connell, castigating the fact that a man whom the Whigs had called a traitor they now had to enter into a pact with to shore up their position in parliament. This was misrepresented in the press and Disraeli was reported as having called O'Connell 'a traitor ... an incendiary'.

4 Dermot Quinn, *Patronage and piety: the politics of English Roman Catholicism, 1850–1900* (London, 1993), p. 62.   5 David Thornley, *Isaac Butt and Home Rule* (London, 1965), p. 381.   6 *Weekly Freeman*, 22 Mar. 1879.   7 W.F. Monypenny and G.E. Buckle, *The life of Benjamin Disraeli, earl of Beaconsfield* 6 vols (London, 1910–20), i, 270.   8 Stanley Weintraub, *Disraeli: a biography* (New York, 1993), pp 186–8.

O'Connell gave as good as he got and referred to Disraeli as 'a vile creature, a reptile possessed of perfidy, selfish depravity and want of principle'. Adverting to Disraeli's Jewish background, O'Connell made a number of anti-semitic remarks culminating in the barb that Disraeli had 'just the qualities of the impenitent thief on the cross'.[9] It is perhaps worth remarking that Disraeli had to suffer from this type of anti-semitism throughout his political career. Even when he finally became prime minister in 1868, Lord Clarendon remarked that of a man in high office one 'desires that he should be honest & well principled & have some consistency and some perception of the difference between right and wrong, in all of which the Jew is notoriously deficient'.[10] Even Cardinal Newman remarked in a pompous and supercilious manner, 'Does not Disraeli's elevation show that when you open the highest places [in government] to mere talent, you must not hope to find in them nobility of mind?'[11]

To return to 1835: Disraeli, to say the least, was not best pleased with O'Connell's strictures. He initially challenged O'Connell to a duel. When O'Connell refused on the grounds that he had once killed a man in a duel and had vowed never to take part in such activities again, Disraeli challenged O'Connell's son, Morgan, who rightly did not see why he should be compelled to fight duels on behalf of his father. Morgan did concede that he had in fact fought a duel with Lord Alvanley, but that was because Alvanley had insulted O'Connell senior. Disraeli responded by publishing a long and scurrilous letter in the press deprecating O'Connell. He topped this off by writing to Morgan:

> Now Sir, I *have* insulted him; assuredly it was intention to do so … And I fervently pray that you, or someone of his blood, may attempt to avenge the unextinguishable hatred with which I shall pursue his existence.[12]

Furthermore Disraeli resolved never to let up in a campaign to blacken O'Connell's name. In the following year Disraeli published a series of letters in *The Times* signed 'Runnymeade', in which he systematically attacked O'Connell, Catholicism, the Irish and the Liberal government. He denounced O'Connell as 'the vagabond delegate of a foreign priesthood … the hired instrument of the papacy, as such his mission is to destroy your Protestant society'.[13] Adverting to O'Connell's religious practices, Disraeli

9 Monypenny and Buckle, i, 288.   10 A.L. Kennedy (ed.), *My dear duchess: social and political letters of the duchess of Manchester, 1858–1869* (London, 1956), p. 345.   11 C.S. Dessain and Thomas Gornall (eds), *Letters and diaries of John Henry Newman*, xxiv (Oxford, 1973), p. 43.   12 Monypenny and Buckle, i, 292.   13 Francis Hitchman

observed that some people marvel at the fact that 'the triumphant demagogue humbles himself in the mud before a simple priest', but, he continued

> There is no hypocrisy in this, no craft. The agent recognized his principal, the slave bowed before his lord, and when he pressed to his lips those sacred robes, reeking with whiskey and … incense, I doubt not that his soul was filled at the same time with unaffected awe and devout gratitude.[14]

To say the least, not a flattering portrait of O'Connell or the Irish Catholic priesthood. Disraeli's real venom, however, was reserved for a subsequent letter addressed to the house of lords in which he said of the Irish:

> They are the foes of England. They hate our free fertile isle. They hate our order, our civilization … our liberty, our pure religion. This wild, reckless, indolent, uncertain and superstitious race have no sympathy with the English character … Their history describes an unbroken circle of bigotry and blood. And now, forsooth the cry is raised that they have been misgoverned! How many who sound this party shibboleth have studied the history of Ireland? A savage population under the influence of the papacy, has, nevertheless, been so regulated, that they have contributed to the creation of a highly-civilised and Protestant empire.[15]

All this seems an unpromising start for a man who was to claim that he had given most of his early political life to winning Irish Catholics for the Tory cause. His maiden speech on entering the house of commons in 1837 was also filled with anti-O'Connell, anti-Irish and anti-Catholic hyperbole.[16] There were, however, other influences on Disraeli at that stage. With the return to power of the Tories in 1841 Disraeli had hoped for office under Sir Robert Peel. The prime minister was, however, not well disposed to Disraeli and refused him a position in his ministry. For his part, Disraeli formed, along with George Smythe and Lord George Manners, a ginger group of backbench Tories in opposition to Peel which became known as 'Young England'. It is difficult to say how much ideological coherence the group had beyond the fact that they 'despised utilitarianism, middle-class liberalism and centralised government'.[17] They were also caught up in a romanticism about

(ed.), *The Runnymeade letters* (London, 1885), p. 115. **14** Ibid. **15** Quoted in G.I.T. Machin, *Disraeli* (London, 1995), p. 29. **16** Monypenny and Buckle, ii, 8–12. He deliberately asked Lord Stanley to give way in the debate so that he could follow O'Connell in the speaking order. **17** David R. Schwarz, *Disraeli's fiction* (London, 1979), p. 81.

England's pre-reformation Catholic past, which found expression in various literary endeavours. Even Lord John Manners in a fit of enthusiasm for the English Middle Ages was able to pen such forgettable lines as, 'Each knew his place, king, peasant, peer or priest, The greater owed connexion with the least, from rank to rank the generous feeling ran, And linked society as man to man'.[18]

More substantially there issued from Disraeli's pen the so-called Young England trilogy: *Coningsby* (1844), *Sybil* (1845) and *Tancred* (1847). In these works Disraeli not only attacked Peel, for having no principles; he also rejected the Whig view of history. More importantly, however, from our point of view, he gave a much more sympathetic treatment of Catholicism that was evident in his Runnymeade letters. Sympathy for Catholicism was not, however, to last, and by the time he wrote *Lothair*, published in 1870, he had returned to his old anti-Catholic and anti-Irish ways. Why that should be we will come to in due course. It is interesting to record, however, the chronology of Disraeli's personal history associated with his early novels. When he began writing *Coningsby* in 1844 he was a 40-year-old MP with few real prospects. He had not yet made a name for himself as an orator, and he had still to live down the scandal of bad debts and a hasty marriage to a wealthy society widow. The marriage alone had made him a figure of some notoriety.[19] By the time *Tancred* appeared, he had become the leader of his parliamentary party in the house of commons and had brought down Sir Robert Peel's administration almost single-handedly. All this in little over three years.

Vernon Bogdanor warns that we should not take the sentiments expressed in Disraeli's novels at their face value.[20] On the other hand, Disraeli himself claimed that, '[m]y books are the history of my life', and Isaiah Berlin observed in relation to Disraeli's fiction: 'A man may not be sincere in his political speeches or his letters, but his works of art are of himself and tell one where his true values lie.'[21]

There are in fact striking parallels between Disraeli's fiction and his public political pronouncements. In *Sybil*, for example, he has his hero, Egremont, say of the way in which English history has been written that: 'Generally speaking, all the great events have been distorted, most of the important causes concealed, some of the principal characters never appear, and all who do are misunderstood and misrepresented.' The Glorious Revolution he dismissed as the Dutch 'invasion' of 1688, in contrast to the Whig idolization of that event.

In the year prior to the publication of *Sybil*, in a speech in the commons

18 Ibid., p. 83. **19** Robert Blake, *Disraeli* (London, 1966), pp 158–61. **20** Vernon Bogdanor (ed.), *Lothair* (London, 1975), p. xxxvi. **21** Quoted in Schwarz, *Disraeli's fiction*, p. 81.

during the adjournment debate on Ireland he had blamed all the troubles of the country on the Whigs. 'To attribute the present condition of Ireland to Protestantism' he declared, 'was an error.' Puritanism, so far as he was concerned, was the cause of Ireland's ills, and he went on to accuse the Whigs of supporting in Ireland 'the tyranny established by Oliver Cromwell'.[22] Equating Anglican Protestantism with Toryism, he remarked that the Tories did not seek to exclude anyone and it was not they who had invented the penal laws. In ringing tones he asserted that the Tories were 'the natural allies of the Irish people'.[23] In a sense Disraeli was giving a revisionist account of Irish history to suit his own political ends.

It is also worth saying that it was in this remarkable speech that Disraeli made his famous analysis of the Irish problem, 'a starving population and absentee aristocracy, an alien Church, and in addition the weakest executive in the world'. He went on to suggest that if in the abstract one were reading about such conditions one would say the remedy for such social dysfunction was revolution. However, such a contingency was ruled out because of Ireland's connection with England. Ironically, many years later these ideas were to find a resonance in an unlikely quarter. Archbishop John MacHale writing in the summer of 1864 could say

> Whilst our rulers extend to all subjects of all the other governments of the world the right to revolt beyond what religion or reason would sanction, so jealous are they of the superior excellence of their own government that to arraign it of tyranny or injustice would be deemed wickedness or infatuation.[24]

For Disraeli, at that stage of his political development the connection with England was logically the cause of Ireland's miseries. In which case it was the government's duty to affect all the changes a revolution would bring about. The moment one had a strong executive, a just administration, and ecclesiastical equality, there would be order in Ireland. Even so Disraeli believed that such a process would take fifty years.

At this point in his career one could say that Disraeli had in many ways grasped the need for far-reaching reforms in Ireland, and saw that such reforms needed to be prosecuted at every level. It therefore comes as something of a surprise to discover that in 1845 he actually opposed the increase of the grant to Maynooth, despite the fact that the other two leaders of the Young England group, Manners and Smythe, supported the move.

22 *Hansard* 3rd series lxxii, 1012. **23** Ibid., 1009. **24** Quoted in Emmet Larkin, 'The Irish political tradition' in Thomas E. Hachey and Lawrence J. McCaffrey (eds), *Perspectives on Irish nationalism* (Lexington, 1989), p. 100.

For his part, Disraeli joined the ultra-Protestants and high tories in trying to defeat the measure – an indication of the worst sort of political inconsistence for personal advantage. By contrast, Ian Machin has argued Disraeli's stance on the Maynooth grant represented 'no consistent opposition to Irish Catholic interests on his part, but was merely the seizure of another chance to attack Peel'.[25] Equally it has to be observed that in their exchange in the commons on the matter Peel pointed out that Disraeli had written to him asking for government office, which the prime minister had refused, and he suggested that this was the cause of Disraeli's opposition to the government proposal and not any fixed principle.[26]

It is also important to bear in mind that Gladstone also abandoned his stated public position in order to vote on the Maynooth question, but in his case in favour of the increase of the grant. Such an action was contrary to the views he had outlined in his two volumes on, *The State in Its Relations with the Church* (1838). Gladstone therefore resigned his ministerial office rather than appear to be inconsistent. When he tried to explain all this to the house of commons Cobden remarked, 'I have been sitting listening with pleasure for an hour to his explanation, and yet I know no more why he left the government than before he began.'[27]

It seems clear that Disraeli was much more concerned with the advancement of his own political position than he was with treating issues of policy on their own merits, or indeed even as part of a consistent political philosophy. He even campaigned against Peel's 'Protection of life: Ireland Bill' of 1846, despite the fact that it aimed to do just what Disraeli had demanded of the government: namely to 'feed the poor and hang the traitors'.[28] His opposition to this measure helped bring down his party leader whom he despised. Ironically, of course, if one takes Disraeli's political outlook as a whole, what we actually see is that when he was in a position of power, for the most part, he followed Peelite policies. Thus, when in 1852 his fellow Tory MP, the ultra-Protestant, Richard Spooner, called for an inquiry into the continuation of the Maynooth grant, Disraeli resolutely opposed him, since Disraeli and other party leaders hoped to increase Tory support in Ireland at the general election that year, and this they succeeded in doing.

No such considerations weighed with him during the passage of the Ecclesiastical Titles Act of 1851. He supported the measure but tried to gain advantage over Lord John Russell's government by appearing to be more 'no-

25 Machin, *Disraeli*, p. 46.   **26** Weintraub, *Disraeli*, p. 254. Disraeli in response lied saying he had never either directly or indirectly sought office from Peel. C.S. Parker (ed.), *Sir Robert Peel from his private letters*, 3 vols (London, 1891–9), ii, 486–9, gives the original exchange of letters.   **27** John Morley, *Life of Gladstone*, 3 vols (London, 1903), i, 278.   **28** Hitchman, *Runnymede letters*, p. 89.

popery' than Russell himself. In November 1850 he attempted to stage a county meeting in Buckinghamshire so as to accuse the government of actually encouraging papal aggression by previous concessions to Catholics. Furthermore he helped to devise a commons motion which was debated in May 1851 and which attributed to Russell's government, rather that to Pius IX, the responsibility for the restoration of the Catholic hierarchy in England.[29] All this was so much political posturing and has to be set against what Disraeli regarded as Russell's political miscalculation in the whole affair. He wrote to Lord Stanley that Russell was 'indulging in his hereditary foible, to wit having a shy at the papists'.[30] Russell's attitude alienated, as Disraeli pointed out, the two props of his government: the Irish Catholics, who were horrified by Russell's reference to Catholic ceremonials as 'the mummeries of superstition', and the Peelites, who reacted with distain to the prime minister's attempts to revive sectarian tensions in England. From this whole affair Disraeli learned, as Lord Blake has pointed out, that Catholic affairs were 'a political liability of the first order'.[31]

So far as Ireland was concerned Disraeli tried, albeit half-heartedly, to move the Tories in the direction of reform when they briefly came to power in 1852. Although chancellor of the exchequer he proposed two bills for the redress of tenant grievances, admittedly to offset the unpopular measure of the extension of income tax to Ireland, but influenced nonetheless by the leaders of the Tenant Right League, Charles Gavan Duffy, William Shee, and Frederick Lucas. Lord Derby, the prime minister, would have none of it writing angrily to Disraeli, 'If we lose the landed gentry of Ireland, especially of the North, we are gone.' In the event the government's budget was rejected by the house of commons and the Tories were gone. Disraeli would make little further effort to influence Conservative policy on Ireland until he had himself attained prime ministerial office.

By the end of January 1867 Lord Mayo, the Tory chief secretary for Ireland, was in an optimistic mood. He talked of meeting the new session of parliament with a good tenant bill, and an education commission to examine the university question, *habeas corpus* restored, and, with spectacular miscalculation, 'the Fenian movement crushed and the country very quiet'. The decision to rescind the emergency legislation was soon reversed and the *habeas corpus* suspension act was reintroduced and all its provisions became law on 26 February. In terms of an attempt at long-term remedial policies the Tories appointed a Royal Commission on the Church of Ireland later that year in the aftermath of the half-hearted Fenian rising. Russell was convinced that if Disraeli succeeded Derby as party leader, he would use the question of

29 Machin, *Disraeli*, p. 93.   30 Blake, *Disraeli*, p. 300.   31 Ibid.

disestablishment of the Church of Ireland as a means of persuading radical liberals to continue their support for the minority Conservative government.[32]

On the other hand, with the Fenian rising and the Manchester and Clerkenwell incidents the government had more immediate concerns in dealing with the potentially explosive Irish situation. Judging by the extensive correspondence that he conducted in relation to the victims of the Clerkenwell bombing, and the fact that he directed the relief effort through his secretary, Disraeli does seem to have been genuinely moved by the plight of those who were killed or injured. Equally there was a good deal of cynicism shown by those around him. Henry Matthews wrote to Montagu Corry:

> I cannot refrain from expressing my delight at your beneficent exertions at Clerkenwell, which do the utmost honor to your chief and yourself. I would have given a great deal to have seen you arrive, like a good fairy, with a bag full of gold & silver, to assist the wretched suffers. It was a counter-expulsion of prompt and delicate charity and reads like an oriental story; as though you were secretary to a Vizier ... rather than to a Minister of Queen Victoria.[33]

In more general terms there were those such as John Bright, not it must be stressed an impartial observer, who believed that the only policy the Tories had towards Ireland was one of terror.[34] Others such as Cardinal Cullen, a strong supporter of tough law and order measures, were beginning to despair of the Tories enacting any political reforms. Archbishop Manning of Westminster could write to Cullen in March 1868 that, 'Mr Disraeli', who had just become prime minister upon Derby's resignation, 'would have an Irish policy if he could; but his followers render it impossible as they always have and always will.'

Nevertheless Disraeli had to flirt with the notion of some policy for Ireland. He commissioned John Lambert, the head of the Poor Law Board, to draw up a memorandum on Irish affairs, and this Lambert presented at the beginning of March 1868. Lambert stressed the need to establish tranquillity in the country with measures which went beyond mere 'temporary palliatives'. The memo rehearsed many typical English prejudices, such as that the Irish could not govern themselves and that they lacked the qualities necessary for industrial enterprise. Lambert did, however, advocate a reform

32 British Library Add. MS 44429 Gladstone papers, Russell to Gladstone, 3 Jan. 1868, f. 3. 33 BLO B/XII/D/6 Disraeli papers, Matthews to Corry, 18 Dec. 1867. 34 That at least is what Bright confided to his diary on 21 November 1867. R.A.J. Walling (ed.), *The diaries of John Bright* (London, 1930), p. 312.

programme which would have found favour even with Cardinal Cullen. The memo recommended disestablishment of the Church of Ireland and the secularization of its endowments, a charter for the Catholic University, and 'perhaps some modification ... in the national system of education, so as to render it more in accordance with the denominational system in England'.[35]

Disraeli was also taking advice from other places. Charles Gavan Duffy had already written to him from Australia in November 1867 urging him to settle the land issue, about which Duffy made various proposals, which had they been enacted would have allowed tenants to buy out their holdings for annual payments. He further commented, with perceptive political sagacity, that 'The Church question and the education question will remain to be dealt with no doubt, but these are the questions of an educated minority, the uneasy classes are uneasy because of perpetual uncertainty of tenure.'[36]

It is not clear if either Lambert's memo or Duffy's letter had any impact on Disraeli's thinking on Ireland. His general policy on the question throughout 1868 was determined by the need to maintain his minority administration with the indulgence of radical liberals while at the same time not alienating the more high church members on his own benches. Disraeli had, however, out-maneuvered Gladstone and the Liberals on the Reform Act of 1867, and might well have done so over Ireland, even on the church question. In the aftermath of the election of 1865 he had written to Lord Derby, 'I do not think any general resolution respecting the Irish church could be successfully withstood in the present parliament. It is a very unpopular cause even with our best men.'[37]

Disraeli had for some time been in negotiations with Archbishop Manning concerning the question of a charter for the Catholic University in Dublin. It is also clear that he had been discussing with him a whole range of issues including land reform and concurrent endowment. So far as the university was concerned Disraeli proposed that the governing body should consist of five bishops, with the president of Maynooth and a large body of laymen. In addition, the state would pay for the establishment costs, but the question of state endowment would be postponed. But Disraeli was insistent that there was to be no attempt to influence the religious opinions of such non-Catholics as might attend the university. Manning had seen a draft of these proposals and had assured Disraeli that the Irish bishops would approve of them.[38] He had written to Cullen: 'Would it not be best to accept [a charter without endowment]? Would not endowment come by force of events?'[39]

35 BLO Disraeli papers B/IX/A/1, 'Legislation for Ireland' p. 13. The memo is dated 1 March 1867. 36 Quoted in Monypenny and Buckle, *Disraeli*, v, 8. 37 Ibid., iv, 405–6. 38 Ibid., v, pp 5–6. 39 Shane Leslie, *Henry Edward Manning, his life and labours* (London, 1921), p. 208.

For their part the Irish bishops had other ideas and wanted not just a charter but full financial support as well. In addition they wished to have a board mostly composed of bishops and clerics, with Cardinal Cullen as the chancellor. Archbishop Leahy of Cashel and Bishop Derry of Clonfert, on behalf on the Irish bishops also insisted with the prime minister, when they visited London on behalf of the Irish hierarchy, that the bishops should have the right to select the books for the university library. Disraeli knew that such proposals would be unacceptable to most members of the house of commons. It was precisely at this point that Gladstone gave notice of his intention to introduce his famous resolutions on the Irish Church question which so captured the imagination of his party and of the Catholic community in both Ireland and Britain.

Only a few days before Gladstone's notice, Disraeli had written to Lord Derby that the cabinet had decided to bring in a land bill and had unanimously approved of his university scheme. He continued:

> With regard to the great difficulty and the real danger, the Church, although there was great difference of opinion in the Cabinet, on the merits of the question there was unanimity that it ought not to be treated except in a new parliament; and also that no pledge should be given of maintaining absolutely unchanged the present state of ecclesiastical affairs.[40]

Disraeli's old ally Lord Stanley confided to him that no one who was not an Irishman had anything good to say about the Church of Ireland. At the same time Disraeli could tell the Tory Lord Cairns, an Ulster Protestant and an Orangeman, that he intended to link the question of Irish disestablishment with that of disestablishment in England and Scotland. Disingenuously he wrote to Queen Victoria that Gladstone's proposals for the first time sought to dissolve the connection between government and religion. If disestablishment were to succeed, he assured the queen, the Anglican Church would break into sects and schisms,

> and ultimately be absorbed by the tradition and discipline of the Church of Rome, and the consequence will be that the Queen's supremacy, the security of our religious liberty, and in no slight degree, our civil rights would be destroyed.[41]

In his speech on Gladstone's resolutions Disraeli was at pains to assert the relationship between the state's authority and divine power. 'If government is

---

40 Monypenny and Buckle, *Disraeli*, v, 13–14. **41** Ibid., pp 31–2.

not divine, it is nothing. It is a mere affair of the police office, of the tax gatherer, of the guardroom.' It was not the best speech Disraeli ever made, and both John Bright and Gladstone recorded in their diaries that Disraeli was clearly the worse for the brandy and water he was drinking throughout his performance at the dispatch box. If the effects of brandy can be invoked in mitigation of his ill temper in 1868, no such excuse can be adduced for his comments in February 1871 during the debate on the suspension of *habeas corpus*. The cabinet had decided upon a select committee to investigate the matter at which Disraeli thundered that Gladstone's policies in effect 'legalized confiscations, consecrated sacrilege, condoned high treason'. He continued: 'we have destroyed Churches, we have shaken property to its foundations, we have emptied gaols, and now we cannot govern a country without coming to a parliamentary committee'.[42]

Not everyone in his party shared Disraeli's intellectual instability. In 1868 Disraeli's contradictory attitudes over the church issue led Lord Cranborne, his fiercest critic on the Tory benches, to say that he would as soon predict which way a weathercock would be pointing as to prophecy Disraeli's attitude to the great questions before parliament.[43] For the rest of the 1868 session leading to the general election in December that year, Disraeli did his best to turn the climate of public opinion in a decidedly ultra-Protestant direction, in the hopes of raising a no-popery scare over the disestablishment of the Church of Ireland. He claimed that high church ritualists and followers of the pope had long been in secret combination and were now in open confederation to subvert Protestantism. To the queen he wrote that the general election would be 'a great Protestant struggle'.[44]

Lord Blake has calculated that this attempt to stir up militant anti-Catholic feeling had no effect on the outcome of the election except in Lancashire, where the blast of no-popery had its usual salutary effect in the Tories' favour. There were, however, some surprises elsewhere not least in Dungarvan, Co. Waterford. Here the future Viscount Llandaff, Henry Matthew, an English Catholic, won the contest for the Tories, at a cost it is said of 800 bottles of whiskey. Matthew would subsequently become the first Catholic in modern times to be a cabinet minister.

Disraeli's attempt to use the lords in 1869 to frustrate Gladstone's bill on the Irish Church was not one of the high points of his political career. It seems strange that for so gifted a politician Disraeli should immerse himself in such blatant anti-Catholic agitation. At the same time such sentiments were very much part of the fabric of British political life throughout the

42 *Hansard* 3rd series cxcvi, 1058.   **43** Blake, *Disraeli*, pp 498–9.   **44** G.E. Buckle (ed.), *The letters of Queen Victoria*, second series, 2 vols (London, 1926), i, 501.

nineteenth, and indeed into the twentieth, century. By 1874 even Gladstone was to indulge himself in vituperative anti-Catholic sentiment with the publication of his *The Vatican Decrees in their bearing on civil allegiance*, in which he questioned the ability of Catholics to be loyal to the state in the light of papal infallibility. The following year saw the publication of his *Vaticanism: an answer to reproofs and replies*, which if anything was even more rhetorically polemical than his efforts the year before. British appetite for this type of anti-Catholic diatribe was such as to earn Gladstone substantial sums from royalties at a time when he was facing some financial embarrassment.[45]

Out of office from December 1868, Disraeli used his enforced leisure to settle some old scores by writing his first novel in twenty-three years. *Lothair* was loosely based, among others things, on the conversion to Catholicism of John Patrick Crichton-Stuart, the 3rd marquis of Bute, in 1868. Montagu Corry had written to Disraeli of the young Bute's accession to the Catholic faith that he was 'joining himself to the scarlet woman'. In Disraeli's eyes *Lothair* was a warning against the twin evils of Catholicism and nationalism, both of which were the products of fanaticism.

In the novel Disraeli paints a very unflattering portrait of Archbishop Manning who appears, thinly disguised, as Cardinal Grandison, a man who deals in deception and is altogether calculating and dishonest. The Fenians too make an appearance. 'Captain Bruges', otherwise known as 'the general', clearly the French General Gustave Cluseret, whom they are hoping to recruit as military tactician, a role Cluseret actually played for the Fenians, is made to say:

> I am sorry it is an Irish affair, though, to be sure what else could it be? I am not fond of Irish affairs: whatever may be said, and however plausible things may look, in an Irish business there is always a priest at the bottom, I hate priests.[46]

Again one might argue that such sentiments do not actually represent Disraeli's view and are mere poetic license. In this instance, however, he was challenged in a review of the novel in the Catholic weekly *The Tablet* to repudiate the blatantly anti-Catholic sentiments of the novel, a challenge he chose to ignore. Furthermore, in the preface to the eighth edition Disraeli referred to Catholic religious practices which had been taken up by the Oxford Movement, as 'medieval superstitions, which are generally only the embodiments of pagan ceremonies'.[47]

45 Roy Jenkins, *Gladstone* (London, 1995), p. 391.   46 *Lothair* (Hughenden ed., London, 1881), p. 48.   47 Ibid., p. xv.

The work enjoyed enormous contemporary popularity. The first edition sold out within two days. On the first day of publication in the United States it sold 15,000 copies and in 1870 alone there were eight editions. There was, however, a down side to all this notoriety. The novel's appearance caused something of a stir within the Tory party and even led to an attempt to replace Disraeli as leader with the 15th earl of Derby in February 1872. This attempted coup occurred not because of the anti-Catholic sentiments the book contained, but rather because it was felt to be beneath the dignity of the leader of the Tory party to write such insubstantial and undignified a story. In an ironic sequel to the whole episode, the marquis of Bute married in 1872 at the fashionable venue for society weddings, the Brompton Oratory, London. It was the highlight of the social calendar that season. Archbishop Manning presided in the sanctuary, Monsignor Capel, who had also appeared in *Lothair*, officiated, and the best man was none other than Disraeli himself.

Meanwhile, the issue of Ireland remained to haunt the British political scene. Having dealt with the church question and the land issue Gladstone turned his attention in the 1873–4 session of parliament to the university question. This was to prove to be for him, as in some ways it had been for Disraeli, his undoing. G.E. Buckle claimed that in the passage of the bill in 1873: 'Once again Manning was deep in the counsel of a British Primer, hopeful of finding a solution, and he was to mislead Gladstone as he had misled Disraeli.'[48] For his part Disraeli dismissed Gladstone's bill as 'all humbug'. He also claimed that the Catholics, having reduced Ireland to a spiritual desert, now wanted parliament to make the desert bloom. Once again a government fell on the university question, but the Tories refused to form yet another minority administration and Gladstone was forced to soldier on until the general election of 1874. As a result of that contest, for the first time in thirty years the Tories were returned with an overall majority in the commons.

In his government of 1874–80 Disraeli had no real policy for Ireland. Indeed, he was determined to 'keep Ireland in the background',[49] and not to engage in any of the areas that had led to Gladstone's downfall. The lack of priority for Irish affairs was seen in the fact that the Irish chief secretaryship was, yet again, not a cabinet post. Furthermore Disraeli confided in Lord Cairns that the ideal person for the job would be someone who had a good horse and had 'a gift of the gab'.[50] On the other hand, some progress was made in Ireland under the competent management as chief secretary of Michael Hicks Beach. The Royal University was set up and there were some

48 Monypenny and Buckle, *Disraeli*, v, 202.   **49** J.P. Parry, *Democracy and religion: Gladstone and the Liberal Party, 1867–75* (Cambridge, 1986), p. 411.   **50** PRO 30/51/1 Cairns papers, Disraeli to Cairns, 6 Aug. 1875, f. 123.

developments on the question of intermediate education. Most of the tone for the administration's Irish policy was, however, set by the Tory viceroy, the duke of Marlborough, who was in the cabinet. Even Disraeli, however, regarded him as something of a 'black sheep'. Malborough did much to conciliate Catholic opinion, mostly through the charitable activities of his wife. Even his son, Lord Randolph Churchill, busied himself as his father's unpaid secretary whilst trying to become the Tory party's expert on Ireland.[51] In a memorable speech at Woodstock in 1877 Lord Randolph criticized the government's lack of policy on Ireland, but, oddly, blamed this on the obstructionist activities of Irish MPs. The speech caused a minor stir in government circles. Malborough sought to explain away Lord Randolph's aberrant behaviour by writing to the chief secretary that since the speech was delivered after a banquet; he supposed his son must have been drunk.

The only real policy the Tories had for the remainder of Disraeli's administration was one of resistance to home rule. This was what they fought the 1880 election on – an election which once again saw Gladstone in Downing Street and the Tories on the opposition benches. During the election the Liberals accused Disraeli of being anti-Catholic and the mortal enemy of Ireland and the Irish.[52]

Given his personal history as something of an outsider, even when he had climbed to the top of the 'greasy pole', it might have been expected that Disraeli ought to have been more sympathetic to the Catholics and the Irish. On his part we have seen that he claimed to have invested considerable time in drawing his party into alliance with Irish Catholicism, but all this was to no avail. What is true, however, is that English Catholics increasingly came to see their natural home in the Tory ranks. Their loyalty to that party was beyond question, a fact well illustrated in the persons and work of such individuals as John Wallis, editor of *The Tablet,* and Herbert Vaughan who at one point owed and edited the same paper and who in 1893 became the archbishop of Westminster and later a cardinal. As Dermot Quinn has remarked, 'Catholic Tories could always be relied upon to come to the aid of the party, no matter how seldom the party came to the aid of them.'[53]

The particular bonds which united many English Catholics with the Tories were in fact of longstanding duration. One essential ingredient in this adhesion of many Catholic English to the Tory cause was a coolness, not to say hostility, towards the Irish. Thus Cardinal Manning in an exchange of letters with Gladstone at Christmas 1890 remarked of his predecessor Cardinal Nicholas Wiseman that '[h]e was a Tory without Irish sympathies

51 R.F. Foster, *Lord Randolph Churchill: a political life* (Oxford, 1981), p. 57. **52** Monypenny and Buckle, *Disraeli,* vi, 516. **53** Quinn, *Patronage and piety,* p. 62.

though himself an Irishman. He came into the ring of the old Catholic Families and never went beyond them. They as you know and see are nine times English.'[54]

In so far as Disraeli had any policy on any matter it was, as Maurice Cowling observed, one of 'consistent opportunism'.[55] His very position as a rank outsider meant that he often exaggerated the prejudices of the English Tory grandee in an effort to become more 'Tory than the Tories themselves'. In arguing against Gladstone's disestablishment proposals, he declared that the scheme would increase papal power in Ireland. Indeed, he claimed that it facilitated the pope's objective of turning Ireland into 'a popish kingdom'. He ended this particular tirade against Gladstone's bill with words which are as chilling in their prejudice as in their prophetic force. 'It is natural', he declared, 'that the papal power', and by this he meant the Catholics in Ireland, 'will attempt to attain ascendancy and predominance. Is it natural that the Protestants should submit without a struggle, to such a state of things? You know they will not.'[56]

One might charitably conclude that Disraeli was detached from Irish affairs. To be less charitable one might say that in so far as he could he used the issue – as many others did – to forward his political career. He exhibited many of the typical English prejudices in dealing with the Irish and even with English Catholics, and ultimately he had little sympathy for or interest in either.

54 BL Add. MS 44250 Gladstone papers, Manning to Gladstone, Christmas 1890, f. 307. **55** Maurice Cowling, *1867: Disraeli, Gladstone and revolution: the passing of the second reform bill* (Cambridge, 1967), p. 303. **56** *Hansard* 3rd series cxcvi, 1058.

Catholicism in Fermanagh, 1795–1850

For Roman Catholic purposes, most of Fermanagh is in the diocese of Clogher, whose administrative centre, despite its name, is actually in County Monaghan. Three parishes, although in the county either in whole or in part (Derrylin, Killesher-Derrylester and Kinawley), are territorially in the Kilmore diocese. In surveying the documentation for Catholicism in Fermanagh[1] in the eighteenth and early nineteenth centuries one cannot but be struck by the amount of material concerned with feuding between priests and bishops. Seosamh Ó Dufaigh has tried to explain this situation by suggesting that intra-Catholic squabbling occurred as the result of a late survival of the tribal feuds which had brought medieval Ireland to an end in the sixteenth century.[2] If the Catholic authorities gave time and energy to fighting among themselves, their attentions, and that of their congregations, were deflected from whatever criticism they may have had of their political rulers.

The most authoritative historian of Catholic Fermanagh to date has suggested that for the most part at this period Catholics in the county were more submissive to state authorities than their co-religionists elsewhere.[3] It has long been argued that the relative weakness of Presbyterianism in the county militated against United Irish activity in the 1790s. More recent research, however, has tended to suggest that Fermanagh Catholics did participate in the political activities leading up to the rising of 1798.[4] On 12 October 1797 three men from Roslea were hanged for United Irish insurgency. Furthermore we know of individual priests such as John McNally, parish priest of East Clones, who were staunch supporters of the United Irishmen.[5] Henry Forde, the Catholic pastor in Enniskillen, was the agent for the United Irish newspaper, the *Northern Star*. Although some priests were obviously keyed to the possibilities of political action as a means of furthering the cause of Catholicism, others were deeply concerned about the prevalence of defenderism and ribbonism in the community.[6]

---

1 Unusually for a Catholic diocese, very many diocesan documents can be inspected at the Public Record Office of Northern Ireland DIO(RC)/1 passim. 2 S. Ó Dufaigh, 'James Murphy, bishop of Clogher 1801–24' in *Clogher Record*, 6 (1968), 447. 3 Peadar Livingstone, *The Fermanagh story* (Enniskillen, 1969), p. 140. 4 B. MacDonald, 'Fermanagh in the age of the United Irishmen' in Sean MacAnnaidh (ed.), *Fermanagh in 1798* (Tempo, 2000), pp 11–43. 5 J.E. McKenna, *Parishes of Clogher* (Enniskillen, 1920), ii, 105. 6 NAI Rebellion papers 620/9, 9 Sept. 1776 records the details of one

In gauging the health and state of Catholicism in Fermanagh there is a sense in which the church was only as good as its leaders. The education of the clergy in many instances was deficient. The north of Ireland generally was slow to recover from the effects of the penal laws, there was a shortage of priests, and Catholic infrastructure, in the shape of places of worship, was greatly underdeveloped. In many instances ordinary Catholics were ignorant of even the most basic tenets of their faith and sat lightly to the prescriptions of canon law and ecclesiastical discipline. Even as late as 1836 Francis McGennis, parish priest of Enniskillen, could write to the future bishop of Clogher of the state of religion in East Aughnamullen that it was 'frightful in the extreme . . . the misguided people here have resorted to a system of terror and vow to spurn all Church authority'.[7]

Given the deprived economic state of most Catholics, ecclesiastical authorities were heavily dependent on the generosity of Protestant benefactors for the building of places of worship. That help was in the main readily given, as the Catholic authorities acknowledged.[8] It is perhaps tempting to think that Protestant assistance for Catholic purposes was a feature of the fact that Catholicism did not present a political threat to the ascendancy position, and therefore Protestants could afford to be generous. It is equally clear, however, that Protestant generosity continued at a time when the Catholics, and especially their priests, had become deeply politicized even to the extent of using chapels for overtly political purposes.[9]

Protestant bankrolling of Catholic projects is all the more remarkable when one considers the explicitly sectarian aspects of the relationship between Catholics and Protestants from the 1770s onwards.[10] The explicitly anti-Catholic prejudices of even 'liberal' observers of the Irish scene cannot be underestimated. The Revd Dr J. Duncan Craig, a well-known Church of Ireland minister could write:

> Entertaining an honest conviction that the great secret of Ireland's misery is to be found in the Ultramontane Roman Catholicism which

Fermanagh priest who had condemned the defenders and now went in fear of his life. 7 PRONI DIO (RC) 1/10A/10, Revd Francis McGennis to Revd Charles MacNally, 22 July 1835.   8 See 'The Relatio status of Bishop James Murphy to Propaganda Fide in Rome, 8 Oct. 1814'. The Relatio, written originally in English, is given in full in Ó Dufaigh, 'James Murphy', p. 460f.   9 *Enniskillen Chronicle and Erne Packet*, 12 Feb. 1824, in which the bishop of Clogher was thanked for the use of the chapel in Enniskillen for a meeting of the Catholic Association.   10 NAI Outrage papers County Fermanagh, 8 Jan. 1835 gives some examples of routine sectarian clashes. Such incursions do not seem to have unduly disturbed the authorities at Dublin Castle. However, an attack by Catholics on Protestants at a fair in April 1835 was especially vicious and the police reported that the Protestants had been beaten in 'a shocking manner' (ibid., 7 Apr. 1835).

broods over her ... [t]he earnest prayer of my heart for them is that they might be led by the guidance of God's Holy Spirit from error into the glorious light of the pure and simple Gospel.[11]

We have by now come to see that the French Revolution and its aftermath changed forever the pattern of Catholic ecclesiastical leadership in Ireland. Until the late eighteenth century, bishops and priests were, for the most part, the products of continental colleges and universities, but from that time on the Catholic clergy on the whole received their education at St Patrick's College, Maynooth. Maynooth in its early years could not, however, provide for all the demands made upon it by the Irish Church. In addition, some of its professors thought that any enlargement of the establishment would reduce both discipline and educational attainment. That at least was the opinion of Dr Charles MacNally, future bishop of Clogher, in his evidence before the commissioners of Irish education in 1827.[12]

By that time MacNally's bishop, James Murphy, had already opened in his diocese a temporary seminary in which candidates had been instructed in philosophy, moral theology, scripture, and 'speculative theology'. Even so, Murphy conceded that the twelve priests who had graduated from the seminary were at best 'tolerably well instructed'.[13] There was a general perception that many of the priests of Fermanagh were not sufficiently well educated.[14] On the other hand, conferences in the sacred sciences were held once a month for seven months of the year. In these meetings further instruction in hearing confessions, moral theology and scripture was given. The bishop himself would examine the curates on their competence in these areas. The more intelligent would be rewarded with a promise that they would become parish priests as soon as pastorates became available.

Murphy's effort to educate and train his clergy was fraught with considerable difficulty. By 1822 he had closed his temporary seminary and was then in a position to send £1000 to Maynooth to establish four new scholarships for priestly candidates from his diocese. The following year he wrote to the college reserving one of these scholarships for a relative.[15] It was precisely this gratuitous nepotism that was to cause the bishop immense difficulties.

By the time of Murphy's episcopate (1802–24), the exploitation of ecclesiastical position to further the interests of one's own family was a regular and common feature of the Catholic Church in Ireland, and Clogher was no exception. Murphy's immediate predecessor, Dr Daniel O'Reilly, was the

---

11 J.D. Craig, *Real pictures of clerical life in Ireland* (London, 1875), pp v–vi. 12 *Eighth report of the commissioners of Irish education inquiry*, HC 1826–7 (509), xiii, p. 142. 13 Ó Dufaigh, 'James Murphy', p. 465. 14 PRONI DIO (RC) 1/4A/12, Revd James McKenna to Revd Charles Cassidy, 2 June 1812. 15 Ibid. 1/4A/25, Murphy to

third O'Reilly to hold the see in succession, as nephew followed uncle in the episcopacy. Indeed, it was Daniel O'Reilly's attempt to have his own nephew Hugh appointed as his successor[16] which led to one of the major rows in Clogher at the end of the eighteenth century.

Murphy himself had signed a petition in 1776 in favour of Hugh O'Reilly's appointment. When this did not happen, and by the time Murphy had received ecclesiastical preferment as dean of the chapter of Clogher, he led that body in a successful appeal to Rome to have Hugh's appointment blocked when Daniel O'Reilly tried to repeat the exercise in 1795. Murphy duly succeeded to the see in 1801 and by 1814 tried to have his own nephew, Patrick Bellew, appointed as coadjutor bishop with right of succession.[17] Bellew was singularly ill read, had neither Greek nor Latin, and it is alleged had studied theology for only eight months. When he was merely a sub-deacon, his uncle had appointed him to a professorship in the temporary seminary he had founded,[18] and in 1811 he was made vicar general of the diocese.[19] Bellew did not live up to his uncles expectations. His fellow priests alleged that he was 'slothful and abused the hospitality of several clergy, physically assaulted a priest', and that he had many quarrels while he was in the seminary.[20]

Murphy was not utterly corrupt in the administration of his diocese. On the contrary, he was something of a disciplinarian. He enforced the rule laid down in the Clogher diocesan statutes that priests must preach to their people each Sunday; failure to do so on three consecutive occasions entailed suspension. He was, as we have seen, acutely conscious of the educational shortcomings of his priests and worked diligently to try to rectify these. He embarked on an ambitious church building programme throughout Fermanagh and the rest of his diocese, and he launched a vigorous campaign against intemperance. This last was especially irksome to his flock since he prohibited the consumption of whiskey, wines, and ales 'under pain of mortal sin'.[21] This prohibition gave rise to a series of complaints about the bishop's severity in carrying out his duties. One exasperated pastor wrote to the bishop early in 1813: 'I never knew any priest to question your lordship in estab-lishing the statute, yet experience, the mistress of laws, seems to many to point out great inconvenience attending it.'[22] Among the inconveniences was

Revd Charles MacNally, 27 Jan. 1823. **16** PRONI DIO (RC) 1/4A/5. **17** PRONI DIO (RC) 1/4B/19. **18** PRONI DIO (RC) 1/4B/13. **19** PRONI DIO (RC) 1/4A/11. **20** PRONI DIO (RC) 1/4B/17. **21** S. Ó Dufaigh (ed.), 'Bishop Murphy's Relatio status, *Clogher Record*, 6 (1968), 470. It is clear if we compare this document with earlier statues of the diocese that Murphy added this stipulation to the diocesan statutes. **22** PRONI DIO (RC) 1/4B/5, Revd Michael McGinn to Murphy, 3 Feb. 1813.

the fact that the laity were staying away from confession, since they could not abstain from alcohol and would not bring themselves to confess that its consumption was a mortal sin.

This was but one of many issues that formed the basis for complaints to Rome about Murphy's conduct of affairs. The archbishop of Armagh, Richard O'Reilly, expressed his horror about the situation in Clogher and believed that the state of religion would suffer 'a deep wound from the scandalous conditions which prevail between a faction of the clergy and their bishop'.[23] Murphy seems to have brought some of the trouble on himself. It was alleged that he was high-handed, demanded too much money for dispensations, and that his only real advisers were members of his own family. Equally, Murphy had a number of difficult and truculent priests to deal with, who would either not respond to reasonable requests from the bishop, or who led scandalous lives and were ill-disposed to amend their ways. Perhaps the most notorious in the latter camp was the Revd Thomas Campbell. Campbell had, among other things 'criminal intercourse with two cousins', and his housekeeper Nancy McCusker was 'generally believed to be his concubine'. Perhaps as a means of deflecting attention from himself, he accused his curate of having an adulterous relationship with 'a Protestant's wife'. This was too much for the good lady concerned who sued Campbell in court and he was duly fined £200.[24]

The greatest opposition Murphy engendered from his clergy came from his attempt to appoint the parish priest of Enniskillen, Edward Kernan, as coadjutor bishop in 1816. Kernan was from a well-to-do Enniskillen family. His brother Randall was a leading barrister in the area and a pillar of the Catholic establishment. Indeed, it was through his good offices that a site was purchased on Darling Street in the town in 1802 for the first Catholic chapel to be built since the Reformation.[25]

On the face of it, Kernan seemed well qualified for the position. He was educated at Portora Royal School and had studied for the priesthood at Salamanca. He had been pastor of Enniskillen from 1799 and was a man of wide learning and considerable pastoral experience. Adversely, he was not especially well liked, either in the town or among the clergy of the diocese. McKenna diplomatically says of Kernan that: 'Although he does not appear to have been a great favourite with the people of Enniskillen, they presented him with a substantial sum of money on his departure, "to buy plate"'.[26] Kernan's departure was, however, delayed for various reasons. Whilst his election as coadjutor had been supported by powerful clerical friends such as Daniel Murray, the assistant bishop of Dublin, nevertheless twenty-four

23 Rafferty, *Catholicism in Ulster*, p. 108.   **24** PRONI DIO (RC) 1/5A/7.   **25** McKenna, *Parishes of Clogher*, ii, 199.   **26** Ibid., p. 200.

priests of Clogher had signed a letter on 26 June 1816 objecting to his nomination.[27] This was partly as a result of Kernan's involvement in a dispute with the Revd John Goodwin who accused Kernan of violating the seal of the confessional. This and an ancillary dispute between Murphy and Peter Maginn, the archdeacon of Clogher, helped poison the atmosphere both against the bishop and his nominee. The Holy See therefore, on the recommendation of an Irish priest in Rome, Bernard McArdle, decided to suspend, temporarily, Kernan's appointment. Kernan's brother Randall immediately played the 'veto card', arguing it was at the behest of the British government that the appointment was delayed. Ó Dufaigh argues that this was 'plausible' but offers no evidence for the suggestion.[28]

In order to resolve all outstanding issues between Murphy and his clergy the Holy See appointed the bishop of Kilmore, Fergal O'Reilly, to conduct an apostolic visitation of Clogher. The letter appointing him states that, among other things:

> You know that the Bishop of Clogher has asked for Edward Kernan as his coadjutor. But there have been so many serious complaints against him that his appointment has been suspended. It has been reported ... that Kernan is very intimate with the Bishop; that he is his adviser and very like him in severity; that he is inexperienced, physically violent and so detested by all that even his own parishioners refuse to pay their dues.[29]

Furthermore it was asserted that he did not speak Irish[30] and, intriguingly, was unacceptable to Protestants.

O'Reilly managed to pour the proverbial oil on troubled waters; the various malcontents made their submission to Bishop Murphy, and Kernan was duly confirmed as coadjutor. However, peace was still a long way off, and James Duffy, one of the ring-leaders in opposing the bishop, wrote to Cardinal Litta, the Prefect of Propaganda Fide in November 1817. He stated that the fact that the priests had made their submission to Murphy was 'merely an act of condescension, humility and an honorary compliment paid to our Bishop on the Restoration of Peace'.[31]

Problems emerged almost immediately. Murphy appointed Bishop Kernan

27 PRONI DIO (RC) 1/4B/45.   28 Ó Dufaigh, 'James Murphy', p. 439 n. 90. In a letter forwarding the petition objecting to Kernan's nomination the dean of Clogher, the ubiquitous Hugh O'Reilly, said that he could have had more signatures of protests had time allowed. Ibid., p. 274.   29 Quoted in Peter Mulligan, 'The life and times of Bishop Edward Kernan', *Clogher Record*, 10 (1979–81), 324.   30 As bishop, however, he compelled one of his priests to learn Irish. PRONI DIO (RC) 1/5A/26.   31 The text of this letter is given in Ó Dufaigh, 'James Murphy', p. 478.

as parish priest of Annyalla. The parishioners did not want him, preferring their own priest, and as late as 1821 Kernan continued to live in Enniskillen although he was no longer pastor there. When he succeeded to the diocese in his own right in 1824, Kernan showed himself to be a hard-working and vigorous shepherd. He visited every parish in the diocese each year and in 1833 confirmed in the Clones area, a parish that straddles Monaghan and Fermanagh, upwards of 6,000 children. Following a general agreement of the Ulster bishops, Kernan tried to enforce a new rule whereby curates in parishes would of right receive one-third of the offerings for their keep, rather than relying on handouts from parish priests. The Clogher pastors, fractious as ever, would not have this, although understandably the curates were much in favour of the new arrangements. The changes in financial arrangements were linked to a plan to reorganize parishes and make them smaller. The parish priests did not hesitate to tell Rome that such changes would be both dangerous and disruptive to the 'Catholic religion in this northern part of Ireland where there are so many sects'.[32] In this instance the bishop's will prevailed, but Kernan by now had a reputation at Rome for making things difficult for himself. He had decided that, since the leaders of opposition to him were to be found in the diocesan chapter, he would let that institution die, by refusing to appoint any new members to it. He further told his priests that diocesan chapters were not in favour in Rome and that the chapter of Clogher had been the cause of all the trouble in the diocese since it was re-established forty years earlier.[33]

Such were Kernan's slightly megalomaniacal tendencies that Charles MacNally, his successor, could say of Clogher that there was in the diocese no ecclesiastical law 'except the arbitrary will of an ignorant and perhaps corrupt bishop'.[34] In this particular instance Kernan was forced to back down and he began once more to make appointments to the diocesan chapter.

Too much emphasis on clerical factionalism can obscure the function of the priest in the early decades of the nineteenth century. His main task, after all, was to assist Catholics in the practice of their faith. As time went on, people's knowledge of the faith improved and the opportunity for access to the ministrations of a priest were multiplied. It is equally clear that the type of Catholicism the inhabitants of Fermanagh were exposed to did not always conform to the established ultramontane exuberance of continental Catholicism. Thus, an Austrian Redemptorist priest conducting a mission in Enniskillen in 1852 could complain that Catholics there had never assisted at benediction of the Blessed Sacrament and had never seen incense used in

32 PRONI DIO (RC) 1/5B/21. From the pastors of Clogher to Cardinal Redicini of Propaganda, 21 May 1834.   33 PRONI DIO(RC) 1/5B/2. This opinion was penned in 1829.   34 Ibid., 1/5B/33.

divine service.[35] Furthermore, although Bishop Charles MacNally could report to Rome in 1852 that pious associations and practices were widespread, such as devotion to the Sacred Heart of Jesus, and the use of the Scapular and 'St Dominic's Cord', nevertheless: 'For fear of irreverence and profanation we do not yet dare to take the risk of permanently keeping the Most Holy Eucharist in any church or chapel.'[36] The quality of religious observance is also linked to the difficult question of how many Catholics actually practised their religion. So far as accessibility to a place of worship was concerned, in the diocese as a whole by 1844 there were seventy-six churches and chapels. Twenty years later there were now only six more such facilities. It is clear that from the beginning of the century much of the money for building Catholic places of worship was provided by Protestants. Protestant generosity in this regard is attested to time and again.[37] The vast majority of the churches and chapels had slate roofs, and, whilst some had pews for the wealthier members of the congregation, most people stood during Mass. A fairly typical description of a chapel is that at Kilroaskagh in the parish of Cleenish. There it was said to be a fine stone building with a slated roof capable of accommodating 600 people. An inscription at the front said that it was 'erected to the honour and glory of the living God and dedicated to St Patrick, 1828'.[38]

Did the majority of Catholics make use of these buildings for purposes of public worship on Sundays and holidays? In a justly famous and seminal article some thirty years ago David W. Miller argued that very many Irish Catholics before the famine did not practise their faith, if that practice is measured by attendance at Mass. It is clear that in some eastern towns practice rates did approach 100 per cent, while in the west of the country practice could fall as low as 30 per cent.[39] Miller's thesis has been attacked by some Catholic scholars who have tended to argue for higher rates of practice, and who have suggested various technical difficulties with Miller's calculations based on canonical requirements to attend Mass. More recently Miller

---

35 S.J. Connolly, *Priests and people in pre-famine Ireland, 1780–1845* (Dublin, 1982), p. 93. 36 Cf. 'Dr Charles MacNally's Relatio Status, October 1853', trans. by Donal A. Kerr and James O'Kane, *Clogher Record*, 13 (1989), 99. The reservation of the Blessed Sacrament and frequent daily visits to pray before it became a staple in Catholic devotional life later in the nineteenth-century. Battersby's *Catholic directory* (Dublin, 1846), p. 249, also indicates that devotion to the Virgin Mary was a prominent feature of Catholic life in Clogher. Various papal indulgences had been obtained in connection with this and other para-liturgical practices. 37 Ó Dufaigh, 'Murphy's Relatio Status', p. 460. 38 A. Day and P. McWilliams (eds), *Ordnance Survey memoirs of Ireland: parishes of County Fermanagh, II, 1834–5* (Belfast, 1992), p. 21. By far the biggest chapel was that at Enniskillen which could accommodate 1,500 individuals. (ibid., p. 56). 39 D.W. Miller, 'Irish Catholicism and the great famine', *Journal of Social History*, 9 (1985), 81–98.

has revisited the question and with the use of complex technology has concluded:

> It is worth noting that in most areas north and west of a line from Dundalk to Killarney Mass attendance was less than 40 per cent of the Catholic population while in areas south and east of such a line it is generally greater than 40 per cent.[40]

The Catholics of Fermanagh fall into this general pattern. The evidence for the routine of parish life can be found in parish registers. Ecclesiastical law forbade marriages in Advent or Lent, so the weeks before these seasons proved very popular as a time for marriage. From 1835 the holding of 'Station Masses' in the homes of wealthier individuals in the diocese became a compulsory practice. Stations were held between St Michael's Day and the end of the Christmas season. Pastors were also instructed to arrange for two days in the Easter season when, with the help of priests from neighbouring parishes, they were to hold stations for confessions. In principle, all this made it easier for individuals to avail themselves of the sacraments in locations closer to their homes. There is, however, not much evidence that large numbers took up these sacramental opportunities.

Insofar as the evidence is available, we can see that from the 1830s there was less superstition among Fermanagh Catholics. The changing social mores, even among the poor, were doubtless attributable to the catechetical work of the priests and their lay helpers. We read, for example, that the popularity of holy wells had begun to diminish. In the parish of Tempo there were three such wells, but from the mid-1830s they were 'somewhat neglected' despite the innumerable stories of miraculous cures attached to them.[41] Some superstitions were, however, more difficult to eradicate. When a priest died, there was often a dispute between his family and his parishioners over the remains. Normally the family wanted to bury the body in an ancestral resting place, but the people 'had some traditions handed down through generations, that if their parish priest was buried outside the confines of the parish famine and pestilence would prevail during the time of his successor'.[42] The attempt to reform the religious and social outlook of the people was nevertheless an uphill struggle. Diocesan regulations insisted that wakes and 'nocturnal dances' were to be vigorously resisted by pastors with a view to their abolition.

---

40 D.W. Miller, 'Mass attendance in Ireland in 1834', in S.J. Brown and D.W. Miller (eds), *Piety and power in Ireland* (Belfast, 2000), p. 174.   41 Day and McWilliams, *Ordnance Survey memoirs*, p. 76.   42 McKenna, *Parishes of Clogher*, ii, 452. McKenna records this practice under the heading of the parish of Devenish West, which includes Garrison. The superstition was, however, not confined to this area.

There were also heavy penalties for priests who assisted at funerals where they knew that alcohol would be served; such an individual would be *ipso facto* suspended.[43]

Other customary practices such as lighting bonfires on St John's Eve were beginning to fall into disuse, whilst St Patrick's Day was beginning to be celebrated with religious fervor.[44] A general feature of Fermanagh Catholicism from the 1810s was that its adherents were increasingly abandoning the Irish language, and although they continued to understand it, especially those over forty, in general they seem to have preferred to speak English.[45]

A major influence on the religious ethos of Catholicism in Fermanagh was St Patrick's Purgatory at Lough Derg, just across the county boundary in Donegal, but still in the diocese of Clogher. The piety connected with the shrine was heavily Marian. Even so, pilgrims were expected to make a general confession and receive holy communion. Fasting on bread and water, the pilgrim could spend three, six or nine days on the island, with one night given to a sleepless prayer vigil. Those who wished to undertake the purgatory had to obtain permission from their own parish priest when beginning the pilgrimage. By the early 1850s Bishop MacNally believed that the best confessions in the diocese were made at Lough Derg; at the same time he felt that the pilgrimage was in need of reform.[46] Although Lough Derg had none of the debaucheries besetting other such pious locations, it was not entirely free of irregularities or superstition. Pilgrims urged one another on to even greater austerities believing that this would ensure that no request to heaven 'good, bad or indifferent' would fail to be granted.[47]

One fairly neutral English Protestant observer was not inclined to denigrate the pilgrimage, believing that the '[d]eity cannot regard with aversion any homage that is rendered in sincerity'. He was equally convinced that many of the clergy did not in practice recommend Lough Derg to their parishioners, since 'the absence of his parishioner and the expense of the pilgrimage, will diminish, rather than increase [the parish priest's own] revenue'.[48]

On the whole, the laity made generous provision for the clergy despite the poverty of many Fermanagh Catholics. In addition to stipends for baptism, marriages and funerals, priests were also paid in kind in the shape of farm produce. There were also special collections at Christmas and Easter.

43 *Clogher diocesan statutes 1789–1824*, paragraph 16.   44 Day and McWilliams, *Ordnance Survey memoirs*, p. 35.   45 William Shaw Mason, *A statistical account or parochial survey of Ireland*, i (Dublin, 1814), p. 636.   46 Kerr and O'Kane, 'Dr Charles MacNally's Relatio Status', p. 101.   47 Carleton, *Traits and stories of the Irish peasantry* (Dublin, 1830–3), i, 173.   48 H.D. Inglis, *Ireland in 1834*, ii, 175.

Naturally enough, the amount of money varied depending on personal circumstances. Offerings could be anything from one shilling from poorer parishioners to one pound or thirty shillings from the wealthier members of the congregation. At least in Tempo, the priests were 'extremely rigid in their exaction of this due. If it be denied or not liberally given, the party so offending is either publicly denounced or privately marked out from his more liberal neighbours.'[49]

Although the laity tended to be less active in the administrative life of the Fermanagh parishes compared, for example, with Newry or Belfast, they could at times act with impunity when they believed their prerogatives were being infringed. Frances Lady Maguire asserted her rights in 1796 to appoint the parish priests of Tempo and Enniskillen. She claimed that Bishop Daniel O'Reilly had illegally usurped her family patronage, and she sued in the court of Rome to have it restored.[50] This was part of a continuing dispute that had begun with Dame Frances' son, Hugh Maguire, in 1793. Hugh was a Protestant although his wife and children were Catholic. The bishop argued that since Maguire had apostatized he lost *ipso iure* the right of patronage.[51] In the end a compromise was arrived at whereby the bishop agreed to the appointment of one of several individuals the two Maguire's (mother and son) had indicated as suitable candidates for the jobs in question.

Further down the social scale, the laity could also be concerned with what they perceived as their privileges in the choice of clergy. There are a number of instances in Fermanagh when parishioners believed they had a right to select their own pastors and therefore reject the bishop's nominee. This often led to scenes whereby the rightful pastor was locked out of his own church.[52] One of the most notorious cases was in Devenish East (Derrygonnelly). James Duffy the curate, had himself elected as parish priest by the parishioners and refused to accept the bishop's appointment of Daniel Boylan to that office in 1815. Duffy's supporters made life difficulty for Boylan, even at one point cutting off one of his horse's ears. Unable to endure the humiliations Boylan resigned and was replaced by Nicholas Smyth. An altercation

49 Day and McWilliams, *Ordnance Survey memoirs*, p. 76. **50** Archives of Propaganda Fide atti clxvi MS f.67 rv. A microfilm of this document, of 18 April 1796, is preserved in the NLI. **51** Perhaps the most fascinating aspect of the affair was Maguire's justification for his adherence to Protestantism. He claimed that he was a Protestant in name only since he had either to 'make an external act of conformity with the false Protestant religion' or see himself and his family 'flung headlong downwards from the summit of grandeur to the bottom of the abyss of poverty, misery and mendacity'. Maguire's' submission to the Roman curia is given in A. Faulkner, 'The right of patronage of the Maguire's of Tempo', *Clogher Record*, 9 (1977), 167–86. **52** This phenomenon became so common that the diocesan statutes of 1835 made the practice a 'reserved sin': Mulligan, 'Life and times', p. 334.

took place between Smyth and Duffy's supporters on 26 December 1816 which resulted in several individuals being sent to prison for public order offences.[53]

We have seen something of the fractious nature of intra-Catholic relations. Those between the Catholic and Protestant communities could exhibit fluctuations between friendliness and hostility. One element which served to heighten inter-community violence was undoubtedly the role of the priest in politics. As has been noted, from the second decade of the century Catholic places of worship were used for the purposes of political meetings. Furthermore, the Fermanagh priests, and indeed even Bishop Kernan,[54] played a prominent part in the campaign for Catholic emancipation. At a meeting in the chapel in Enniskillen in November 1825 a resolution was drawn up to petition parliament in favour of emancipation. A committee of six was established to work on the petition – four priests, including James Shiel the parish priest of Enniskillen, and two laymen, one of whom was Randal Kernan, the bishop's brother.[55]

It could be argued that since most of the religious disadvantages Catholics had laboured under had been removed,[56] clerical involvement in issues such as emancipation was simply political and could not be related to the sacred function of the priest. On the other hand, it is possible to suggest that the protection of the Catholic community from government abuse, in any form, was proper to the role of the priest and therefore political activity was compatible with his duties. In December 1824 the *Erne Packet* carried an article examining this problem. It lamented the role that priests had played in collecting the O'Connell rent, and concluded that 'the functions of a Minister of Christ are but ill suited to the aspirates of political disputes'.

The campaign for emancipation roused Protestant antipathy to the Catholic community as a whole, an antipathy that at times boiled over into violence. In 1825 Fermanagh Protestants organized a petition against an emancipation bill going though parliament that year.[57] When the measure was defeated, by the house of lords, in May 'respectable Protestants' rejoiced by lighting bonfires and firing shots. Less respectable ones, such as those in the Brookeborough area, 'conducted themselves in a manner extremely insulting to the Roman Catholics of the place'.[58]

Not all Fermanagh Protestants were against the Catholic claims. In the

53 McKenna, *Parishes of Clogher*, ii, 429.   54 Once emancipation was granted in 1829 Kernan seems no longer to have taken an active part in politics.   55 *Erne Packet*, 10 Nov. 1825.   56 A point that Bishop Murphy himself made in his report to Rome in 1804, in the course of which he remarked that so far as the operation of Catholicism was concerned there was 'no obstruction or hindrance of any kind from our mild government'.   57 *Erne Packet*, 17 Mar. 1825.   58 *Erne Packet*, 2 June 1825.

aftermath of the hotly contested 1812 election, Gerard Irvine, the high sheriff of the county, refused to sign a requisition calling a public meeting to pledge the newly elected members to oppose Catholic emancipation, declaring that 'his hand would never sign what was repugnant to his heart'.[59]

Inter-community tensions had long been a feature of county life and could be quite unassociated with politics. The Orange order and the ribbonmen were both early arrivals in Fermanagh and their respective activities kept the sectarian pot boiling for many years.[60] On 24 July 1838 it was reported from Belleek that 100 men had gathered on the Belleek–Pettigo road 'for the purpose of attacking and preventing Orangemen of that place from walking in procession had they attempted to do so'.[61] One of the more surprising instances of religious conflict occurred in Enniskillen in September of that year. The 38th regiment had just arrived in the town on the night of Sunday 9 September. Various individuals assembled at the corner of the street leading to the army barracks and shouted sectarian insults at the soldiers, most of whom were Catholics. Among the insults hurled were 'to hell with the pope' and 'no surrender'. The soldiers joined by some Catholic civilians shouted in turn anti-Protestant slogan such as 'to hell with the Orangemen', and 'we will have a surrender'. These scenes were repeated the following evening with violence exchanged between the parties. We are told that 'the soldiers were on this night very violent'.[62]

Much of the Catholic–Protestant violence was of a routine, perhaps 'recreational' nature. Market fairs seemed especially to be a catalyst for violence, quite often associated with the consumption of alcohol. But even fairly innocuous occasions such as sporting fixtures could become the focus for violence as sectarian partisanship intruded into social life. On one occasion, two Protestants and one Catholic were beaten to death as tempers flared at a race meeting. Sixteen Catholics were arrested and charged with a variety of offences and, although the chief constable of Enniskillen freely admitted that Protestants were also responsible for perpetrating the disturbances, none was arrested.[63]

The failure of the authorities to deal even-handedly with both communities was a long-held grievance. On 22 June 1810 three Protestants broke into and stole vestments from the Catholic chapel in Enniskillen. They destroyed the vestments and disposed of them. Although they confessed to their crimes

59 McKenna, *Parishes of Clogher*, ii, 199. **60** See for example the evidence of Edward Tierney, crown solicitor for the north-west circuit in *Minutes of evidence taken before the Select Committee of the House of Lords appointed to enquire into the state of Ireland since 1835*, HL 1839, (11), ii, 607. **61** NAI Outrage papers, County Fermanagh, 1838. **62** Ibid. **63** NAI Outrage papers, County Fermanagh, 11 Mar. 1835

and there were no mitigating circumstances, they were declared not guilty by 'a jury of Orangemen'.[64]

The county authorities could also show themselves hostile to Catholicism in other ways. Edward Kernan, the future bishop, had acted as chaplain to Enniskillen gaol for many years without payment. When it was decided in 1812 that a salary could be paid, the grand jury, rather than appoint Kernan, chose instead a renegade friar, Fr Stephen Keen, despite the fact that strictly speaking under the terms of Catholic canon law Keen could not function as a priest. To add insult to injury, when Keen died in June 1812 one of the curates at Enniskillen was appointed in his place, despite the fact that Kernan had once again applied for the job.[65] It must be said that Kernan was a sufficiently awkward character for the ill feeling against him to be personal rather than necessarily predicated on religious grounds.

Relations between Catholics and Protestants, as we have seen, were not always hostile. Not only did Protestants give money for Catholic purposes; they also attended Catholic services and listened to the Catholic clergy preach. At times, individual Protestants had Catholic priests as lodgers in their homes. Thomas Bogue, the curate at Tempo, resided in the home of a well-to-do Protestant family, which was then subject 'to continuous persecution for harbouring him'. Bogue went on to be a champion of O'Connellite politics, although he also did sterling work as a priest. He built the church at Roslea and established six primary schools between 1822 and 1832. Not all such instances of priests having the hospitality of Protestant families worked out for the best. Patrick Cairns, a curate at Garrison, had his residence in the home of Thomas Carson and ended up marrying Barbara, his landlord's daughter.[66]

These examples of ecumenical harmony notwithstanding, Catholic-Protestant relations were often marked by violence and bloodshed. One great source of tension was the proselytizing activity brought about by the 'second reformation'.[67] Lord Enniskillen became a great patron of the movement in Fermanagh and between October 1826 and January 1827 Catholics in towns such as Enniskillen, Lisnaskea, Killesher and Pettico, conformed to Protestantism. There is some indication that Catholics who were seduced by Protestant neighbours or business contacts into eating meat on Fridays thought they had thereby become Protestants.[68] Attempts to convert

---

64 *Erne Packet*, 23 Sept. 1810.   **65** McKenna, *Parishes of Clogher*, ii, 217–8.   **66** Ibid., p. 451.   **67** Desmond Bowen, *The Protestant crusade in Ireland, 1800–1870* (Dublin, 1978) provides a comprehensive treatment of the issues involved. The relevant section of David Hempton and Myrtle Hill, *Evangelical Protestants in Ulster society, 1740–1890* (London, 1992) is also a useful starting point.   **68** Livingstone, *Fermanagh story*, pp 160–1.

Fermanagh Catholics continued into the 1850s. Bishop MacNally records that, although proselytizing was widespread throughout the diocese, for the most part the efforts of the Protestants were largely unsuccessful. He mentions, however, that some of the poorer Catholics had been converted by the 'Society for the education of the people through the medium of Irish'. One of the techniques used by the society was the subterfuge that the individuals concerned could keep their conversion a secret from their Catholic neighbours. MacNally, however, reports that the 'abject imposture being discovered, we publicly exposed it'.[69]

Catholic and Protestant grievances could at times coalesce and thereby produce surprising results. The tithe war of the 1820s was not simply a Catholic and Dissenter protest against the exactions of the established church. The Church of Ireland rector of Gallon was very much an absentee parson, having also a cure of souls in the parish of Clogher. Never the less his proctors still demanded the tithes. The farmers in the area, of all religious persuasions, in the years 1818–20 refused to pay anything. The case came to court and Randal Kernan for the defence argued, perhaps disingenuously, that since the pastor in question, the Revd John Benjamin Storey, had never so much as said the Lord's Prayer for the people of Gallon for more than twenty years; he did not deserve tithes for his services. The magistrate dismissed Storey's claims, and the parishioners 'Protestants and Catholics alike united in their rejoicing'.[70]

Such cross-community co-operation in the face of injustice and adversity was seen again during the famine, when apart from the first year, Fermanagh suffered greatly. In the period 1845 to 1858 the county lost some 40,000 people, about 25 per cent of its population. Catholics and Protestants came together in large numbers all over the county to plead for government relief in September 1846. The authorities could not cope with the scale of the crisis. To give but one indicator: Enniskillen workhouse was established in 1845 and was intended to accommodate 260 people. By May 1847 it had 1,433 inhabitants. Bishop MacNally could write to the president of Maynooth about famine conditions:

> It would be impossible to give an idea of the deplorable state of our
> poor people. In this neighbourhood fever and famine are making
> frightful ravages among the people. They are lying in the fields and the
> people are so terrified that none but the clergy can be induced to

69 Kerr and O'Kane, 'Dr Charles MacNally's Relatio Status', p. 97.   **70** *Erne Packet*, 2 Mar. 1820. The judgment was reversed on appeal and a long and tortuous struggle ensued.

approach them … It is wonderful how the clergy can bear their unceasing labours attending the sick and the dying.[71]

By that time MacNally was well on his way to being a typical political bishop. He had clashed with the archbishop of Armagh, William Crolly, about the involvement of priests in politics. Crolly had been rapped over the knuckles by Rome about a whole range of politicking by Irish priests, including protests over the charitable bequests act of 1844. Crolly was now determined to eliminate priestly political machinations. When MacNally failed to keep his priests in line, Crolly sought to chastise them. The bishop responded that his priests would 'receive with due and becoming deference such admonitions as your Grace may feel it your duty to address them'.[72] His new-found radicalism sits at odds with his earlier career when he had shown himself to be a staunch upholder of crown and constitution. He was one of a group of Maynooth professors who had signed the 'Sorbonne manifesto', refuting the claims of Bishop James Doyle that if there was a rebellion in Ireland the clergy would in effect side with the rebels because of the radicalized educational influence they received at St Patrick's College. MacNally and his associates indignantly maintained that they inculcated in students a sense of 'allegiance to our gracious sovereign, respect for the constituted authorities and obedience to the law'.[73]

In his evidence before the Education Commissioners in 1827 MacNally not only declared that any attempt to separate Ireland from England would be mischievous but he also said that the opinion of all those in Maynooth was favourable to the Union.[74] His political opinion had now turned full circle and he became an ardent supporter of all O'Connell's demands.

In this MacNally might be said to be a true barometer of Catholic sentiment in Fermanagh. We have seen that at the beginning of the period here briefly surveyed, Catholics reflected the same ambiguities towards political issues as their co-religionists elsewhere in the country. Whatever support there was for the United Irishmen, it was relatively contained. The church in the shape of its officials, by and large, resisted United Irish sentiment, as they did the incursions of the Orange order and the activity of the ribbonmen. Relations between the communities, whilst not perfect, were relatively harmonious, but, given the near equal distribution between

71 Maynooth College Archives, Renehan papers, MacNally to Renehan, 9 Mar. 1847.
72 PRONI DIO (RC) MacNally to Crolly, 17 Feb. 1845.   73 Donal A. Kerr, 'Charles MacNally: O'Connellite bishop–reforming pastor', *Archivium Hibericum*, 37 (1982), 11–20, see also P.J. Corish, *Maynooth College, 1795–1995* (Dublin, 1995), pp 61–2.
74 *Eighth report of the commissioners of Irish education inquiry*, HC 1826–7 (509), xiii, p. 142.

Catholics and Protestants, that harmony could easily be disrupted. Although the church was very much aware of its general indebtedness to Fermanagh Protestants for financial support across a whole range of activities, it was also increasingly alert to the political aspirations of its own wealthier members, aspirations that were perceived as a threat by Protestants.

As time went on, Catholics, and the leadership of the church, began to have a greater sense of confidence; Catholic interaction with the state had about it a more demanding and strident note. There is a sense, even in the early part of the century, that the church's involvement in politics was undertaken for religious and not directly political motivation. Such political advances as were achieved at emancipation in 1829 were mirrored by religious developments, and this is especially striking in Fermanagh. The growth of Catholic infrastructure went hand in hand with better education for priests, who gave more of their time to the religious formation of their parishioners.

Given the culture of dependence between priest and people, much of the religious improvement was necessarily spearheaded by the clergy. There was a certain purging of the more overtly superstitious elements in the practice of Catholicism over the fifty years or so that we have been considering. But old habits died hard; even for the priests, attempts at reform and renewal did not always work. Bishop Charles MacNally spoke of the habitual drunkenness of some clergy and for others '*sollicitantes in tribunali*', seeking sexual favours in the confessional, was the major weakness. For such individuals he could not proceed with the exact canonical penalties, given 'our position in this country' and the opprobrium the church would have from Protestants if such practices became widely known. Instead he sought to send such refractory priests to the missions, especially the United States, in the hopes that a change of environment might bring about some improvement in their moral condition.[75] Ultimately, of course, Catholicism endured and developed because of the commitment of the ordinary faithful, who persevered in their faith and practised their beliefs, despite political and social constraints and in the face of the weaknesses and infidelities of their institutional leaders.

75 Kerr and O'Kane, 'Dr Charles MacNally's Relatio Status', p. 99.

7

Cardinal Cullen, early Fenianism
and the MacManus funeral affair

The political threat posed by the growth of Fenianism in Ireland in the late 1850s and early 1860s has generally been underplayed by much present-day historiography. Even some contemporaries were not disposed to see American Fenianism as much of a danger to the constitutional stability of Ireland. The Dublin police authorities decided to recall Sub-inspector Thomas Doyle from his surveillance work in America in July 1860. By that time Doyle had sent dozens of reports on Irish-American revolutionary activity. On this basis the authorities knew that John O'Mahony and Michael Dohney, both of 1848 notoriety, were prominently involved in the Phoenix and Fenian conspiracy.[1] They also knew the general points of the 'phoenix theory' that England's difficulty was Ireland opportunity, that men were being recruited and drilled in large numbers in the US for a possible invasion of Ireland, that O'Mahony's theory was 'to root out the Government, to cut down the landlords, and to confiscate the land of Ireland', and that John Mitchel had gone to Paris as an agent of the 'phoenix confederacy' in the US.[2]

On the whole, however, the reports were not such as to excite too much concern by the Irish executive; hence Doyle's recall. He did not return to Ireland until January 1861, owing in part to bureaucratic confusion. Many of his reports contained clippings from the New York Fenian newspaper *The Phoenix*. Dublin Castle may have decided that it was cheaper simply to intercept this paper in Ireland.[3] While not being especially alarmed at the reports from America, it is equally clear that the Irish government kept up

1 The term 'Fenian' occurs in Doyle's reports for example on 27 Sept. 1859, 15 Nov. 1859, 23 Mar. 1860 and a number of instances after June 1860. This is at odds with Brendan MacGiolla Choille's judgment that, 'Before the end of 1863 it is unlikely that the historian will find in the registered papers (or indeed in any of the contemporary State papers) documents which mention persons in Ireland as fenians *ipso nomine* or activities under the title of fenianism': 'Fenian documents in the State Paper Office', *IHS*, 16 (1968–9), 266. Sir Robert Anderson, *A great conspiracy* (London, 1910), p. 37, records that many of the early Fenian reports were not registered but kept in a special cupboard in Dublin Castle. Anderson made use of these for his manuscript 'The Fenian conspiracy'. See note 8 below for a discussion of this neglected source.   2 NAI Fenian police reports, Box 1, Doyle's reports, 9 Aug. 1859 and 23 Nov. 1859.   3 NAIFPR Box 1. Report of sub-inspector Bernard Potter of Bandon, 13 June 1861. Such a practice was, however, technically illegal.

clandestine surveillance operations, as is evidenced from the frequent letters from the under-secretary in Dublin to the Treasury in London requesting funds for 'secret service' work.[4] However, by June 1861 Dublin Castle, in the person of the under-secretary Sir Thomas Larcom, was sufficiently concerned to have Doyle's reports edited as a 'Précis of information respecting [an] association in the United States entertaining designs hostile to the British government'.[5] All this activity notwithstanding, some government officials were inclined to give the impression that the country was by then more peaceful than it had been for decades, a general estimation supported by influential sections of the press. The events surrounding the reburial in Ireland in Dublin on 10 November 1861 of Terence Bellew MacManus, one of the leaders of the abortive rebellion of 1848, did little to disturb the Irish government's complacent attitude.

On the surface there seemed no reason to think that the funeral had any relevance to the political affairs of the period, other than as a sentimental tribute to a half-forgotten member of a ludicrous attempt at rebellion, which had been notoriously badly organized. By contrast, Fenians were to come to see the events surrounding the burial as a great fillip to their fortunes. The Fenian newspaper, the *Irish People*, returned to the topic on a number of occasions during its brief existence, describing how important the event was in the evolution of the movement.[6] Many years later Joseph Denieffe recalled how he had passed on to O'Mahony a letter of James Stephens early in 1862 in which Stephens asserted that a successful revolution could have been staged on the day of the funeral had there been adequate American support.[7] The government official who knew most about the workings of Fenianism, Robert Anderson, also came to accept that the funeral was an enormous recruiting occasion for the IRB, during which the 'Fenian oath was adminis-tered and eagerly taken'.[8] For its part, the Catholic Church in Ireland, despite some division of opinion among the hierarchy, regarded the whole display as

---

4 NAICSO Letter book 264, 19 Sept. 1858, 20 Sept. 1860 and *passim*. On each occasion the amount remitted exceeds £1,150. 5 NLI Larcom papers MS 7697. 6 *Irish People*, 5 Dec. 1863 and 12 Feb. 1864. Here in the course of an article on the funeral the paper used a phrase, a slight variation of which was to have enormous significance for future generations of militant nationalists. The paper enjoined the Irish people to depend on no one but 'themselves alone'. 7 J. Denieffe, *A personal narrative of the Irish Revolutionary Brotherhood* (New York, 1906), pp 71, 168 and 170. 8 NLI Larcom papers MS 7517; 'The Fenian conspiracy', p. 96. This history of Fenianism was drawn up by Anderson at the request of Lord Mayo, probably in 1867. Curiously more than sixty of the initial pages are missing from the Larcom papers, although a rough draft of some of them is preserved in NAIFPR box 4. A heavily edited version of the document, which is almost 500 pages long in two volumes, appeared as 'Fenianism: a narrative by one who knows' in the *Contemporary Review*, 19 (1872), 301–16 and 624–46.

an attempt to incite enthusiasm for anti-clerical and revolutionary ideas, and for the most part it held aloof from the proceedings.

The church's lead in this was given by Paul Cullen, the archbishop of Dublin. It is a mistake to think that Cullen was neutral with regard to the funeral, and that he would have allowed a religious service provided he had received some reassurance that it would not have been exploited for political purposes.[9] Whatever the government thought about the matter,[10] most clerical opinion saw the event as a rally in favour of rebellion and tried to undermine its significance. Cullen, writing Bernard Ullathorne, bishop of Birmingham, made clear that the expressed purpose of the funeral's organizers was 'to proclaim their adhesion to the principles of revolution, for which [MacManus] suffered, and their admiration for his conduct in taking up arms against the government in 1848'.[11] In fact, the committee charged with arranging the funeral had made it no secret that they saw it primarily as a political demonstration. The printed letter distributed in Dublin during MacManus' lying in state at the Mechanics' Institute invited mourners to come to his funeral and support the cause for which he had suffered.[12] On the day before the funeral, *The Tablet* editorialized that MacManus' obsequies were being used as a protest against the Irish government and, while the paper recognized that there was discontent in the country, it was confident that it was not such as to give rise to revolution.[13]

Cullen amid talk of doing honour to the 1848 rising made it clear that he was not going to ally himself with sentiments which smacked of rebellion. In a letter to Bishop Laurence Gillooly of Elphin, he reiterated his conviction that the whole affair was orchestrated to 'turn away people's minds, and fill them with a wild revolutionary spirit'.[14] Two weeks later he again wrote to Gillooly:

> Everyone here knew that the funeral was intended as a declaration in favour of the rebellion of 48. One of the gentlemen who came to ask for a high Mass stated distinctly that the object was to proclaim that we adopted the principles for which MacManus suffered. All the

9 A thesis advanced for example by R.V. Comerford, *The Fenians in context: Irish politics and society 1848–82* (Dublin, 1985), pp 77–8. **10** NAICSO *Registered papers* 1861/8418, Larcom was sufficiently concerned to consult the law officers on the question. They counseled that the funeral should be allowed to proceed with the least possible interference. **11** DDA Cullen papers, Letter book No. 3, Cullen to Ullathorne, 13 Nov. 1861. **12** A copy of this hand bill is preserved with the police report on the funeral in NAICSO Registered papers 1877/3591. **13** *The Tablet*, 9 Nov. 1861. **14** NLI Gillooly papers mf p7622 series B, Cullen to Gillooly, 12 Nov. 1861, f. 44.

addresses were in the same [vein]. How could I in such circumstances order a Mass?[15]

Cullen received support for his attitude to the funeral from both churchmen and prominent lay people. William Monsell, the Limerick MP, told him that had it not been for the archbishop's conduct the Catholic cause would have been gravely compromised. He further attributed Ireland's 'weakness' to the 1848 rising.[16] Thomas Furlong, the bishop of Ferns, wrote to Cullen that every person of sense in Ireland approved of his conduct and that had he acted otherwise he would have given the solemn sanction of religion to 'one of the most silly and mischievous attempts at revolution on record'.[17] Despite the overwhelming support for Cullen's position from the Catholic establishment, there was need for caution. Thus Bishop Gillooly, while sharing Cullen's attitude, nonetheless warned him that it would be as well to have a priest of the Dublin diocese give a full account of the affair, since there were 'very many good people to whom that refusal [of the obsequies] is still a subject of surprise and regret, (it was after all tantamount to an excommunication), and by some it has ... [been] attributed to your Grace's political opinions'.[18]

The difficulties in Cullen's position were complicated by the fact that MacManus had been given the last rites of the Church by the archbishop of San Francisco, Dr Joseph Alemany. He had also conducted a funeral service for MacManus, as had the archbishop of New York, John Hughes. Even in Ireland the bishop of Cloyne, William Keane, had allowed the body to rest in the chapel of the hospital run by the Sisters of Mercy in Queenstown. Furthermore, the students at St Patrick's College Maynooth gathered to chant a requiem office for the dead patriot. One hostile contemporary source commented on this that rarely had the students 'assembled on such solemn occasion with such heart-felt good will ... and while they prayed that his soul might rest in peace, they wished every success to the cause which he repre- sented'.[19] In addition, eleven priests from the Ennis area of Co. Clare wrote their local dean asking him to call together all the clergy to offer a high Mass and the office of the dead for MacManus.[20] Most notoriously of all, Patrick Lavelle, parish priest of Partry, Co. Mayo, contributed to the funeral and persuaded two other priests, his curate Peter Geraghty, and Fr Ulick J. Bourke of St Jarlath's College, Tuam, to do likewise. Lavelle also wrote a quite extraordinary public letter, amounting to a denunciation of Cullen,

15 Ibid., ff 51–2.   16 DDA Cullen papers, Monsell to Cullen, 14 Nov. 1861.   17 Ibid., Furlong to Cullen, 7 Nov. 1861.   18 Ibid., Gillooly to Cullen, 16 Nov. 1861. 19 *Morning News*, 6 Nov. 1861. Scholarly opinion is divided as to the extent of sympathy for Fenianism at Maynooth.   20 *The Tablet*, 2 Nov. 1861.

observing that MacManus was being denied 'the honours acceded to every Castle-slave, time-serving hypocrite, and whigling sycophant'.[21] In the days before the funeral, this letter was printed upon huge posters and placarded all over Dublin.

Cullen realized that by taking the stand he did he would make himself unpopular in the country at large. He told the rector of the Irish College Rome, Tobias Kirby:

> I suspect that informers & spies are engaged in this work to divert public attention from real grievances & to get up odium against me if I refuse a funeral ... I will not do anything to approve of the folly of [William] S[mith] O'Brien and forty eight whatever odium I may incur.[22]

This was a point he stressed to several of his correspondents including Bishop Ullathorne. By opposing revolutionary sentiments Cullen believed he would have to 'encounter the hostility of the multitudes, but nothing will induce me, I trust in God, to go against the dictates of conscience, or to sanction a revolutionary spirit'.[23]

The struggle between Cullen and the Fenians, as this was to be worked out over the next decade, concerned the form and content of political life in Ireland. The failure to move the political debate forward from the 1850s, the debacle over independent opposition, the Sadlier and Keogh defections, and the obsession with Catholic education, almost to the exclusion of any other issue not directly related to ecclesiastical concerns, were all informed by Cullen's socio-political outlook.[24] It is a mistake to see Cullen's perspective on revolution simply as a result of political expediency. This is a view misleadingly propagated by E.D. Steele.[25] Equally it is a travesty to think that Cullen wanted Ireland to be like the Papal States, and ruled by ecclesiastics.[26] The Thomistic and Suarezian traditions underlying much of the theoretical outlook on church–state relations with which Cullen and his contemporaries were familiar are clearly set out in Suarez's *Opera omnia: de Legibus*, v and vi, published at Louvain in 1612. Cullen's theological training taught him to respect the two swords theory of the relationship between church and state.

21 *Freeman's Journal*, 6 Nov. 1861.   22 Emmet Larkin, *The consolidation of the Roman Catholic Church in Ireland, 1860–70* (Dublin, 1987), p. 65.   23 DDA Cullen papers, Letter book No. 3, Cullen to Ullathorne, 13 Nov. 1861.   24 This in turn was also influenced by contemporary political thinking in Rome. Cf. DDA Cullen papers, Kirby to Cullen, 6 Dec. 1861.   25 Cf. E.D. Steele, 'Cardinal Cullen and Irish nationality', *IHS*, 19 (1974–5), 240.   26 Patrick O'Farrell, *Ireland's English question: Anglo-Irish relations 1534–1970* (London, 1970), p. 243.

In addition, his adulation of O'Connell hardly supports the view that he wanted an Irish theocracy. This is not to deny that he saw no role for priests in politics, but he hoped that their influence would be to restrain the more ardent and radical elements in Irish politics and to help head-off any suggestion of revolution.

At a meeting in Dublin's pro-cathedral in January 1850, to sympathize with the plight of Pius IX who had been forced to flee from Rome by the advent of Italian revolutionaries, Cullen declared that Catholics 'repudiate and condemn resistance to lawful authority and denounce treason and rebellion wherever they may spring up'.[27] He emphasized this point in a letter to Kirby in the wake of the MacManus funeral, claiming that the whole affair was a '*pronounciamento*' in favour of revolutionary principles. Furthermore he told his Roman correspondent that to have supported MacManus' funeral would be to have condemned 'all our doings in favour of the pope and in support of established authority'.[28] Unlike the British government, Cullen was not double-minded enough to resist revolution at home and support it abroad. The basis of his opposition to revolution was religious principle. Thus on 29 November he wrote to Gillooly in Sligo that in rejecting the request for a funeral he did so in order to demonstrate a repudiation of those 'revolutionary principles, which are destroying religion everywhere they prevail'.

Time and again Cullen's correspondence and pastoral letters returned to the denunciation of revolution. Emmet Larkin is surely mistaken in his belief that Cullen's condemnations did not foreclose on a revolution in a just cause where there was a reasonable chance of success.[29] While the principle here enunciated by Larkin conforms to teachings of Roman Catholic theology in the matter, it is extremely unlikely that Cullen ever felt that the conditions for a just revolution could be fulfilled in Ireland. Again in his letter to Ullathorne in November 1861 he asserted that he considered it contrary to gospel principles to, in any way, foster a spirit of opposition to authority, 'especially in a country like this where resistance to one of the most powerful governments in the world on the part of our unarmed and undisciplined peasantry, could not be recommended except by men devoid of commonsense'. Furthermore, recent papal teaching corroborated Cullen's views. Although Pope Gregory XVI had accepted (in his brief, *Sollicitudo ecclesiarum*, 1831) the *de facto* position of the emergent South American republics, he was nevertheless innately conservative when faced with revolutions in Europe. On 9 June 1832 he issued an encyclical *Cum primum* chastising the Polish clergy

27 *Ireland and the Holy See: a retrospective. Illegal and seditious movements in Ireland contrasted with the principles of the Catholic Church as shown in the writings of Cardinal Cullen* (Rome, 1883) p. 7.   **28** DDA Cullen papers, Letter book No. 3, Cullen to Kirby, 12 Nov. 1861.   **29** Larkin, *Consolidation of the Roman Catholic Church*, p. 78.

and people for having attempted a revolution against the authority of the Tzar, and reminding them that 'We are taught most clearly that the obedience which men are obliged to render to the authorities established by God is an absolute precept which no one can violate'. The pope then went on to quote the scriptural proof texts which he believed denied the legitimacy of revolution, *Romans* 13: 1 ff, and *I Peter* 2: 13.[30] Cullen had been in Rome during the attempted revolutions of 1830 and 1848 and these experiences together with his own family history and his deference to Gregory, confirmed a lifelong antipathy to disorder in church or state.

Cullen's problems in coming to terms with early Fenianism were complicated by a number of factors. In the first place, he was dealing with a government headed by a prime minister, Palmerston, of decidedly anti-Catholic inclinations. Although he had supported Catholic emancipation, Palmerston nonetheless distrusted Catholics and thought that they should have no right to high office in a Protestant country. Much of his religious policy was influenced by his evangelical son-in-law Lord Shaftesbury, and possibly by his situation as a major Irish landlord. This in turn influenced the government's attitude towards the Roman question and Italian unification.[31] In this matter, the actual experience of the attitude taken by the British government to the unification of Italy caused Vatican officials to be less sympathetic to British political problems in Ireland than would otherwise have been the case. Hence Kirby's comment, 'In general it is well to remember that rebellion & its promotion is reprobated by all as usual; still whoever writes or acts against *perfida alba* is sure to be sympathized with by all ... The sentiments of people here have greatly changed on this point since the time of Greg[or]y XVI [died 1846].'[32]

In addition to Palmerston's hostility, the chief secretary, Sir Robert Peel, the third baronet, also increasingly made clear his irritation with Irish Catholics, and they in turn repaid the compliment. Peel was convinced that such unrest as existed in the country was the result of the activity of priests whom he described as the 'real offenders' against stability and order in Ireland.[33] In an undated letter to Cullen, William Monsell observed that 'we have had Chief Secretaries as ignorant as he. Perhaps we have had some as bigoted – but we certainly never had one at once so self-sufficient, so heedless of consequences & with so little ... self restraint'.[34] Furthermore *The Tablet* accused Peel of having a 'determined hostility to the Catholic religion'.[35]

30 Claudia Carlen (ed.), *The papal encyclicals, 1740–1878* (Ann Arbor, 1990), p. 234.
31 Denis Judd, *Palmerston* (London, 1975), pp 32–6; Jasper Ridley, *Lord Palmerston* (London, 1970), pp 500f; H.C.F. Bell, *Lord Palmerston*, 2 vols (London, 1936), ii, 34–7.
32 DDA Cullen papers, Kirby to Cullen, 6 Dec. 1861.   33 NAI State paper office, Anderson papers, Fenian Police Reports Box 4.   34 DDA AB4/41/3 Cullen papers,

A further complication for Cullen and his circle in their dealings with government and in trying to keep Fenianism at bay was the fact that the administration was unwilling to concede that the years 1861–3 constituted a period of unusual economic hardship. Time and again Irish Catholics and Liberal MPs protested in vain that certain areas of the country were near to experiencing a minor famine.[36] Continual rain had caused crop failures and had waterlogged peat supplies, the only source of fuel for many. The government regarded representations on such matters as nothing more than attempts to stir up trouble. Peel was adamant that reports of distress were exaggerated. He accused Cullen of having extracted certain passages of his speeches from Hansard and 'with Jesuitical ingenuity ... endeavour[ed] to construe them into an accusation against myself'.[37]

These problems were in addition to other difficulties facing Irish Catholicism in the early 1860s. The evangelical revival of 1859 led to a concerted campaign, in some Protestant circles, of proselytizing among Catholics. Although the numbers and the extent of such activity was probably quite limited, it did attract much press attention and added to Catholic discontent. The education issue was a continuing thorn in the church's side despite some minor victories for the hierarchy at government expense. In 1853 the church had forced the board of national education to withdraw approval of the books *Lessons on the truth of Christianity*, and *Christian evidences*, for use in model schools, thus precipitating the resignation of the author from the board, the Anglican archbishop of Dublin, Richard Whately. This ensured that the Catholic catechism could henceforth be used for the religious instruction of Catholic children in national schools. Cullen had also by the end of 1860 forced the government to equalize the denominational representation on the education board, although the bishops made clear that they regarded the equalization as a government ploy which fell well short of their demands for a Catholic system of education paid for by the state. Much educational activity lay outside clerical control, and those institutions which did come under the hierarchy's sway, such as the Catholic University, were not a conspicuous success. In the case of the university, this was partly because of Cullen's own mismanagement of circumstances.[38] All this

Monsell to Cullen. Adverse comment was not confined to Catholics. Sir Robert Anderson, an uncompromising Unionist, described Peel as 'a political Bohemian who regarded his sojourn in Ireland as a picnic, and meddled but little in the work of his office': *A great conspiracy*, p. 49. **35** 23 Nov. 1861, 737. **36** Cf. *Hansard* 3rd series clv, 268–9; 548–9; 567 and 573. There are also many letters in the Catholic diocesan archives in Armagh and Dublin which show that an extensive amount of assistance was sent in these years from Britain, North America and Australia to relieve the distress in Ireland. **37** *The Tablet*, 23 Nov. 1861. See also L.M. Cullen, *An economic history of Ireland since 1660*, 2nd ed. (London, 1987), p. 137. **38** Fergal McGrath, *Newman's*

contributed to the sense that the Catholic Church was not able to influence government policy in Ireland to the extent that the bishops thought was its right. In this regard, it lived very much in the shadow of the Anglican Establishment.

The government's support for Italian revolutionaries, and the idealization of the anti-Catholic Garibaldi,[39] was not only deeply offensive to many Irish Catholics, but also briefly threatened to shatter the Catholic–Liberal alliance. Liberal foreign policy had led Cullen, to support the Tories in 1859. The election that year witnessed the return of the largest number of Tories to parliament from Ireland since the Union. This was part of a systematic campaign by English Catholics to establish a permanent alliance with the Tories, a campaign championed by *The Tablet* and taken up, temporarily, by Archbishop Henry Edward Manning in the hope of further concessions on the question of Catholic education in Ireland.[40] So far as *The Tablet* was concerned, the 'close connection between Catholics and the Liberal party was an evil'.[41]

Irish politics was in such a state of flux that by early 1862 the Liberal chief whip, H.B.W. Brand, wrote to Palmerston that Irish Catholics were the natural enemies of Liberalism, and he urged the prime minister to begin to cultivate Irish Protestant support which he believed ought naturally to be given to a Liberal government. There is some evidence that Palmerston may have heeded this advice since he instructed the lord lieutenant, Lord Carlisle, not to be led by the Catholic attorney general, Thomas O'Hagan, into distributing patronage among Catholics, but rather to reserve preferment for Protestants.[42]

If such proof were needed, the 1861 census showed the clear numerical superiority of Catholics over Protestants in Ireland. Despite this, Catholics were at a clear disadvantage socially and politically. Protestants still exercised enormous and disproportionate control in membership of grand juries and the magistracy, on poor law boards, in the police and army. Most MPs were Protestant, and the rulings of the board of charitable bequests were often felt to be, perhaps unjustifiably, to the disadvantage of the Catholic community. The queen's colleges were increasingly administered by Protestants, though in this instance Catholics could blame none but themselves since the church

university: idea and reality (London, 1951), pp 501–2.   **39** The adulation of Garibaldi was to provoke serious rioting in London in September 1862, when working class Irish Catholics fought pitched battles with their English Protestant counterparts: Sheridan Gilley, 'The Garibaldi riots of 1862', *Historical Journal*, 16 (1973), 697–432.   **40** Robert Grey, *Cardinal Manning: a biography* (London, 1985), pp 222–3.   **41** *The Tablet*, 14 Dec. 1861.   **42** University of Southampton Palmerston papers, Private letter book 1862–5, Palmerston to Carlisle, 9 Feb. 1863.

refused to support the system. Politically, it is also clear that the country was ruled 'in answer to a British strategic imperative rather than any imagined duty to the people'.[43] For Cullen and his supporters all this tended to create the impression that Ireland was being governed by Protestants in the interest of Protestants. Indeed, Catholic frustration with the administration led Patrick Leahy, archbishop of Cashel, to characterize it as 'a wicked anti-Catholic, anti-Roman, anti-Irish, anti-everything dear to us government'.[44]

Given the situation, the Catholic Church, from its perspective, was remarkably supportive of the institutions of the state. If the church felt threatened from without by the Protestant state, the growth of 'secret societies' in the Catholic community intimidated it from within. When Fenianism emerged as a dynamic force in Irish society in the early 1860s, it competed with the Catholic Church for the affections of working-class potential revolutionaries, who along with the marginalized intelligentsia formed the backbone of the Fenian organization. Although many Fenians seemed not to experience too much difficulty in reconciling Catholicism with membership of a secret society, the church tried to disabuse its adherents of such notions. Cullen's pastoral letter for Advent 1861 declared that members of secret societies were 'under the severest penalties, and are, *ipso facto*, excommunicated; their lot is miserable, indeed, for they are cut off like rotten branches from the Church'.[45]

The outbreak of the American civil war and the possibilities of hostility between Britain and America, presented yet more problems for both church and state, as Irishmen joined the armies in America, in some instances to gain useful military experience. The 'phoenix theory', which was widely known, was even debated in public by former colleagues of the 1848 rising, and mounting tension on the international scene raised hopes in some advanced nationalist circles in Ireland and America.[46] A letter from Richard More O'Ferrall, MP for Co. Kilkenny, to Cullen neatly summaries a number of the concerns facing Irish Catholicism at the time of the MacManus funeral.

> I fear that the American news will cause great disturbance here by exciting hopes that would end in ruin and bloodshed. How fortunate it is that the MacManus demonstration received no clerical countenance

43 Charles Townshend, *Political violence in Ireland: government and resistance since 1848* (Oxford, 1983), p. 102. **44** Leahy to Kirby quoted in Desmond Bowen, *Paul Cullen and the shaping of modern Irish Catholicism* (Dublin 1983), p. 265. **45** Patrick Moran (ed.), *The pastoral and other writings of Cardinal Cullen* (Dublin, 1882), i, 869. **46** 'Correspondence between John Martin and William Smith O'Brien relative to a French invasion' (Dublin, 1861). A copy of this document is preserved in NLI Larcom papers MS 7697.

in any quarter. I am inclined to believe that some undertaking has been given by the Irish in the southern army that if the north declared war with England the Irish in the Southern army would desert them. There can be no doubt that the deputation that accompanied MacManus' remains came for a bad purpose ... The evil principles which Palmerston & Co. have patronised in Italy will be exemplified here and they will hang Irishmen for the crime they honoured [in] Italy. Mitchel's writings have done great mischief among the half educated young men and I fear will lead many to destruction.[47]

Against this background we can begin to look at a number of specific details of the funeral and evaluate Cullen's reactions accordingly. Undoubtedly the greatest embarrassment for Cullen was what appeared to be the approbation by Archbishop Hughes of New York for MacManus' cause. In the course of his sermon at MacManus' requiem Mass in the old St Patrick's Cathedral in New York, Hughes commented:

Love of country has generally been understood as that by which men defended their native or adopted soil, and supported the government when that government is lawful and not oppressive. If government should degenerate into oppression and tyranny, then would come the love of country – but not government ... Some of the most learned and holy men of the Church have lain it down with general sanction that there are cases in which it is lawful to resist and overthrow a tyrannical government.[48]

Hughes' example was contrasted favourably with Cullen's among more ardent nationalist opinion. In a subsequent dispute about the affair, Hughes defended himself by claiming that he had conducted the funeral because the archbishop of San Francisco had written to him saying that MacManus had died a good Catholic. In the situation he had done no more than his duty. But

47 DDA Cullen papers, O'Ferrall to Cullen, 1 Dec. 1861. Mitchel's *Jail Journal* had been recently published and had scandalized sections of Catholic opinion. *The Tablet* on 9 November quoted the *Journal* to the effect that Ireland would get its independence despite the priests. Cullen had read the work and was suitably horrified by its contents, particularly given its Carlylean influence.   48 The full text of this remarkable sermon is given in Rutherford, *The secret history*, i, 187–91. Extracts can also be found in Michael Cavanagh, *Memoirs of Thomas Francis Meagher* (Worcester, MA, 1892); Richard Pigott, *Recollections of an Irish journalist* (Dublin, 1883), and Desmond Ryan, *The Fenian chief: a biography of James Stephens* (Dublin, 1967).One place from which it is conspicuously absent is Laurence Kehoe (ed.), *The complete works of the Most Reverend John Hughes D.D.*, 2 vols (New York, 1864–5), hereafter *Hughes*.

he added: 'this I could not accept as a compliment, if intentionally or acciden-
tally, it implied any censure upon the conduct of others'. He also implied that
at his insistence the New York funeral was a less exuberant affair than the
organizers wanted.[49] In a further letter to the *Cork Examiner* on 29 November
1862, Hughes remarked that when MacManus had been buried in Dublin a
'misunderstanding' grew up between the clergy and the funeral organizers.
The news reached New York where it was greeted with 'deep regret' by the
archbishop. He added that when in Rome in the winter of 1861–2 he heard of
the resentment against Cullen because of his attitude to the funeral and this
left 'a deep impression' on his mind. But neither in Ireland nor in Rome had
he discussed the matter with Cullen.[50]

Hughes had been forced to defend himself publicly in this way by yet
another imprudent gesture, apparently implying he supported the National
Brotherhood of St Patrick, which in effect was a front organization for the
Fenians. In the course of his stay in Dublin in August 1862 he received a
delegation from the Brotherhood, which included among others, The
O'Donoghue MP (as so often playing both sides in the revolutionary divide),
Denis Holland, editor of the *Irishman*, and Peter Gill, editor of the *Tipperary
Advocate*. In the conviviality of such company Hughes talked about how
much gratification it had given him to conduct MacManus' funeral, and he
outlined again the Church's general teaching on revolution. His closing
remarks, however, proved the most controversial. 'Gentlemen', he told the
delegation,

> there are events occurring which are calculated to bring the wrongs, the
> miseries, the sufferings of the Irish people under consideration
> elsewhere … But if the time comes, it will not be to redress your
> wrongs merely – for the world is selfish … it will originate in an effort
> to settle other more general grievances; through them no doubt Ireland
> may have her opportunity.[51]

Hughes' remarks were being taken down in shorthand by Holland, apparently
unknown to him although this was disputed, and when they were published
the archbishop was indignant. He asserted that he had been mislead as to the
nature of the delegation which he was to receive, and outraged that his private
remarks should be published by his guests. He repudiated the whole
proceedings even to the extent of denying that he knew that the Brotherhood
was a condemned organization, or the meaning of the phrase 'nationalists of
Ireland'[52]

49 *Hughes*, ii, 530.   50 Ibid., p. 538.   51 Ibid., p. 528.   52 *The Tablet*, 16 Aug. 1862.

Hughes' response was not simply the result of embarrassment over unguarded remarks of an advanced nationalist nature. He had just completed a delicate diplomatic mission, on behalf of the Union government in Washington, to France and the Holy See, concerning European support for the North against the Confederate States,[53] which had been undertaken soon after the *Trent* affair.[54] In November 1861 he wrote to Cullen that if his mission to Europe was successful it would have very great importance for all concerned. He asked Cullen to meet him in Liverpool where he hoped to tell Cullen much that would be of interest to the 'land of my birth', which 'same things I could not write with equal propriety'.[55]

After his meeting with Napoleon III in Paris he again wrote to Cullen saying that it would not be appropriate to commit the contents of his conversation to paper, but that all went satisfactorily from his point of view.[56] He also told Cullen in this letter that he had it on good authority that the British government was puzzled that he had not landed in Ireland since they imagined his mission was to stir up trouble in that country. Certainly the government was concerned about the suspicion that Irishmen were being illegally recruited into the Union army, something heartily denied by the Union States consul in Dublin.[57] There is also some suggestion that Hughes himself may have tried to encourage recruitment on the grounds that the military experience thus gained would be of use later in Ireland. Hughes' genuine alarm then has to be set within the context of a tense diplomatic situation. It was one thing as the archbishop of New York to say what he did over the MacManus' remains in the autumn of 1861, and quite another as an agent of a foreign and possibly hostile power to appear to give credence to revolution in Ireland.

Hughes' primary purpose in Ireland in the summer of 1862 was to preach at the laying of the foundation stone of the Catholic University at Drumcondra on 20 July. Vincent Comerford, oddly, sees this as Hughes' effort to make amends to Cullen for his role over the MacManus affair.[58] In fact, Cullen had invited Hughes to preach at the ceremony almost immediately after MacManus' funeral, when his own feelings were still aggravated.

---

53 *Hughes*, i, 13. See also DDA Cullen papers Kirby to Cullen, 14 Dec. 1861. 'Dr Hughes is expected here [in Rome] towards Xmass. The object of his mission is well known.' Washington feared that the Vatican might support the South. Later in the civil war Pius IX did send a blessing to the Confederacy. **54** The *Trent*, an English-registered ship, had been intercepted by the United States navy on 8 November 1861 while carrying two confederate representatives to Europe. The agents were arrested and taken to the US. A similar incident had sparked the Anglo-American war of 1812. **55** DDA Cullen papers, 17 Nov. 1861. **56** Ibid., 1 Jan. 1862. **57** NAICSO Register papers 1861/12487. Consul Henry B. Hammond to chief secretary's office, 29 Mar. 1862. **58** Comerford, *The Fenians in context*, p. 79.

Whatever his personal embarrassment about Hughes' shenanigans apropos of MacManus' funeral, Cullen seems never to have adverted to annoyance about it in any of his extant correspondence. Furthermore, the Irish church was heavily dependent on money from America for many of its ecclesiastical and charitable enterprises. It is most unlikely that Cullen would have snubbed Hughes in any way that would have jeopardized a lucrative source of funds.[59]

The sermon Hughes preached at Drumcondra was, despite the obligatory swipe at the government's educational policy, a model of conciliation and loyalty. He told his auditors that in the not too distant future the British Empire would need the services of well educated and highly cultured Catholics both in the army and government of the colonies. The Catholic University was the means of supplying such individuals.[60] His words on this occasion were neither revolutionary nor belligerent.

We now must examine a number of difficulties surrounding the funeral itself which have tended to cause confusion. The first problem was who was actually in charge of the funeral proceedings. The need to include MacManus' former Young Ireland colleagues presented major difficulties for the Fenian orchestration of the funeral. Fr John Kenyon, a veteran of 1848, by his initial agreement to be associated with the reburial, lent both a religious and advanced nationalist credibility to the proceedings. There is evidence that Kenyon was asked initially to deliver the oration at the funeral. James Stephens, the Fenian founder, asked to see a text of what Kenyon proposed to say, and having read it vetoed the oration and instead asked Captain Michael Smith of the California delegation to speak. This high-handedness on Stephens' part occasioned a major row between the funeral committee and the former Young Irelanders. Fr Kenyon and John Martin tried to persuade MacManus' sister Isabella, to have her brother's body taken away from the funeral committee and entrusted to them. This she refused to do.[61]

As we have seen above, it is quite clear that Cullen did not at any point intend to provide a funeral for MacManus, but neither did he refuse the request outright. The first letter Cullen received from E.J. Ryan, secretary of the MacManus funeral committee, asked him 'to order a solemn funeral service' for the dead patriot and if it met with his approval to receive a delegation to discuss the details. His first inclination was to refuse the request that he receive a delegation, but clearly he thought better of it. Cullen in his

59 The Irish hierarchy was thrown into high dudgeon in 1865 when the bishop of Boston, John B. Fitzpatrick, refused permission for collections in his diocese to be taken up for projects in Ireland. See Archives of the Archdiocese of Armagh, Dixon papers vii, folder 7. 60 *Hughes*, ii, 359–60. 61 The details can be followed in Denieffe's, *Recollections*, pp 166–7, where he gives in full Stephens' letter of 16 November explaining the circumstances of the incident.

public dealing with the committee was anxious to stress that there had to be some clear and objective reason for a public funeral. When the committee was unable to present him with a satisfactory reason, he refused to permit a public Catholic burial. One possible explanation for his equivocation was that the burial was a private family matter as well as being a public event. He had no wish to hurt or cause offence to MacManus' sole surviving relative, but at the same time he had no desire to encourage revolutionary fervour.

Although often portrayed as a hard-faced ecclesiastical politician, which undoubtedly he was, Cullen was also a pastor. Isabella MacManus had personally appealed to Cullen asking that her brother's remains might be given the final blessings of the church. She wrote to Cullen on 15 October saying that she had heard a rumour,

> that your Grace declines to give the use of one of the churches in Dublin for the celebration of the funeral obsequies ... I cannot bring myself to believe [this] unless I hear from your Grace that the sacred services are to be denied to my poor brother.

She also pointed out that her brother had died a good Catholic, and therefore by implication in full communion with the Catholic Church and hence entitled to a Catholic burial.[62] This letter obviously gave Cullen pause for thought and he tried to avoid answering it. Having heard nothing, possibly because of Cullen's negotiations with the committee, MacManus wrote again on 21 October repeating her request. Cullen replied eight days later telling her that is was not usual for a bishop to prescribe such a funeral except in the most extraordinary cases, 'and where the Church wd. be anxious to honour one who had rendered signal services to religion or his country'. These conditions did not apply in the present case.[63]

The MacManus committee, however, was persistent and at least wanted an official graveside ceremony with ecclesiastical approval. It wrote to the chaplain at Glasnevin cemetery and asked him to conduct the burial service. The priest there, Brendan Delany, referred the matter to Dr Murray, Cullen's secretary, who drafted the response: 'before I give a definite answer it is necessary for me to know whether there will be an oration at the interment, and if so by whom it is to be delivered'.[64] Comerford interprets this to mean that the chaplain would have conducted the service provided no oration was given. He comments: 'This move must have been inspired by Cullen; in any case it shows the over-simplicity of the notion that the archbishop had from

---

62 DDA Cullen papers, MacManus to Cullen, 15 Oct. 1861.   63 Ibid., Letter book No. 3, 29 Nov. 1861.   64 Ibid., 340/1/I.

the outset placed a ban on all ecclesiastical involvement in the MacManus obsequies.'[65]

In fact it can be argued that Cullen's actions were simply a delaying tactic. He had already made himself unpopular by the refusal of a church service, and clearly in the emotionally heightened atmosphere of the burial itself he wanted to avoid further immediate public opprobrium. He now employed a typical ecclesiastical damage-limitation strategy. There was no need to announce what would take place at the cemetery until he absolutely had to. Delany was approached on the morning of the funeral itself, 10 November, and the committee gave him the details of what was to take place in the cemetery. He wrote to Murray at 9.45 a.m. that the oration would be given by Captain Michael Smith, as arranged by Stephens, and that Smith would be introduced by Fr Patrick Lavelle.[66] At this point Cullen forbade the graveside ceremony which in the event was performed by Lavelle and a priest of the Birmingham diocese, Fr P. Courtney.

It is impossible to consider Cullen's attitude to MacManus' funeral without seeing that he regarded the sentiments it represented as fundamentally hostile to the interests of the Catholic Church in Ireland. *The Tablet* in commenting on his leadership of the Irish Catholic Church in November 1861, observed that he urged the Irish people to be good and faithful citizens, and no grievances, or afflictions, ought to induce the people to chant the praises of sedition or rebellion.[67] This is a reasonably accurate assessment of Cullen's mind-set. His principal concern was for the progress and wellbeing of the Roman Catholic Church in Ireland and not any romanticized view of Irish nationalism. On the other hand, he did believe that the British government at times worked for the destruction of the church in Ireland. Thus for example, he was convinced that the government deliberately allowed secret societies to flourish so that they would subvert the Catholic faith.[68] In trying to cause disaffection between the priests and their people, he wrote to Archbishop Spalding of Baltimore, the government was operating on the old maxim of divide and rule.[69] Whatever the basis for this assertion, there can be no doubt that the church as an institution could represent a formidable impediment to any government policy that it chose to oppose. It is also apparent, however,

---

65 *Fenians in context*, p. 78. His source for the chaplain incident is T.N. Underwood. Cf. NLI O'Brien papers MS 447, Underwood to William Smith O'Brien, 1 Jan. 1862. 66 DDA Cullen papers 340/1/I, Delany to Murray, 10 Nov. 1861. It is therefore clear that Lavelle's role was not as impromptu or unexpected as has been suggested. See John O'Leary, *Recollections of Fenians and Fenianism* (Dublin, 1896), i, 169; Ryan, *The Fenian chief*, p. 177; and Larkin, *Consolidation of the Roman Catholic Church*, p. 72. 67 *The Tablet*, 23 Nov. 1861. 68 Cullen to Kirby, 4 Mar. 1864, quoted in Bowen, *Paul Cullen*, p. 267. 69 DDA Cullen papers, Letter book 3, Cullen to Spalding, 12 Nov. 1864.

that Cullen was temperamentally and theologically predisposed to favour the government of the day.

For their part the Fenians maintained that government must be evaluated by its results and not by metaphysical considerations. Furthermore they also insisted, in the circumstances of Irish political culture, on the need to differentiate between the sacred and secular in Irish affairs. These principles provided a challenge to both government and ecclesiastical thinking. Although he was to set his face firmly against Fenianism, Cullen was simultaneously engaged in a struggle with the British administration to secure for the country what he took to be the rights and liberties of Catholicism. The Fenians, as the promoters of revolution, were in his estimation, like their 1848 predecessors, advocates of disorder and irreligion, and so he opposed them, as he did any such manifestation. Only in this light can we understand his *modus operandi* with regard to the MacManus funeral.

8

The Catholic Church and Fenianism, 1861–70: some Irish and American perspectives

In his memoirs Benedict Kiely draws attention to a poem of Alice Milligan in which Milligan indicates how the Fenians have for so long been the bogeymen of Irish Unionist imagination:

> Come in! for it's growing late,
> And the grass will wet ye!
> Come in! or when it's dark
> The Fenians will get ye.

Kiely observes:

> For the ghosts of the Fenian men of 1867 were still on the hills. It was time for all good Protestants and persons loyal to the English crown to be abed. So the little flock of children ran helter-skelter to the nursery fire to listen to dreadful tales of that night in March with loyal folk waiting to see a great army of men come, devastating. An army of papists waving a green flag, and black police and redcoats flying behind them.[1]

Milligan's nanny, however, had the last word on the papist army since she assured her charges:

> But God (Who our nurse declared
> Guards British dominions)
> Sent down a deep fall of snow
> And scattered the Fenians.[2]

If the Fenians are the great dark shadows that stalk as so many wolverines Protestant unionist mythology, one suspects that this has as much to do with Catholicism as with militant Irish nationalism. Home Rule is, after all, Rome Rule.

1 Benedict Kiely, *Drink to the bird: a memoir* (London, 1991), p. 133. 2 Alice Milligan, 'When I was a little girl', *Poems* (Dublin, 1954), pp 2–3. Cf. Sheila T. Johnston (ed.), *The harper of the only God* (Omagh, 1993), pp 50–1.

No one wishes to deny that perhaps the majority of Fenians were practising Catholics. It is, however, important to bear in mind that the Catholic Church waged a bitter and acrimonious campaign to disrupt any notion of the compatibility between membership of the Fenian brotherhood and the Roman Catholic Church. Moreover, it is worth considering that many historians regard the specific contribution of Fenianism to the development of Irish nationalism to be precisely that it insisted that Catholicism and nationalism were not materially equivalent terms.[3] Furthermore, some of the leading lights of Fenianism were of course Protestants: Thomas Clarke Luby; Thomas Neilson Underwood; Dr David Bell, a renegade Presbyterian minister; and perhaps even John Martin, who if not directly sworn into the movement was certainly sympathetic and influential. My aim here is, in general terms, to outline the ways in which the Catholic Church on both sides of the Atlantic sought 'to disabuse those ignorant persons who think they can remain good Catholics while they join secret seditious associations which the Church has never ceased to condemn'.[4]

The advent of Fenianism as a serious political threat in the 1860s coincided with the re-emergence of the 'Catholic question' in British politics. Developments in Italy determined the Whig–Liberal government upon a foreign policy antithetical to the interests of Catholics in Britain and Ireland.[5] It was as an indirect result of his Italian policy that Palmerston had been forced from office in 1858,[6] but the inability of the Tories to make any substantial gains in April 1859 ensured that Palmerston once again became prime minister. At this stage, 17 of the 25 new Tory seats were from Ireland, testimony to the strength of Catholic resentment at the Whig–Liberal attitude to the government of the Papal States.

English public opinion was genuinely sympathetic to the revolutionary struggles of the Italians, the Czechs, and the Poles,[7] but saw no correlation between those struggles and similar movements in Ireland.[8] It may not be

3 Cf. F.S.L. Lyons, *Ireland since the famine* (London, 1971), p. 133.   4 *Ireland and the Holy See: a retrospective 1866–83: Illegal seditious movements in Ireland contrasted with the principles of the Catholic Church as shown in the writings of Cardinal Cullen* (Rome, 1883), p. 3.   5 J.L. Altholz, 'The political behaviour of English Catholics, 1850–67', *Journal of British Studies*, 4 (1964–5), 99.   6 The attempt on Napoleon III's life was planned by Italian exiles in London, owing to the French ruler's failure to fulfill his promise over Italian unification. His protests forced Palmerston to introduce the conspiracy bill over which he was defeated: William D. Jones, *Lord Darby and Victorian conservatism* (Oxford, 1956), p. 226.   7 Nicholas Mansergh, *The Irish question, 1840–1921* (3rd ed., London, 1975), p. 80.   8 There were exceptions to this and not just the obvious ones, such as John Stuart Mill. At a later stage Lord Tennyson wrote to Gladstone to plead for the lives of the 'Manchester martyrs', and Swinburne saw that the *Risorgimento* was the same in Ireland as in Italy. Intriguingly, Swinburne wrote a poem about the Manchester men, subsequently dropped from his collected works. See

entirely coincidental that Garibaldi and Mazzini, having received enormous support from the governing classes in Britain, tended to denigrate Irish nationalism. By the 1860s Italian nationalism was in some respects thoroughly anti-Catholic, and this doubtless helped commend it to British tastes. However, the pervasive anti-Catholicism of much British political life[9] also inadvertently played into the hands of the Fenians. Opposition from the Catholic Church to what were perceived to be anti-Catholic polices, in education for example, help to create a climate of opinion in Ireland in which opposition to the British government seemed generally acceptable, despite the injunctions of pastors to the contrary. Thus David Moriarty, bishop of Kerry, was inclined to blame Paul Cullen's too spirited defence of Catholic interests as a factor in stirring up trouble.[10]

Despite some attempts to portray Cullen in a decidedly more nationalist light,[11] the judgment of Edward Norman that Cullen's politics must be seen as essentially religious has about it a ring of truth.[12] His primary concern was for the advancement of the Catholic Church in Ireland, and he was prepared to align himself with whatever political institutions best served those interests.

Cullen's undoubted dominance of the Irish hierarchy set the tone for much of the political outlook of official Irish Catholicism in the Fenian period. As the movement grew in the course of the 1860s, it was clear that Fenianism presented both a political and a religious challenge to the Irish church. It competed with the church for influence over the mass of the rural and urban working class, and it questioned the church's right to any say in the political arena. Time and again the Fenian newspaper, the *Irish People,* railed against clerical involvement in Irish political affairs.[13] Emmet Larkin is therefore mistaken in his view that the Fenians confined themselves to complaining that

Shane Leslie, *The Irish tangle for English readers* (London, 1946), pp 115–16.   **9** Edward Norman, *Anti-Catholicism in Victorian England* (London, 1968), p. 21, remarks that anti-Catholic sentiments were among the most important political catalysts in nineteenth century Britain.   **10** AICR Kirby papers, Moriarty to Tobias Kirby, 1 May 1864. Moriarty's exact words were: 'Some of us by our abuse of Govt., drive the people into disaffection and the spirit of rebellion. We cannot blame them if they are more logical than canonical in their conclusions.'   **11** E.D. Steele, 'Cardinal Cullen and Irish nationality', *IHS*, 19 (1974–5), p. 256; Desmond Bowen, *Paul Cullen and the shaping of modern Irish Catholicism* (Dublin, 1983), pp 255–9. Bowen is also anxious to stress what he takes to be Cullen's bigotry.   **12** Edward Norman, *The Catholic Church in Ireland in the age of revolution* (London, 1965), p. 10. This view finds echo in P.J. Corish, 'The radical face of Paul Cardinal Cullen', in Corish (ed.), *Radicals, rebels and establishments* (Belfast, 1985), p. 175.   **13** See for example *Irish People*, 27 Feb. 1864, p. 217. 'Ireland cannot possibly be saved if the people are not taught to draw a clear line of demarcation between ecclesiastical authority in spiritual matters, and ecclesiastical authority in matters which are not spiritual'.

the church was exceeding its power in condemning them, but never went so far as to maintain that the church had no right to political influence.[14] On the contrary, the *Irish People* regularly and bitterly complained that the clergy overstepped their proper role in society by presuming to extent their domain into political matters.[15] It was this radical departure in seeking a separation between church and state which generated such alarm in Cullen and his supporters, and caused them to see the Fenians in the same light as anti-clerical Italian revolutionaries. There were, at most, some intellectual affinities with the latter,[16] but the Fenians were not anti-clerical in the strict sense.

The fortunes of the Fenian organization were by early 1861 at a low ebb. However, the reburial of Terence Bellew McManus, in Ireland, helped rally Fenian fortunes – largely through the activity of its front organization, the National Brotherhood of Saint Patrick. But that event also demonstrated differences of opinion between leading American and Irish churchmen over how to deal with revolutionaries. This provoked an outburst from the radical journal *Mooney's California Express*, which in January 1862 carried a poisonous attack on the clergy. 'The Irish priesthood', it declared, 'are, for the sake of thirty thousand pounds a year [a reference to the Maynooth grant] sworn in as a species of police force for England. Our eyes were opened by the MacManus funeral to the sickening fruits of the alliance between Church and State.'

That North America should by the 1860s be a centre of Irish discontent can hardly have come as a surprise to the British government. As early as the mid-1850s, the British Minister in Washington had found it necessary to report to London on the nefarious activities of various Irish groups in cities as far apart as Boston, New York, Chicago and Cincinnati.[17] The treasonable sentiments of the Irish in America were bound up not only with the often harsh experiences which caused them to flee Ireland in the first place, but also with the less than ideal situations in which they found themselves in the great American republic.

Of all the institutions which offered continuity for the immigrant between life at home and in the new world, none was more important or powerful than

---

14 Emmet Larkin, 'Church, state and nation in modern Ireland', *American Historical Review*, 80 (1975), 1276.   **15** There are too many reference to advert to them all but a representative sample will include the *Irish People*, 9 Apr. 1864; 7 May 1864; 14 May 1864 (where it is asserted that 'submission to certain Irish bishops in political matters is equivalent to slavery'); 4 June 1864.   **16** James Stephens, the founder of the Fenians, seems to have been sworn as a Carbonaro in Paris, and he regarded the Italians as having a genius for revolution. See Oliver MacDonagh, *States of mind: a study of Anglo-Irish conflict, 1780–1980* (London, 1983), p. 80.   **17** PRO FO 5/640 John Compton to Lord Palmerston, 4 and 12 Feb. 1856.

the church. Bereft of other means of social support, immigrants looked to the church for reassurance, and for a focus to preserve and express a sense of identity. The immigrants often looked to the church to play the role of Irish nationalism at prayer, but not only was the American Catholic Church unwilling to play such a part, it also deeply distrusted the more radical Irish nationalist spirit in the United States.[18] Much of the church's concern was not with the rights or wrongs of the situation in Ireland, or with the circumstances which gave rise to Fenianism, but rather with Catholicism's own position in wider American culture. This involved not only struggles over the 'know nothing' movement, but also over the need for acceptance of Catholicism as a legitimate force in the United States during and in the aftermath of the American civil war. Fenianism highlighted tension within the church over such issues as support for the confederacy or the union and the exercise of authority by bishops and priests over the political opinions of practising Catholics. The Fenian convention in Chicago in November 1863 specifically railed against 'all interference with the legitimate exercise of our civil and social privileges ... under the American constitution on the part of any man, or class of men ... who claim to represent or receive instructions from any foreign potentate'.[19]

The attitude which the American bishops assumed in regard to the Fenians varied from outright hostility to a desire to let well enough alone in the hopes that Fenianism would simply die of its own accord. In June 1864 the Catholic newspaper in Philadelphia carried an article which served to embarrass the bishops over their obvious differences concerning the Fenian question. With a taunting attitude the editor remarked, 'One bishop says it is a secret society; another patronizes it by a contribution; and a third illustrates in a letter to bishops that it has the freedom of Ireland in its hand. What is it? That is the question.'[20] As the bishops themselves were aware, such differences of approach did 'more harm than good'.[21] For his part John Duggan, bishop of Chicago, had already condemned the organization following the Chicago convention of 1863. He did so under the terms of decree nineteen of the Chicago diocesan synod of 1860. Duggan regarded the Fenians as members of a secret society and hence that they fell under the general ban of the church.[22] Bishop James Wood of Philadelphia issued a pastoral letter on 19

18 There were exceptions to this general pattern. One such was Fr Edward O'Flaherty, pastor in Crawfordsville, Indiana, who was the Fenian head centre for the state. Such were his exertions that during his life Indiana was known as 'the banner state of Fenianism'. See John Savage, *Fenian heroes and martyrs* (Boston, 1868), p. 56. 19 *Irish American*, 21 Nov. 1863. 20 PAHRC Wood papers 51–204j-Aso. 21 AAB 34-S-5 Spalding papers, Bishop John Luers to Archbishop Martin Spalding, 24 Mar. 1864. 22 APF *Scritture Riferite nei Congressi America Centrale* 20, f. 888. He confirmed this view in a letter to Spalding late in 1864 in which he remarked: 'I never doubted after the

January 1864 saying that the Fenians were a condemned secret society, and Archbishop John Baptist Purcell of Cincinnati reiterated his view that if the Fenians succeeded in Ireland they would give her a government worse than the one she already possessed.[23] Archbishop Martin Spalding of Baltimore, on the other hand, regarded such outbursts from his episcopal colleagues as both 'foolish and mischievous'.[24]

Most of the bishops throughout the years 1863–4 were content to follow the practice of the bishops of the New York ecclesiastical province, as explained by Archbishop John McCloskey:

> With regard to the Fenians, it was considered best to preserve the course we have thus far been pursuing of making no public denunciation, nor any final decision, further than to advise our clergy to use every effort to discourage them, & to prevent their people joining them.[25]

On behalf of the American bishops Spalding submitted the matter to Rome in October 1864, requesting a judgment about the canonical status of the Fenian movement. There was a good deal of hesitation there, and indeed even in the United States, about the propriety of an authoritative public pronouncement against the Fenians. In his petition, Spalding briefly indicated what he took to be the history of Fenianism, and how it was linked to the '*Juvenis Hiberniae*' movement which had opposed Daniel O'Connell and had staged the 1848 rising. He also pointed out that the stated aim of the organization was to overthrow by military means the union of Great Britain and Ireland. More importantly, from the perspective of moral theology, he alleged that the Fenians were bound under secret oath to prompt obedience to the president of the organization, the head 'centre'.

This official approach by the titular head of the American bishops was complemented by a number of individual applications that the Holy See had received that year from priests and bishops, asking for a ruling on whether or not the Fenian Brotherhood was a lawful organization. There was considerable delay at Rome in answering this question, since, as Spalding explained, '*Roma, mora, amor*'.

first examination of the Fenian Brotherhood that it is a secret society coming under the censures of the pontifical constitutions'. AAB Spalding papers, 33-S-12.   **23** *Catholic Telegraph*, 22 Feb. 1865. Purcell had condemned the Fenians the previous year.   **24** AAB Bayley papers 42-O-6, Spalding to Bishop Bayley, 3 Mar. 1865.   **25** AAB Spalding papers 35-D-10, McCloskey to Spalding, 25 Aug. 1864. One major issue for Spalding was in the light of the Chicago Fenian convention should the American church now regard the Fenians as an organization proscribed under ecclesiastical law. See AUND Purcell papers II-5-b, Spalding to Purcell, 13 Sept. 1864.

In the meanwhile, the Fenians continued to cause pastoral and other difficulties for the church in the United States. In January 1865 several American Catholic newspapers published a report which claimed that Rome had written to the American bishops saying that '*Feniani non sunt inquisitandi*'. The bishops immediately denied this, but several of them did write to Rome asking if the reports could be true. It was not until the following August that the Holy See denied this, and at the same time issued a document 'by order of His Holiness', agreeing with those bishops who were of the opinion that the Fenians fell under the terms of the decree of the Holy Office of 5 August 1846, which prohibited membership of secret societies. However, Rome decided that this intelligence should not be published at large, but merely communicated to priests, the implication being that priests were to use their influence through the confessional to prevent people from joining the organization or to get them to leave if they were already members.

Although the American bishops in their dealings with Rome received this ruling with their customary deference to the wishes of the Holy See, among themselves their reaction was somewhat mixed. Purcell who was among those who had pressed for a public condemnation, now found himself thoroughly confused. He may perhaps have contributed to the overall confusion, having written to Rome that should the Holy See find it necessary to censure the Fenian leaders publicly, no mention should be made of their 'zeal' for collecting funds for church purposes.[26] He now complained that the Fenians were rampant everywhere, and yet Rome was prepared to treat them 'gingerly, tenderly, paternally'. He was also of the opinion that that Fenians seldom went to confession and hence believed that the ruling would have no effect.

That the Roman authorities were prepared to tolerate very different approaches to the Fenian question in Ireland and America is indicative of the different political circumstances facing the church in both countries. It remained true, however, at least in Cullen's eyes, that Fenianism in Ireland would not finally be stopped until its financial support from America had been cut off.[27] Cullen also tried to impress upon his American correspondents the specifically religious dimension of the Fenian threat:

> The worst of all is that great evil is inflicted on religion. The American Fenians have paid for the support of a newspaper, and for the spreading of a system, which pretending to assail England, is immediately and powerfully directed against the Catholic Church.[28]

26 APF *Scritture* 20, f.1124 Purcell to Cardinal Barnabo.   27 AUND Purcell papers II-5-b, Cullen to Purcell, 2 Dec. 1865.   28 AAB Spalding papers 33-O-8, Cullen to

This aspect of the affair continued to haunt the American hierarchy. Again Purcell complained to Spalding that 'we are in danger of losing a vast number of Irish Catholics to Fenianism'.[29] This perhaps also ties in with the opinion of many commentators, who were inclined to observe that the Irish in America were generally less deferential to the clergy than those who remained in Ireland, and this may well have been one factor in the 'softly, softly' approach of some American churchmen to the whole problem. Indeed, the American consul in Dublin saw all this in slightly more melodramatic terms. When writing to the secretary of state, William Seward, he claimed that the relative freedom in America loosened 'the bonds of mental slavery by which their faith enthralls them in this land of ignorance and superstition'.[30]

The American church's battle with Fenianism also fed into self-questioning about North American Catholic identity. To give but one example: Judge G.H. Hilton of Cincinnati could complain of Archbishop Purcell that

> [a] mitre & years of contact & American attrition never could remove the Divine Paddy out of [him] ... Not that I am prejudiced to the Irish or Irishman in his proper place ... But out of its proper place it is abominable: narrow, provincial & hateful.[31]

By 1865 John Farrell, bishop of Hamilton, Ontario, took the opportunity of the proclamation of the jubilee, in connection with the encyclical *Quanta Cura* and the *Syllabus of Errors*,[32] to 'warn all confessors not to administer the sacraments to members of societies calling themselves Fenians or Hibernians, but to treat them as *ipso facto* excommunicated'.[33] Such sentiments did not win much influence for Farrell with Hibernian and Fenian circles in the Ontario area. By that time an enormous row was already brewing in the Canadian church between Archbishop John Lynch of Toronto and the archbishop of Halifax, Thomas Connolly, owing to Lynch's effusions on the question of the status of the Irish in North America. Connolly was concerned

Spalding, 16 Jan. 1866. **29** Ibid., 36A-R-8 Purcell to Spalding, 19 Jan. 1869. **30** American National Archives William B. West to Seward 6 Oct. 1864, *United States Consul Dispatches*, Dublin T199 (roll 4). **31** AUND Brownson papers I-2-a, Hilton to Orestes Brownson (undated). **32** A significant element in both documents, at least for the church in the United States, was highlighted by Archbishop McCloskey of New York. Not only did he think that the encyclical was ill-timed, but that 'it places us in a state of *apparent* antagonism, as far as our principles are concerned, to the institutions under which we live': AAB Spalding papers 35-E-1, McCloskey to Spalding, 17 Feb. 1865; Spalding seems to have agreed with this analysis although in practice he defended both documents. See his *Acta episcopalia*, p. 13. **33** ARCAT Lynch papers LAD-02–22, Bishop John Farrell, *Publishing the Jubilee*.

that too much emphasis on the wrongs of Ireland not only encouraged Fenianism, but could also adversely affect the position of Catholics in British North America. In particular, he warned Lynch that if, in the context of a possible Fenian invasion of Canada, there was any hint of support from Catholic prelates for the Fenian cause, the whole Canadian Catholic people would be 'attended by disastrous results'. Stressing his contempt for Fenianism Connolly added that there was:

> [n]ot a day in the last 600 years when Ireland could have risen success-fully and never was there so little chance as at the present moment ... I cannot approve of the *impossible* and I abominate *whining* and *screeching* and contemptible threats against the *Bloody Saxon*.[34]

With such potentially divisive and contradictory attitudes among senior churchmen, it is perhaps understandable that the American prelates wanted to avoid wrangling over Fenianism, and that even their most public declarations were hedged with so much ambiguity. Gradually, however, the issues for the Fenians and the church also changed. In the light of possible Fenian raids on Canada, Purcell wanted to know if it was permissible to give Christian burial to Fenians killed 'fighting against England'.[35] For its part, the church in Ireland felt more acutely the menace posed by Fenianism, but at the same time saw the American element as the main problem. As Cullen explained to Spalding:

> If the Fenians in America were to succeed in driving our half starved and unarmed people to revolt, the massacres of Cromwell w[oul]d be renewed and all that religion has gained during the present century would be lost in six months. I think we are rather in a dangerous position, and that measures ought to be taken to check the progress of Fenianism.[36]

Despite the turmoil of the previous year, by October 1866 Gladstone, for one, was convinced that Fenianism in Ireland was no longer formidable. At least so he told Pope Pius IX. The pope, for his part, 'spoke warmly against Fenianism' and assured Gladstone of his hostility to it and that of the Irish clergy.[37] The importance of Fenianism as an issue in British–Vatican relations had been underlined earlier that year in an exchange between Odo Russell,

---

34 Ibid., LAE-06–14, Connolly to Lynch, 12 Mar. 1865. **35** AAB Spalding papers 36A-R-6, Purcell to Spalding, 20 Jun. 1866. **36** Ibid., 33-O-5, Cullen to Spalding, 2 Mar. 1865. **37** H.C.G. Matthew (ed.), *The Gladstone diaries*, iv (Oxford, 1978), p. 473. The entry is dated 22 Oct. 1866.

the unofficial British diplomatic representative at Rome, and the pope. Pius explained to Russell that the principles of Fenianism had been condemned in his latest encyclical and that he hoped Fenianism would soon be completely suppressed.[38] Russell also took the opportunity to complain to the papal secretary of state, Cardinal Giacomo Antonelli, that the Irish clergy were the fomenters of political strife. They tended to blame all the wrong of Ireland on the English, whereas Russell maintained that 'all the misfortunes they had brought upon themselves by their own idle Celtic habits'.[39] Antonelli rejected the idea that priests were the 'active apostles of disaffection', and was sure that they opposed all secret societies in accordance with papal teaching. In a subsequent interview in February 1866 Antonelli demanded to know the names of priests whom the British government alleged were sympathetic to Fenianism and who heard confessions of Fenians. Russell, however, refused to name any, saying that Antonelli had his own sources of information on the subject, not least the fathers of the Irish College in Rome, who seemed to be 'wonderfully well aware of Fenian proceedings in Ireland'.[40]

Government alarm was matched by that in some ecclesiastical circles. The political situation was sufficiently confused for the clergy to have often contradictory attitudes to contemporary events. As a means of trying to come to terms with their inability to control revolutionary propensities among their flocks, bishops, seeking an explanation, tended to fall back on the anti-clerical nature of Fenianism. Cullen, for example, told Tobias Kirby, rector of the Irish College Rome, that in any revolution he himself would be the first to be attacked, acknowledging how much a consolation this intelligence was to the Protestants of Ireland.[41]

The main problem in all this for the church was that Fenianism might become a permanent barrier to the influence of priests over their people, or more especially of the Catholic Church's influence with the Protestant state. Alarmingly for the church, when the Fenians issued their proclamation of the Irish Republic in March 1867, among other things they demanded the complete separation of church and state.[42]

Meanwhile the redoubtable David Moriarty, bishop of Kerry, had once again lived up to his reputation as a Castle bishop by roundly condemning the attempted February 1867 rising in his famous 'hell is not hot enough nor eternity long enough' sermon. Lord Naas, the Irish chief secretary, used the opportunity during the debate on the second reading of the *habeas corpus* suspension act on 21 February, to praise the Catholic clergy for using their influence 'to prevent the people from taking part in this conspiracy'. He

38 PRO FO 43/96a Russell to Clarendon, 22 Jan. 1866 f. 57. **39** PRO HO 45/7799; pt 1, pouch 2, f. 720. **40** PRO FO 43/96a; ff. 166–9. **41** AICR Kirby papers Cullen to Kirby, 20 Jan. 1866. **42** *The Tablet*, 9 Mar. 1867.

quoted liberally from Moriarty's sermon in which the bishop hoped that 'God's heaviest curse, His withering, blasting, blighting curse', might be visited on the Fenian leaders.[43] Naas's sentiments of approbation of the clergy were to be re-echoed by *The Times* in the aftermath of the second Fenian rising in March. An editorial called attention to 'the remarkable loyalty shown by the Roman Catholic bishops and clergy in holding themselves aloof from the conspiracy'.[44]

The rising confirmed for Cullen and his circle all their worst fears of Fenianism. Archbishop Patrick Leahy in a pastoral letter of 12 March castigated Fenianism as 'most sinful in itself, and condemned by the Church under the heaviest penalties'. Moriarty issued a circular letter to his priests telling them to 'inform your flock that all persons joining the Fenian society whether sworn or un-sworn incur a papal excommunication'.[45] Cullen could not resist making the point that since Lord Naas had stated in the house of commons that twenty-nine of the captured Fenians proved to be national school teachers, he hoped this might help 'to convince our rulers that education without religious control is well calculated to promote revolution.[46]

In some respects this was the heart of the problem for churchmen in dealing with Fenianism and the British Protestant state. Catholic Ireland as an instrument for the propagation of Catholicism could only play that role within the British empire. The cross followed on the coat-tails of imperial expansion, partly because of the percentage of Irish Catholics in the British army. These soldiers were accompanied by priests, for most of the century unpaid, and they built Catholic churches everywhere from Brisbane to Barbados. But the church's place in Ireland was undervalued and to some extended unacknowledged by the Protestant state. Clearly this was beginning to change, but Fenianism threatened the emergence of the church as a regulator of social morals, and undermined its scope for political influence – not so much because of Fenian insistence on the separate duality of the temporal and spiritual spheres, or because it in fact encouraged infidelity to Catholicism (after all many Fenianism still remained practising Catholics),[47] but rather because it obscured the church's agenda. Fenianism would clearly never be satisfied with the reformism demanded by the church to enable institutional Catholicism to take its rightful place in Irish society, and to pose as the one defender and promoter of the interests of the Irish people. Of course, the irony is that it was precisely the impetus given to reform by the Fenian movement which secured two of the three most important elements in the

43 *Hansard*, 3rd series, clxxxv, 734 and 738. 44 *The Times*, 18 Mar. 1867. 45 *Cork Examiner*, 11 Mar. 1867. 46 AICR Kirby papers Cullen to Kirby, 12 Mar. 1867. 47 Hence Mark Ryan's comment, '*Next to my religion* Fenianism has been the greatest thing in my life': *Fenian memories* (Dublin, 1945), p. xxiii. My italics.

church's agenda for mid-nineteenth-century Ireland: disestablishment of the Church of Ireland and a land bill.[48] Those reforms by 1867 were still some time off; meanwhile both church and state had to deal with the menace of Fenianism as best they could.

In the aftermath of the Manchester executions, a spontaneous outpouring of indignation and revulsion found expression in mock funeral demonstrations and demands for public masses for the dead patriots. The Cork demonstration took place on 1 December with 7–8000 walking in procession 'accompanied' by 5000 others.[49] As in so many places the Catholic churches in Cork were placarded, asking worshipers to pray for the souls of Allen, Larkin and O'Brien. Cullen was furious that priests should take part in such public demonstrations, and still more that public masses were offered for the Fenians. As he explained to Tobias Kirby:

> The poor men who suffered at Manchester are made heroes and martyrs of because they belong to that class which is undoubtedly under the ban of the Church. They were not honoured or prayed for because they were good men or died penitent, but because they were Fenians. The great processions were got up not for prayers, but as a display in favour of Fenianism.[50]

Cullen was deeply critical of fellow bishops such as MacHale of Tuam who said public Masses for the Manchester men. He was no doubt horrified to read in the *Weekly News* that his erstwhile comrade in arms, Bishop MacEvilly, had permitted a public mass in Ennistymon, Co. Clare. However as MacEvilly explained, all the young people in the area, 'young men and girls too', were red hot Fenians who demanded the Mass and for the sake of peace he permitted it.[51] The most important demonstration was in Dublin on 8 December 1867. Cullen wrote to Kirby that the demonstration was head by John Martin 'a Presbyterian who cares little about prayers for the dead. The only object in getting up High Masses and offices is to promote Fenianism.'[52]

By the time Gladstone was returned to Downing Street in December 1868 he was determined to make Ireland a central focus of his government. The

48 The third element, denominational education, at least at the university level, was not satisfactorily resolved until the foundation of the Royal University. 49 NAI Fenian papers F series, box 3, F4994. 50 AICR Kirby papers, Cullen to Kirby, 7 Feb. 1868. 51 DDA Cullen papers, MacEvilly to Cullen, 1 Jan. 1868. By contrast he pretended to Kirby in Rome that he knew nothing of the Mass in advance and that it was all the fault of the local parish priest. AICR Kirby papers, MacEvilly to Kirby, 3 Jan. 1868. 52 Ibid., Cullen to Kirby, 7 Feb. 1868.

two questions which he decided needed immediate attention were the church and the land issues. The established position of the Church of Ireland was an especially thorny problem from many perspectives. The point, however, is that Gladstone in dealing with the church and land questions thought he was in some way dealing with the Fenian issue.

When by March 1870 disestablishment had not brought peace to Ireland, Gladstone could scarcely conceal his anger. He detected, he wrote Cullen, a sinister force 'having for its object perpetual war between England and Ireland' and making use of the disguise of agrarian crime, 'seeks to triumph by the double means of convincing Great Britain that reasonable legislation will not be accepted, and of alarming us into the destruction or suppression of constitutional freedoms'.[53] He therefore called upon the Catholic Church to use its influence to prevent a 'contest' between the two countries, and in morose tones warned that 'the crisis is a solemn one, and it is becoming more solemn everyday'. Cullen flung the challenge back in Gladstone's face, telling him that remedial legislation was not the way to deal with lawlessness. 'Nothing good can be affected for Ireland, until something shall have been done to prevent the ravages of an infidel and revolutionary [organization] subsidized and maintained to a great extent by foreign gold'.[54]

One of the main issues facing both church and state at the end of the 1860s was the problem of the exact role and influence of the clergy in radical politics. At one end of the spectrum of ecclesiastical opinion we have David Moriarty who was convinced that the priests by and large rejected Fenianism only on pragmatic grounds. He wrote to William Monsell that the 'clergy will preach against the rebellion on account of the evils it will bring on the people, but I am sure that if there was a fair chance of success it would be lawful nay "*dulce et decorum*"'.[55] At the other end, Cullen was convinced that the priests would obey the injunctions of the church with regard to its teaching on secret societies and revolution.

It was often assumed by British politicians that because the clergy were financially dependent on their people, they to some extent must therefore share the political expectations of those who financed them. Furthermore, given that they were drawn, for the most part, from the same class as the mass of the population, it was also believed that they naturally shared the same prejudices and social ambitions as those of their kith and kin. This phenomenon has led many historians to suggest that the church itself,

53 BL Add. MS 44425 Gladstone papers, Gladstone to Cullen, 6 Mar. 1870, f. 192.
54 Ibid. Cullen to Gladstone, 12 Mar. 1870, f. 244.   55 NLI MS 8319 Monsell papers Moriarty to Monsell, 2 Mar. 1868. To be fair to Moriarty he did think that if the pope ordered the clergy to speak out against Fenianism they would do it: Archives of the English College Rome Talbot papers, Moriarty to Mgr George Talbot, 10 Jan. 1868.

through the clergy, was not only a passive supporter of Irish nationalist (indeed at times advanced nationalist) opinion, but also perhaps the most significant instrument in the creation of modern Irish nationalism as that emerges in the nineteenth and twentieth centuries.[56]

There are many problems with such a thesis, not the least is the fact that the police and, as we have seen, a substantial percentage of the army stationed in Ireland were drawn from the same class. If the clergy were simply a prism through which shone the myriad light of undimmed Irish nationalism, then it would be reasonable to assume that the same iridescence would be mirrored in all members of that class. That this was not the case is attested to time and again. In the debate in the house of lords on the March 1867 insurrection, Viscount Lifford adverted to the conduct of the police whom, he maintained, might be taken as 'a type of the Irish people'. They were the sons not of the middle classes, but of small farmers, and had been brought up 'with all the feeling and prepossessions of that class', and yet during the Fenian distur-bances they had behaved with 'a gallant loyalty'. He concluded that whatever disloyalty there was in Ireland, it could not be very deep.[57]

As to the loyalty of the army, the army commander-in-chief, the duke of Cambridge, declared in the lords that despite what was said to the contrary, in any revolutionary situation the soldiers would exhibit no feelings 'except of the right sort'.[58] Both he and the army commander in Ireland, Lord Strathnairn, were convinced that Irish Catholic soldiers had in general 'rendered good service against the Fenians'.[59] Of course soldiers and policemen were employees of the state. Their loyalty may, in part, be regarded as a function of their employment, of the 'don't bite the hand that feeds you' variety. That loyalty was not, however, an absolute, and there are sufficient indicators from government sources to show that treasonable activity was a problem in the army, and to a lesser extent in the police. By contrast, the most striking aspect of the issue is not the relative disloyalty of the clergy, but, on the contrary, how much they in fact acted as upholders of the duly constituted authority of the state.

In analyzing the role of the clergy in politics, perhaps it is more helpful to

56 See for example R.F. Foster, *Modern Ireland* (London, 1988), pp 339–41, 370, 453; Donal A. Kerr, *A nation of beggars?* (Oxford, 1994), pp 143–65; J.J. Lee, *The modern-ization of Irish society, 1848–1918* (Dublin, 1992), pp 42–9; S.J. Connolly, *Priests and people in pre-famine Ireland* (Dublin, 1982), pp 13–4, 261–2; Oliver MacDonagh, 'The politicization of the Irish Catholic bishops', *Historical Journal*, 18 (1974), 37–53. **57** *Hansard*, 3rd series, vol. clxxxvi, 459. **58** Ibid., 465. **59** BLO Disraeli papers B/VII/116 Cambridge to Sir John Pakington, 7 Jun. 1867, p. 4. This printed report for the cabinet was marked 'strictly confidential'. Cambridge does add that 'if there had been a rising in 1865, before military Fenianism had been properly dealt with, something disagreeable might and would have occurred'.

think in terms not of Irish nationalism, but what one might term 'Catholic nationalism'. Absenting from the instances when it was blatantly hostile, the Protestant state for various reasons was either unwilling or unable to concede to institutional Catholicism that place in British, and more particularly in Irish, society that church officials thought it ought to have. At the level of episcopal leadership, the bishops, as diviners of the political and social aspirations of Catholic Ireland, were anxious in very instance to promote the interests of church members. Their desire to see Catholics advance socially in Ireland was connected to their desire to exercise that degree of influence which they believed they should have as regulators of the faith and morals of the great majority of the Irish people. Hence their great delight when Thomas O'Hagan was appointed lord chancellor[60] and subsequently raised to the peerage, and they used every opportunity to bring their influence to bear on him, as is clear from even the most casual acquaintance with his correspondence.[61]

The bishops' preponderant desire was to steer the ship of state into a decidedly Catholic harbour. This in itself did not imply separation from the United Kingdom; indeed, bishops were sufficiently sensitive political animals to see the great advantages accruing to Catholic Ireland from its position at the very heart of the British empire. At the same time this is not to deny that some priests were clearly either actively or passively supporters of Fenianism. They, however, cannot be taken to represent the generality of clerical opinion in the 1860s. When the lord lieutenant, Lord Spenser, requested that a list be drawn up of names of priests who had 'uttered language either in support of Fenians or in favour of landlord violence' the list contained twenty-one names.[62] Two years earlier Cullen in writing to the under-secretary at Dublin Castle told him that all the bishops 'were most respectful to all charged with the burden of government, and they are ever ready to inculcate obedience and submission to the constitutional authorities in accordance with the teaching of the gospel'.[63] Why then did successive governments seem to be fixated on clerical influence? Part of the problem was a failure of government to actually control events in Ireland. In casting around for scapegoats, it was natural to fix on the clergy, to blame them not just for the lack of order, but accuse them

60 PRONI O'Hagan papers D 2777/7/3/18, Bishop Moriarty to O'Hagan, 10 Dec. 1868. Moriarty told O'Hagan that his appointment was 'the complete emancipation and final triumph of the our Catholic nation'. Cullen's only reservation was that O'Hagan was 'weak on mixed education'. AICR Kirby papers, Cullen to Kirby, 10 Dec. 1868. **61** See for example PRONI O'Hagan papers D 2777/7/6/A/35 Cullen to O'Hagan in which Cullen pleads to have G.W. Abraham appointed a Dublin city magistrate in preference to M.J. Barry. **62** NAI Fenian papers R series, box 10, 5126R, Spenser to Sir Thomas Burke, 27 Nov. 1869. **63** DDA Cullen papers Letter book No.4, Cullen to Sir Thomas Burke, 23 Feb. 1867, f. 381.

of initiating disorder. Indeed, the process that led to the condemnation of Fenianism by the pope was initially a plea for the condemnation of clerical political agitation.

Since the 1840s there had been a suggestion that successive government policy amounted to trying to rule Ireland through Rome.[64] But what the government actually wanted was, in one sense, to rule Ireland through the priests, as clearly the best placed individuals to maintain any semblance of order. The failure to achieve this had as much as anything else to do with the fact that the Catholic clergy perceived the state as anti-pathetical to them and their religion. This attitude was not without some justification.[65] The problem which Fenianism posed for the church was precisely that it did not, unlike the British state, foresee a role for the church in politics. The revolutionary aspect of Fenianism was that it wanted to short-circuit the church's political ambitions. Priests were to be confined to their sacred function and not allowed to trespass into the secular sphere. Bishop James Walshe's characterization of the Fenians as the Lollards of the 1860s was therefore splendidly apposite, since they disputed the church's right to determine the religious activity of the people in its political aspect.[66]

By the end of 1869, owing to the Fenian amnesty and tenant-right agitation, the security situation in Ireland had considerably deteriorated. This forced the government to move along the twin-track approach of further concessions and coercion. But it was precisely at this point that both church and state in Ireland decided to ask for another Roman intervention to deal finally with the troublesome Fenians. By December Lord Clarendon, the foreign secretary, had written to Odo Russell in Rome pleading with him to consider in what way pressure might be brought to bear on the Irish bishops, then in Rome for the first Vatican Council, in an effort to curb the growth of radicalism among the clergy. A petition in favour of an amnesty for Fenian prisoners had attracted the signatures of about half of all the priests in Ireland. Clarendon remarked to Russell, 'the men whom the priests extol as heroes and martyrs and whose liberation they excite the populace to demand are Fenians, restless adventurers who murder and rob, and who seek by intimidation to disorganise the country and subvert the government'. Lord Spenser, however, took a different view and wrote to Clarendon that the Irish clergy had given great support to the government in its fight against Fenianism and mentioned in particular the effort of three bishops, Cullen, Leahy and Moriarty.

Partly because of the priests amnesty petition, but also because of an attack

64 J.L. Hammond, *Gladstone and the Irish nation* (London, 1964), p. 250.   65 Norman, *Anti-Catholicism in Victorian England*, esp. pp 13–124.   66 AICR Kirby papers, Walshe to Kirby, 9 Mar. 1867. Walshe was bishop of Kildare and Leighlin 1856–88.

on Cullen by Fr Patrick Lavelle over the ecclesiastical status of the Fenians, the Irish bishops drew up a request that the Holy See condemn Fenianism by name. Russell, following instructions from London, sought an audience with the pope and also pressed him to condemn the Fenians. Russell's audience with Pius IX took place on 13 January 1870. The day before, the cardinals of the Inquisition met and determined, in keeping with Catholic teaching on secret societies, that the Fenians were a condemned organization. Gladstone recorded in his diary following a cabinet meeting on the 28th that the government had received a dispatch from Russell telling them of the pope's decision explicitly to condemn Fenianism. The pronouncement '[w]ill be read from the altar throughout Ireland. Irish Bps. agreed: do not wish to be compromised by announcing it. To be read in U.S. also'.[67] But when the condemnation was in fact made public in Rome that day, the American bishops, by and large, were ill disposed to the pronouncement. The Fenians had been condemned in Ireland and America and yet the American bishops had not been consulted. Russell, writing to Clarendon, said that the American bishops were annoyed with the decree because it would 'establish an open feud between the Fenians and the priesthood which would have been better avoided in America, they think'.[68] Cullen wrote to his secretary Dr Conroy:

> The American bishops (at least some of them) are displeased with the Irish bishops for getting the holy office to act in this case. Dr Spalding says we have done a great mischief. I told him the story of the frogs and the boys, and that what was sport in America was death to us and to religion in Ireland ... Dr Wood ... fully agrees with us – he says he condemned the Fenians publicly and always refused them absolution. Hence he had very little trouble with them.[69]

He later told Conroy that the American church would not have had so many bishops at the Vatican Council had Fenian doctrines been more widely propagated in North America. Cullen also saw a direct relationship between the fact that so many American bishops were against the promulgation of the decree on papal infallibility and the fact that they were weak on Fenianism.

For their part, the Fenians simply ignored the decree. In Ireland they tried to convince the more scrupulous among them that since the document mentioned Fenians, while the organization in that country was known as the Irish Republican Brotherhood, the papal condemnation could not apply to them. In America, many bishops and priests did not promulgate the decree,

67 Matthew, *Gladstone diaries*, vii, 229. 68 PRO FO 3/106, Russell to Clarendon, 31 Jan. 1870, f. 198. 69 DDA Conroy papers Cullen to Conroy, 28 Jan. 1870.

and for years later letters were written to the Vatican asking if the Fenians had been condemned or not.

We have seen that the political circumstance in which Catholicism found itself in Ireland and North America conditioned the church's response to the threat from Fenianism. In America, the separation of church and state was such that Catholicism could have no direct political ambitions, and priests did not customarily tell Catholics how to vote at elections. Nonetheless, Fenianism, by keeping alive for a North American audience the centuries-old conflict between Ireland and England, destabilized the church's attempt to integrate Catholicism more fully in the American social scene. Internally, the problem posed by Fenianism was that it potentially placed a barrier between the priest and his flock, by refusing to accept the spiritual sanction of the incompatibility between membership of the Fenian society and the Roman Catholic Church. Fenianism also, because of its high profile, brought to the fore an identification between Catholicism and Irishness which the American church wished to avoid.

By contrast, the problem in Ireland was almost the reverse. There the Fenians resisted the church's demands for a direct political role in the life of the nation. The irony of the Irish situation was that the state was so consti-tuted that willy-nilly the church had a direct political effect on the life of the country, not as great an influence as it would have wished but substantial and powerful nonetheless. After all, Gladstone' first government was brought down in 1873 because of the opposition of the Irish Catholic bishops to his university bill. The Fenians were the only political movement in Ireland which sought to disrupt the relationship between organized religion and the state. Its political threat was a direct challenge to both state and church. This also represented a spiritual danger for Catholicism, since the Fenians rejected the assertion that it was impossible to be a Catholic and a Fenian.

9

Gladstone and the disestablishment of
the Church of Ireland: an overview

By the end of his days Ireland had in a real sense become a major preoccupation for Gladstone.[1] It was the issue which had come to dominate his four administrations and, despite the fact that he visited the country only once, he had, perhaps, more direct impact on the affairs of that nation than any other British statesman in the nineteenth or twentieth centuries.[2] Yet for all this when he came to form his first government it is alleged by Sir Philip Magnus that he had no real knowledge of the Irish people, and his ignorance was shared by the whole of his cabinet and by the mass of the British people.[3] This typically forthright assertion in quite inaccurate. Two members of his first cabinet were former lords lieutenant of Ireland, and John Bright, president of the board of trade, had made an important fact-finding visit to the country in November 1866, in the course of which he developed a keen interest in the welfare of political prisoners.

In fact, even at a relatively early state in his public life Gladstone was not unaware of the importance of the Irish question in British politics. He had written to his wife in October 1845, at a time when he had no special interest in the country, that Ireland was a cloud in the west, 'that coming storm, the minister of God's retribution upon but half-atoned injustice'.[4] The beginnings of Gladstone's attempts to atone for the injustice of England's historic

---

1 On 23 September 1897 after a distance of nearly thirty years, Gladstone wrote of his first cabinet that it was Ireland 'which mainly and almost entirely filled the political horizon': John Brooke and Mary Sorensen (eds), *Autobiographica I* (London, 1971), p. 97.   2 It must be said, however, that scholars are divided on Gladstone's attitude to Ireland. H.C.G. Matthew was of the opinion that Ireland was for Gladstone at best a preoccupation, not an interest or an intellectual attraction. Cf. *Gladstone: 1809–1874* (Oxford, 1986), p. 192. By contrast J.L. Hammond, *Gladstone and the Irish nation* (London, 1964), p. 70, could observe that Gladstone threw himself into the Irish problem as the main task of his life.   3 Philip Magnus, *Gladstone: a biography* (2nd ed. London, 1960), p. 196.   4 A. Tilney Bassett (ed.), *Gladstone to his wife* (London, 1936), p. 64. John Vincent sought to demythologize this letter by explaining that it was written at a time of great emotional stress and that since as a whole it is not concerned with Ireland the Irish references cannot be taken as an accurate indication of Gladstone's mind on the matter. Whatever the strength of Vincent's other arguments about Gladstone's lack of interest in Ireland; on this point his thesis is both weak and unconvincing. See 'Gladstone and Ireland' in *Proceedings of the British Academy*, 62 (London, 1977), 201.

treatment of Ireland, was to deal with the church question. During the election campaign in October 1868 he told supporters in Lancashire that:

> In the removal of this establishment [of the Church of Ireland] I see the discharge of a debt of civil justice, the disappearance of a national, almost a world-wide reproach, a condition to the success of every effort to secure the peace and contentment of that country.[5]

Clearly the proposal was surrounded by controversy, not simply because of the understandable opposition of members of the Irish Church, but because it involved so many diverse elements: charges of inconsistency on Gladstone's part, the displeasure of the queen, still an important consideration at this stage in British politics, Catholic intrigue, and a parliamentary and constitutional crisis of the first order. Gladstone's disestablishment of Anglicanism in Ireland can be variously estimated. It can either be seen as a pragmatic step as part of the pacification of Ireland in the face of the continuing Fenian threat, as a simple question of political and social justice, or as the culmination of Gladstone's own personal, political and theological odyssey.

For those inclined to cynicism it can be argued that Gladstone acted decisively to unite and secure the fortunes of the Liberal Party at a time when it was in disarray and propping up a minority Tory administration. The Irish church question was the one issue which commanded widespread agreement on the Liberal benches in parliament. Gladstone saw his opportunity and seized it for party political motives as well as from fear that Disraeli and the Tories might decide to act on the issue and so once again, as over the reform act, out-manoeuvre the Liberals.[6]

Irrespective of how Gladstone liked to present the measure, it was, perhaps, Lord Stanley who best penetrated to the heart of the matter, when he had clause five of the Act of Union read at the beginning of the debate on Gladstone's famous resolutions of March 1868. There it is stated that:

5 W.E. Gladstone, *Speeches in south-west Lancashire* (London, 1868), p. v. 6 See Robert Blake, *Disraeli* (London, 1966), p. 496; J.P. Parry, *Democracy and religion: Gladstone and the Liberal Party, 1867–75* (Cambridge, 1986), pp 261–2 & 265–6; E.D. Steele, 'Gladstone, Irish violence and conciliation', in Art Cosgrave and Donal McCartney (eds), *Studies in Irish history presented to R. Dudley Edwards* (Dublin, 1979), pp 26of. In fact at a cabinet meeting on 2 March 1868 the Tory government had decided to take no action on the church question until the next parliament. Cf. John Vincent (ed.), *Disraeli, Derby and the Conservative Party: journals and memoirs of Edward Henry Lord Stanley, 1849–1869* (Hassocks, 1978), pp 331–2.

> The Churches of England and Ireland, as by law established, be united
> into one Protestant Episcopal Church to be called 'The United Church
> of England and Ireland'. And that the doctrine, worship, discipline and
> government of the said Church shall be, and shall remain in full force
> forever.

The significance then of disestablishment in its political aspect lay in the fact
that it demonstrated the possibility of altering the Union. Gladstone's act of
1869 was the essential key which ultimately opened the way for the radical
modification of the Union that occurred in 1921. Already in 1865 the Irish
MP W.J. O'Neill Daunt had written to John MacHale, archbishop of Tuam,
indicating that Irish disestablishment would facilitate repeal of the Union by
removing 'a most potent cause of the denationalization of Irish Protestants'.[7]
During the passage of the disestablishment bill through parliament,
Archbishop Tait of Canterbury took a similar line, saying that the measure
would encourage Irish ultramontanes to press for repeal.[8] This is not to imply
that Gladstone in any sense saw the measure as a first step towards home rule.
His conversion to that cause came at a later date, and even then he did not
regard home rule as altering the Union. The vital point about the 1869 disestablishment act was that the British parliament of its own volition, admittedly
under varying pressures from Ireland, amended the terms of the act of
Union. It was a lesson that both Irish radicals and reactionaries were to note
for the future.

Gladstone's penchant for popular causes, amounting to crusades, was for
the most part modified by his instincts for knowing when popular agitation
would be to his own advantage. Hence Disraeli's charge that the pretext for
the resolutions was but a 'monstrous invention of a crisis got up by the right
honourable gentleman opposite for the advantage of his party'. Nonetheless
the election of November 1868 was fought largely on the church question.
Gladstone hoped to capitalize on the 'rainbow coalition' of Scottish
Presbyterians, English non-conformists, radical politicians and Irish
Catholics on this single issue of Irish disestablishment. Although he had
cultivated English non-conformists since the mid-1860s his dealings with
them scarcely amounted to a meeting of minds. As V. Alan McClelland
observes, 'that the Church and the state were separate alien powers incapable
of coalition, the fundamental principle pursued by British non-conformity,
he could not endure'.[9] That the uncertain amalgam of religious and political

7 Bernard O'Reilly, *John MacHale, archbishop of Tuam: his life and correspondence*, 2
vols (New York and Cincinnati, 1890), ii, 543. 8 P.T. Marsh, *The Victorian church in
decline: Archbishop Tait and the Church of England, 1868–1882* (London, 1969), p. 22.
9 'Gladstone and Manning: a question of authority', in Peter J. Jagger (ed.), *Gladstone,*

groups would triumph in the 1868 general election was far from clear. Indeed, Disraeli hoped that a blast of 'non-popery' would have the usual effect on the British electorate, to the advantage of the Conservative party. He had written to Queen Victoria in March that, 'the abhorrence of popery, the dread of ritualism and the hatred of the Irish, have long been smoldering in the minds of the nation'.[10] On this occasion Disraeli had seriously miscalculated. Lord Blake was of the opinion that Disraeli's anti-Catholic election addresses with their hard-line insistence on the prerogatives of the Irish establishment helped the Tory cause only in Lancashire and alienated two groups which traditionally supported the Conservatives – English Catholics and Wesleyan Methodists.[11] By contrast, the Liberals were returned with a majority of 112 in the house of commons, half of that number being supplied by Ireland. It was perhaps the first truly party political government in modern history. Gladstone immediately set upon his mission to pacify Ireland with a religious enthusiasm. The question however is: Were the charges of intellectual inconsistency, on Gladstone's part, merely party political barbs, or had the new prime minister sold his conscience for the sake of a commons majority?

In April 1865 he told his wife's brother-in-law, George Lyttleton, that after the Maynooth grant episode of 1845 he no longer had 'any resistance to the idea of disestablishment of the Church of Ireland'. But, he continued, 'I have held this embryo opinion in mind as there was no cause to precipitate it into life, and waited to fortify it or alter or invalidate it by teachings of experience'.[12] This was to be consistent with the statement he made in the commons during the debate on his resolutions in March 1868. Against the charges of recent intellectual conversion on the church question Gladstone stated that 'a change of mind which extends itself over a quarter of a century ... is hardly to be esteemed a sudden change'.[13]

Even as prime minister, Gladstone was to react swiftly to any suggestion that his policies on Ireland were simply the product of expediency or designed to deal with contingent political problems. In response to Lord Grey's speech in the lords on 26 April 1869 accusing him and his supporters of bringing forward the church measure because their eyes had been opened to 'the urgency of the Fenian conspiracy', Gladstone would admit that the Fenian outrages had an influence only on the timing and not the principles of his Irish policy.[14] On the other hand, he candidly wrote to the home secretary, Sir George Grey, that the government's 'purpose and duty is to endeavour to

politics and religion (London, 1985), p. 149.   10 *The letters of Queen Victoria*, 2 vols (2nd series 1862–78), i, 517.   11 Blake, *Disraeli*, p. 513.   12 Quoted in John Morley, *The life of William Ewart Gladstone*, 3 vols (London, 1903), ii, 238.   13 *Hansard*, 3rd series, 1868, cxci, 474.   14 BL Add. MS 44536 Gladstone papers, Gladstone to Earl Grey, 29 Apr. 1869, f. 152.

draw a line between the Fenians & the people of Ireland, & to make the people of Ireland indisposed to cross it'.[15]

Previous attempts to raise the disestablishment issue in parliament had been dismissed by Gladstone as 'not practical politics', and this is the line he took as late as the summer of 1865 when writing to the Warden of Trinity College, Glenalmond. Nor indeed before the November 1868 election was he entirely sure of the exact nature of what the settlement of the church question ought to be. There is some evidence that he considered the possibility of a 'leveling up' of all the churches in Ireland, in other words a concurrent endowment. Such a policy was, however, anathema to the nonconformists and to the Irish Catholic bishops, who had rejected such a suggestion in October 1867. It does seem clear, however, that the principle of the Irish establishment was one which Gladstone had long since felt to be untenable.

Gladstone was able to justify his change of principle by pointing out that it was the lesser of two evils. Despite popular perception of his position on state religion, he had never in fact held that *simpliciter* the state ought to maintain the established position of the Anglican Church. Indeed, he approvingly quoted Macaulay's review of his 1838 work to the effect that Gladstone's theory rested on the fundamental proposition that 'the propagation of religious truth is one of the principal ends of government as government. If Mr Gladstone has not proved this proposition, his system vanishes at once'.[16] Frustratingly he does not address this substantive issue in his 1868 *Chapter of autobiography*. Here he seems content to maintain that it is impossible to give a theoretical blueprint of the relationship between church and state which is valid for all time. By then he simply argued the pragmatic case that the Irish church cannot profess to be the church of the nation (while he neglects the point that this was never the case in its history), nor was it even the church of the poor, and thus its claim to establishment must fail. In the circumstances of Ireland in the late 1860s, 'the attempt to maintain an establishment becomes an error fatal to the peace, dangerous perhaps even to the life of civil society', given this the church is no longer 'the temple of civil society, but its cemetery'.[17]

There can be little doubt that Gladstone had in fact abandoned his position on church–state relations as he had expounded them in 1838. The important point, however, is that this was not purely opportunistic, a simple pragmatic departure to gain electoral advantage. Almost as soon as he had outlined his principles in 1838, he came to see that their application to the conditions of social and political life in the United Kingdom was anachronistic.[18] The diffi-

15 Ibid., 28 Mar. 1869, f. 134.   16 *A chapter of autobiography*, pp 21–2.   17 Ibid., pp 60–1.   18 A.R. Vidler, *The orb and the cross* (London, 1945), p. 29.

culty for Gladstone's opponents was that too often his evolution of principles looked as if it was determined by popularity at the hustings rather than by moral conviction. Equally, however, one might argue that in sponsoring the disestablishment of the Irish church, Gladstone exposed himself to the wrath of the Tory establishment, a wrath which could easily have prematurely ended his political career. As we shall see, he came perilously close to abandoning the whole disestablishment enterprise, because of opposition in the lords, a move which surely would have precipitated the fall of his government.

That parliamentary opposition in the lords was to be expected, Gladstone at some level took for granted. Neither did he expect that the Church of Ireland itself would surrender without a fight. There is, however, something refreshingly innocent, or especially crafty, about Gladstone's letter to Archbishop Richard Trench of Dublin in December 1868 inviting the opinions of Irish Anglicanism on how best to proceed with the government's legislative proposal.[19] 'All views and wishes,' he told Trench, 'which may be entertained by the Primate and the Irish bishops and by the other leading clergy in general, will at all times have my most respectful attention.'[20] Such respectful attitudes did not prevent the prime minister refusing the bishops' request to meet in convocation on the disestablishment issue. Gladstone did not see why the government should provide them with such a forum from which to attack his government's policy. However, had the meeting been designed to come to terms with the bill, then Gladstone would have recommended to the crown that convocation be summoned. By mid-January he appears to have amended his position somewhat. He then told Samuel Wilberforce, bishop of Oxford that, 'Trench seems to be a dreamer of dreams: and talks of negotiating at a time when all negotiation will have gone by.'[21]

The refusal of Church of Ireland co-operation had serious repercussions on the attitude of the English church. On the other hand, Archbishop Tait, of Canterbury, following his meeting with the prime minister on 19 February, came to the conclusion that it was best to concede the principle of disestablishment and concentrate on getting the most favourable financial terms possible for the Church of Ireland. To this end both the archbishop of

---

19 It is important to stress in this context that although Gladstone took advice from a range of individuals, including Lord Granville, Sir John Acton and Archdeacon Stopford of Meath, the parliamentary bill he presented to the Commons in March 1869 was very much his own work. See BLO MS C475 Lord Clarendon to Odo Russell, 8 Feb. 1869, f. 215–16. 20 D.C. Lathbury (ed.), *Correspondence on Church and religion of William Ewart Gladstone*, 2 vols (London, 1910), ii, 156. 21 H.C.G. Matthew (ed.), *The Gladstone diaries*, vii (Oxford, 1982), pp 14–15.

Canterbury and the archbishop of York, abstained in the crucial second reading in the lords on 19 June, and the bishop of St David's, Connop Thirwall, actually voted in favour of the measure. On the whole, the English clergy, if more detached, were filled with as little enthusiasm for the measure as were their Irish colleagues. One factor in this was that the fate of the Irish church today might be that of the English church tomorrow.[22]

That said, not all Irish opinion was equally hostile. The bishop of Down was the only Irish prelate who took (in Gladstone's terms) a 'rational' attitude to the legislation, urging his diocesan synod to moderation in its opposition to the measure. But in this regard Down was very much the exception. The archbishop of Armagh, Dr Marcus Beresford, warned that if the bill became law it would cause Protestants to leave the country, and, worse still, it would be the death blow to Irish Protestantism. He also voiced the opinion of many Irish Anglicans by declaring that he condemned the proposal from first to last and looked upon it as nothing more than a confiscation. Gladstone wrote Lord Spenser, the lord lieutenant, that he felt such opposition to be lamentable and that the Irish bishops had 'spurned a great responsibility at a time when a man like the archbishop of Canterbury advised moderation ... I think they overestimate their resources. We shall see.'[23]

Most of the Irish Anglican arguments against disestablishment were sectarian in nature, emphasizing that the abolition of the state church would leave the country in a condition where Roman Catholicism would be religiously and politically supreme.[24] But a number of technical arguments were also advanced to the effect that disestablishment was a violation of the Act of Settlement and the Act of Union, and a repudiation of the spirit of the Catholic emancipation act, in which it was solemnly declared that the established church would not be interfered with.

Even the avuncular former dean of Cork, William Connor Magee, whom Disraeli had made bishop of Peterborough in the dying days of his administration at the behest of the queen, initially resolved that there was nothing for it 'but to fight the battle to the bitter end'.[25] However, when the lower house of the Convocation of Canterbury drew up an address to the queen asking her help in preventing disestablishment, Magee dismissed it as 'preposterous'.

After the massive majority for the bill's first reading in the commons on 24 March 1869, Gladstone again made overtures to the Church of Ireland

22 Donald Akenson, *The Church of Ireland: ecclesiastical reform and revolution 1800–1885* (New Haven, 1971), p. 250; Marsh, *Archbishop Tait*, p. 22; Parry, *Democracy and religion*, p. 132. 23 BL Add. MS 44526 *Gladstone papers*, Gladstone to Spenser, 6 Feb. 1869, f. 111. 24 N.D. Emerson, 'The last phase of the establishment', in W.A. Phillips (ed.), *History of the Church of Ireland*, 3 vols (London, 1933), iii, 319–20. 25 John C. MacDonnell, *The life and correspondence of William Connor Magee*, 2 vols (London, 1896), ii, 175.

bishops in the hope of arriving at some understanding with them. The intention here was tactical in view of the impending battle with the upper house of parliament. It would have been an enormous boost to the government's position had it been able to rely on some semblance of support from the Irish church. But the prime minister's approach was once again spurned, the Irish bishops, in a statement more vitriolic than accurate, declared the bill to be 'offensive to God and the greatest national sin ever committed'.[26]

The opposition in Ireland was not confined to the established church. Although there was some overlap between Catholic and Presbyterian interest vis-à-vis the established position of Anglicanism, this very fact led some Presbyterians to voice outright opposition to the proposals. The former moderator of the Ulster Synod of the Presbyterian Church, Henry Cooke, was concerned that disestablishment would further weaken pan-Protestant hegemony in the face of Romanism.[27] The Presbyterian general assembly in the summer of 1868 voted in favour of concurrent endowment, but the majority was a narrow one, 182 ministers and 28 elders in favour, as opposed to 134 ministers and 46 elders who wanted complete disendowment.[28] This division to some extent reflected Presbyterian concern for the limited state support which they received through the *regium donum*. In the event, Gladstone's bill proposed the abolition of the grant, but successful negation on the part of Irish Presbyterian authorities secured in excess of £1,000,000 compensation for that church. Charles Morell, the moderator of the general assembly, had pleaded with Gladstone to be generous in compensating the Presbyterians for the loss of the revenues to their seminary in Belfast, especially given the 'princely' endowments which would remain at the disposal of Trinity College Dublin for the training of Church of Ireland clergy.[29]

The opposition of the Irish Anglican bishops, although at times vociferous, could not compete with the realities of Irish political and religious life. The 1861 census had revealed that Irish Anglicanism represented only one-eighth of the total population of the country, less than 700,000 people. There were some parishes where despite the fact that a minister was paid for the performance of religious duties there were no church members to whom to minister. At the very least the church was in serious need of reform. It was to

26 Morley, *Life of Gladstone*, ii, 262.   27 K. Theodore Hoppen, *Elections, politics and society in Ireland, 1832–1885* (Oxford, 1984), p. 266.   28 W.D. Killen, *The ecclesiastical history of Ireland*, 2 vols (London, 1875), ii, 537 ff; R.F.G. Holmes, *Our Presbyterian heritage* (Belfast, 1985), p. 132. Peter Brooke, *Ulster Presbyterianism, the historical perspective, 1610–1970* (Dublin, 1987), does not give the details of the crucial general assembly debate on the matter, though of course he does advert to the divisions in Irish Presbyterianism over the affair.   29 See BL Add. MS 44418 Gladstone papers f. 243.

meet precisely this problem that Lord Derby had been instrumental in setting up the Royal Commission on the Irish Church temporalities in 1867. The time for reform, however, was long past, and while Gladstone's administration could see off the posturing of a church about to face abolition as a state body, the real test lay in the passage of the bill through parliament. With such a decisive majority in the commons, the major obstacle was obviously the Tory-dominated house of lords.

The first and most serious opposition Gladstone encountered was, however, from Queen Victoria. Although not an intensely religious person, in contrast it must be said with Gladstone, she was nonetheless concerned to uphold the prerogatives of the crown in both church and state. Gladstone wrote to Lord Granville as early as April 1868 stating that he was aware of the queen's 'displeasure' at his having introduced the resolutions in the commons. At the same time he was inclined to blame Victoria's advisers for what he took to be the queen's implacable hostility. In fact, as Victoria wrote to Granville, reports of her anger were inaccurate. She did, however, express her fear that the whole enterprise would become mixed up with 'a party movement', which would make a settlement more difficult.[30]

When Gladstone became prime minister in early December 1868, Victoria made her position clear to him. Her secretary gave Gladstone a memo on 4 December in which it was stated that the queen entertained 'a very strong opinion in favour of the Irish Church'. When Gladstone saw her two days later, Victoria expressed her hope for the Irish Church that 'some connection however slender with the Crown should be maintained'.[31] Although she freely admitted that she did not understand Gladstone's proposals, in many ways she fought a rearguard action to have whatever change the government envisaged kept to a minimum. A letter at the end of January 1869 set forth her views in no uncertain terms:

> Mr Gladstone knows that the Queen has always regretted that he should have thought himself compelled to raise the question as he has done; and still more that he should have committed himself to so sweeping a measure. Regret, however, is now useless, and the Queen can only hope that it may all end in the passing of a measure satisfactory to the country, and to which she can conscientiously assent.[32]

---

30 Edmond Fitzmaurice, *The life of Granville George Leveson Gower: second earl Granville*, 2 vols (London, 1905), i, 525. 31 Matthew, *Gladstone diaries*, vi, 645. 32 G.E. Buckle (ed.), *The letters of Queen Victoria*, 2nd series, 1862–1878, 2 vols (London, 1926), i, 578.

The queen disliked the principle of disestablishment, and could not see why even if the church were disestablished it should not keep all its endowments. Victoria also hoped that even after disestablishment the Church of Ireland would still maintain some organic and organizational unity with the Church of England, a point which Gladstone confessed he did not at all understand.[33] The queen had various additional fears – that the Church of Ireland would fall into schism, and that internal difficulties would result in rival candidates competing for vacant bishoprics, as had been happening at the Cape in South Africa. At the very least she was insistent that more time was needed to deal with such an important question. On this point, however, Gladstone made clear that it was in the best interests of the Irish church to proceed with the matter as expeditiously as possible. The queen's greatest fear was the possibility of a constitutional crisis, and when this loomed in the summer of 1869, in the shape of a confrontation between the commons and the lords, she worked assiduously to avert it.

Gladstone introduced the disestablishment bill in the house of commons on 1 March in a speech which lasted three and a half hours, and of which, according to Disraeli, not a word was wasted. The second reading was carried on 24 March by a majority of 118 votes. Gladstone immediately informed the queen, convinced as he was that the large commons majority would cause the lords to think twice about rejecting the measure. Roundell Palmer, a Liberal who turned down Gladstone's offer of the lord chancellorship because he could not in conscience support the proposal, gave the most effective speech against the bill in the commons. His main argument was against disendowment and this proved to be the issue on which the two houses of parliament were to clash.

The bill's most difficult moment in the lower house came over the question of Maynooth College. It too was to be disendowed but fourteen years' worth of grant was to be given in a lump sum as compensation, amounting to £309,040, and in addition a further £12,704 of debt which the college owed to the board of works was to be remitted. The commons, in a committee of the whole house, considered this question on 6 May, and spent longer debating this than any other clause in the bill. Gladstone was especially anxious lest there might be substantial non-conformist opposition to the proposal. In the event, as he confided to his diary, 'The final division on the prickly point of 107 was the most creditable (I think) I have ever known.'[34] The third reading in the commons took place on 31 May and was carried with a majority of 114. It then passed to the lords.

The stormy passage of the bill in that place had been long expected.

---

33 Ibid., p. 582.   34 Matthew, *The Gladstone diaries*, vii, 65.

Disraeli, having no possibility of obstructing the measure in the lower house tried to use the lords to block it. His motives here, as in the general election, were purely tactical. He thought that the recently found Liberal Party unity would simply not hold and that the party might once again fall apart, giving the Tories yet another opportunity for government.[35] He soon realized, however, that such a scenario was impossible and changed tack, asking the archbishop of Canterbury to lead the opposition in the lords, and thus trying to give the impression that the Tories had only the interests of the church at heart.[36]

However, before this politicking took place sundry attempts had been made to try to work out some compromise. The queen had written in February to Lord Granville, the colonial secretary and the leader of the Liberals in the upper house, suggesting an agreement which had the backing of Bishop Magee of Peterborough, and which the bishop believed would be acceptable to most of the English episcopal bench. Granville replied that Magee's proposed compromise seemed too much like concurrent endowment. This would have no support from the cabinet, and would be unacceptable to the more radical Liberals. Such a course was politically impossible and flew in the face of the government's election promises.[37]

When it became clear in June that a sizeable number of Tory peers were determined to throw out the church bill at its second reading,[38] the queen again intervened this time with, the former Tory leader and prime minister, Lord Derby. She wrote to Derby on 7 June:

> The Queen has never concealed her opinion as to the measure – which remains unaltered; but after the Dissolution last autumn, and the large majorities with which the Bill has been passed in the House of Commons, for the House of Lords to throw it out, and place itself in collision with the House of Commons would be most dangerous, if not disastrous ... Most earnestly does the Queen appeal to Lord Derby to try to prevent this dangerous course from being pursued. She would ask him to show this letter in confidence to Lord Cairns.[39]

35 John Fair, *British interparty conferences: a study of the procedure of conciliation in British politics, 1867–1921* (Oxford, 1980), p. 22.   **36** J.D. Clayton, 'Mr Gladstone's leadership of the parliamentary Liberal Party, 1868–1874', unpublished D.Phil. thesis (Oxford, 1960), p. 208.   **37** Fitzmaurice, *The life of Granville*, ii, 7.   **38** This was a departure from their agreed position. Thus Lord Cairns, the Tory leader in the lords, told a meeting of the shadow cabinet in April that the Conservative peers 'would not throw out the bill on the second reading, through they might amend it in detail'. John Vincent (ed.), *A selection of the diaries of Edward Stanley, 15th earl of Derby: between September 1869 and March 1878* (London, 1994), p. 340. Stanley commented, 'this is right and wise'. Ibid.   **39** Buckle, *Letters of Queen Victoria*, i, 604–5.

Derby refused to use his influence to ensure the second reading. Cairns, however, proved more amenable to royal persuasion, although himself an Ulsterman and ardent champion of the Irish church. Perhaps, however, some attention was also paid to Gladstone's veiled threat that, if the lords rejected the second reading, then the tolerance of the country 'in the dignity and efficiency and permanence of that Assembly' might begin to wear thin.

There were a number of important speeches both for and against the second reading which deserve some note. Magee, although convinced that the measure ought to pass, gave a thunderous speech in defence of the endowments of the church. Archbishop Trench made 'a melancholy and almost inaudible "keen"', to which no one listened. Lord Clarendon, the foreign secretary, drawing on his own experience of having been lord lieutenant of Ireland, said that the bill was both just and necessary. Like Gladstone he also warned of the danger to the lords as an institution if the bill were rejected. The bishop of St David made an intervention so long-winded and off the point that Wilberforce of Oxford remarked that he now realized why Thirwall's history of Greece was in ten volumes.[40] William Alexander, bishop of Derry, gave, in Lord Kimberley's words, '[a] powerful but coarse and slightly vulgar declamation ... (he) evidently forgot that he was not on a platform at a meeting of Orangemen'.[41] The bill was given its second reading at 3am on 19 June by a margin of 179 to 146 votes, a government majority of thirty-three. Thirty-two Tories voted with the government and two Liberals against. There were eighteen pairings. Sixty Tory peers and ten Liberals who were in a position to vote simply stayed away.

The best explanation for the strength of Tory resistance is that given by the bishop of Peterborough. In a letter to the Revd John MacDonnell on 7 June 1869 he observed that the peers faced a dilemma:

> They must fight on the land question, in which they have a deep personal interest; they could not & ought not to begin by yielding on the church question, in which they have less personal interest, lest it should be said that they sacrificed their convictions when it cost them little so to do, and maintained them only when sacrifice would cost them much.[42]

The bill having now passed its second reading became subject to the lords' amendments, which in fact completely distorted the will of the commons.

40 R.B. McDowell, *The Church of Ireland, 1869–1969* (London, 1975), p. 46. **41** Ethel Drus (ed.), *Kimberley diary* (London, 1958), p. 5. Kimberley was lord privy seal at the time and a former lord lieutenant of Ireland. **42** MacDonnell, *Life of William Connor Magee*, ii, 227.

The preamble was changed to allow for the financial surplus remaining after compensation was paid for disendowment, to be applied for religious purposes. Somewhat inauspiciously, on 12 July the lords also approved of concurrent endowment by a majority of seven. After having been given its third reading in the upper house, the bill was returned to the commons, which promptly disposed of the more offensive amendments on 16 July. Parliament was now thrown into a state of crisis.

Meanwhile, Henry Edward Manning, archbishop of Westminster, had written to Gladstone to assure him that the lords had made no impression on the mind of the country by their amendments. 'They are too transparently the work of the ascendancy party.'[43] This was a critical period, and Gladstone claimed that he felt himself sustained only by the prayers of non-conformists and Catholics.[44] Despite the prayerful support at this stage in his great work, Gladstone's nerve began to fail. The cabinet met on 17 July and asked the prime minister to see the queen again. Victoria suggested negotiations with the archbishop of Canterbury using the dean of Windsor as an intermediary. Gladstone told the dean that the cabinet would sanction £170–180,000 of further compensation to what was already on offer, amounting to more than eight million pounds.

Disraeli now made a compromise proposal which would give the Church of Ireland a further lump sum of between £900,000 and one million pounds. The cabinet was not disposed to this proposal and Gladstone in particular felt that his government had made all the reasonable concessions that were possible. On 21 July Gladstone warned the archbishop of Canterbury that, if the lords finally rejected the bill, the commons would not be as generous in future in considering Church of Ireland claims to compensation. The real crisis for him seems to have occurred on the 20th when the bill, again before the lords, was further amended to their lordships' previous specifications. The prime minister, fearing all was lost, decided to let the bill drop. He also indicated in his diary that he was prepared to take the matter to the country in a general election.[45] He was, however, out-voted in cabinet, with Granville making clear that if the bill were dropped he would resign.[46] Granville then persuaded the cabinet to go for an adjournment in the debate.

On 22 July Gladstone had 'taken to his sofa' emotionally exhausted from the strain of the whole business. Lord Granville was thus left to negotiate with Lord Cairns and by 5 p.m. a settlement had been arrived at. Cairns agreed to an improved settlement for the clergy, although less generous than he had hoped for, and he agreed to drop the lords' amendment on concurrent endowment. The preamble, however, was to be accepted by the government

43 BL Add. MS 44419 Gladstone papers f. 87.   44 Matthew, *Gladstone diaries*, vii, 96.
45 Ibid., p. 103.   46 Fitzmaurice, *Life of Granville*, ii, 12 note 1.

as per the lords' amendment since it was sufficiently ambiguous whether or not the surplus could be used for religious purposes, and in any event it would be for parliament to decide how it should be spent. The bill then passed through the lords and was returned to the commons where it passed all stages on the government's recommendations. It received the royal assent of 31 July. Of some sixteen million pounds involved in the disendowment, some nine millions would go to the disestablished Church of Ireland. One and a half millions were set aside to satisfy the claims of the Presbyterians and Maynooth College. A little over a million pounds was paid to the Presbyterian Church and the rest, as we have seen, went to the seminary at Maynooth. The substantial amount remaining was to go to charitable purposes to be determined by parliament. This is clearly at variance with the assertions of D. George Boyce that, after having provided for the security of Church of Ireland clergy with one half of the endowments, 'the other half was raised to compensate the Presbyterians for the loss of their state grant and Maynooth for its parliamentary grant'.[47]

On 24 July Archbishop Manning wrote to Gladstone commenting, in a somewhat histrionic fashion, on the successful passage of the bill:

> I can find no exaggeration in saying that this is the greatest act of the legislature towards Ireland in our history. The act of Union, and the Repeal of the Penal laws alone approach it ... I believe that in its bearing upon Ireland, and upon the British Empire it will have inaugurated a new period of legislation and government, vital to our safety.[48]

In reply, Gladstone thanked Manning for his constant support throughout the passage of the bill, and asked that his thanks be conveyed also to Cardinal Cullen in Dublin.[49] Such exchanges were by no means unusual. The extent of Catholic agitation and pressure on Gladstone for the dismantling of the Church of Ireland is a matter to which we must now turn our attention.[50]

Shane Leslie advanced the surprising thesis that the persisting influence of Archbishop Manning and Cardinal Paul Cullen had more direct impact on persuading Gladstone of the need for disestablishment than had the threat of Fenianism.[51] According to Leslie, Gladstone raised the issue of the Fenian

---

47 D. George Boyce, *Ireland 1828–1923: from ascendancy to democracy* (Oxford, 1992), p. 44.   48 BL Add. MS 44419 Gladstone papers, Manning to Gladstone, 24 July 1869, f. 92.   49 Shane Leslie, 'Irish pages from the postbags of Manning, Cullen and Gladstone', *Dublin Review* (October 1919), 177–8.   50 Akenson, *The Church of Ireland*, p. 228, is mistaken in his belief that apart from minor details relating to Maynooth, Gladstone had little contact with Catholics over the disestablishment issue.   51 The Protestant Defence Association had protested in January 1868 that the Catholic

crisis as an artifice to deflect any suspicion of an undue influence from either Manning or Cullen.[52] Incredible as this may seem, there is nevertheless some evidence that Gladstone advanced in his resolutions speech of March 1868 points that were put to him by Manning and which had already seen the light of day in Manning's pro-disestablishment *Letter to Earl Grey*, published in early March.[53] It has also been suggested that Manning's influence on Gladstone against the Irish establishment pre-dates the former's conversion to Catholicism.[54]

Cullen's *animus* against the Church of Ireland was of a long-standing nature. As archbishop of Armagh in 1850 he described it as 'effete and bearing all the marks of the decrepitude of age and of approaching inevitable dissolution'.[55] He had lent his formidable authority to the foundation of the National Association in December 1864 because one of the chief issues the Association was pledged to campaign on was the end of the Anglican establishment. Like Gladstone he had come to see a link between ending Fenianism and the disestablishment and disendowment of the Irish Church. He regarded the position of the Anglican Church as both a badge of oppression and 'an insult'.[56]

In July 1867 Cullen asked Sir John Gray, the Protestant owner of the *Freeman's Journal* and Liberal MP for Kilkenny, to find out Gladstone's position on the disestablishment issue. At that stage Gladstone seems to have been quite open, according to Gray, either to disestablishment or concurrent endowment. Several months later, writing to Gray, Gladstone declared that in fact his leanings in the matter were towards concurrent endowment, but added that he would not let his personal feelings interfere with 'whatever may be seen to be the most hopeful mode of delivering [Ireland] from a great mischief and a great scandal'.[57] The following month the Catholic bishops issued their declaration against concurrent endowment, and this seems to have tipped the balance against the proposal, since it could clearly not be possible to proceed with such a policy against the wishes of the Catholic Church in Ireland. Both Cullen and Manning sent Gladstone copies of the

clergy were conspiring to have the Church of Ireland disestablished as a first step to destroying Protestantism in Ireland: P.M.H. Bell, *Disestablishment in Ireland and Wales* (London, 1969), p. 70.   **52** Leslie, art. cit., p. 163.   **53** Edward Norman, *The Catholic Church in Ireland in the age of rebellion, 1859–1873* (London, 1965), p. 339.   **54** V. Alan McClelland, *Cardinal Manning: his public life and influence, 1865–1892* (London, 1962), p. 171.   **55** *Letter to the Catholic clergy of the archdiocese of Armagh* (Dublin, 1850), p. 2.   **56** Leslie, art. cit., Cullen to Manning, 8 Aug. 1867, p. 168.   **57** BL Add. MS 44413 Gladstone papers, Gladstone to Gray, 6 Sept. 1867, ff. 134–5. This is at variance with the late Professor Matthew's judgment that for Gladstone, 'The notion of the State being involved in the support of various denominations which were doctrinally irreconcilable he profoundly abhorred …': *Gladstone: 1809–1898* (Oxford, 1997), p. 193.

bishops' resolutions, which, among other things, declared that it was the establishment 'to which, as their fountain-head, are to be traced the waters of bitterness which poison the relations of life in Ireland and estrange one another Protestants and Catholics, who ought to be united as a people' – an astonishing aspiration for the Catholic bishops to make in those pre-ecumenical days. The more overtly political aspect of these sentiments were re-echoed in a letter of Manning to Gladstone on 28 March 1868 in the light of the leader of the opposition's commons resolutions. Then Manning asserted:

> The Irish Establishment is a great wrong. It is the cause of alienation between Ireland and England ... Even the land question is exasperated by it ... The fatal ascendancy of race over race is unspeakably aggravated by this ascendancy of religion over religion ... I say this not as a Catholic but as an Englishman & a good subject who desires to see the two countries confirmed by a complete reconciliation.[58]

It would perhaps be inaccurate to say that Cullen and Manning kept up a relentless campaign against the Church of Ireland, but equally one must not underestimate the encouragement and support they gave Gladstone in prosecuting disestablishment. Manning not only told Gladstone that he was the only man who could gain Ireland's confidence in such a way as to prevent it becoming republican; he also pledged himself, on Gladstone's becoming prime minister, to work with him 'in a case in which my whole heart can go with you'.

It was Manning who urged Gladstone to consolidate the victory of the resolutions vote by turning the majority there gained to 'practical purposes'. And it was Manning who assured Gladstone that the extraordinary coalition of interests, Catholic, radical and non-conformist, could only hold together if disestablishment and disendowment were pursued with full vigour. In responding to this point Gladstone told Manning, 'Your last note was of much value, and shewed me at once with what an accurate eye you had measured the situation.'[59]

Cullen and Manning had both advised Gladstone to overturn the amendments which the lords had introduced into his bill. Cullen assured Gladstone that the bill in the form proposed by the lords would do no good in Ireland.[60]

---

58 BL Add. MS 44249 Gladstone papers, Manning to Gladstone, 28 Mar. 1868, ff 34–5. **59** Ibid., Gladstone to Manning, 24 July 1869, f. 82. **60** BL Add. MS 44421Gladstone papers, Cullen to Gladstone, 14 July 1869, f. 151. The bluster against concurrent endowment did not prevent Cullen from here asking Gladstone for some of the Church of Ireland cathedrals. A request to which Gladstone strongly declined to

On the day after the bill's second reading in the lords, Manning wrote saying that in the interests of peace in Ireland the amendments would have to be revoked. He was even of the opinion that it would be better to lose the bill than have it enacted in its amended form.[61] Gladstone assured both men that the government had no intention of allowing the lords to have their way on either the concurrent endowment question or the issue of the disposal of the residue.

Not all Catholics were equally convinced of the evils of concurrent endowment. Aubrey de Vere, the convert and Liberal MP, favoured the arrangement as did, at an earlier stage, David Moriarty, bishop of Kerry, Lord Gormanston and John Henry Newman.[62] But the internal debate among Catholics in Ireland and Britain was also influenced by thinking from Rome. The Vatican secretary of state, Cardinal Giacomo Antonelli, assured the British minister at Rome that the Holy See could not approve of the idea of concurrent endowment. At the same time he assured the minister that papal policy could not approve of disestablishment either.

On the other hand, Pope Pius IX indicated that in broad terms he was pleased with Gladstone's bill,[63] as were the Irish clergy in Rome, but not it seems the English Catholic priests in the eternal city.[64] Ireland was very much the exception in Roman thought on the relationship between church and state. For the most part it was Manning, rather than Cullen, who directed the Holy See's policy on the matter. The foreign office had made it clear how much it distrusted Cullen, and this made the Vatican wary of at least some of Cullen's pronouncements. Clarendon in a tempestuous outburst had complained to Pius IX that Cullen was 'the bitter and pertinacious enemy of the English government and never misses an opportunity to do mischief'. He wrote to Russell at Rome of Cullen:

> It is really too bad that this viper should be permitted to create diffi-
> culties [over the Church bill] in addition to those that already exist. I
> shall be grateful if in gentle language you could convey to the Cardinal
> [Antonelli] and to Manning the utter disgust we feel at the conduct of
> Cullen and Co., who, as I need not say, give the tone to the whole
> priesthood of Ireland.[65]

accede.   **61** BL Add. MS 44249 Gladstone papers, Manning to Gladstone, 16 July 1860, f. 80.   **62** Charles S. Dessain and Thomas Gornall (eds), *The letters and diaries of John Henry Newman*, xxiv (Oxford, 1973), p. 182.   **63** PRO FO 918/4 Odo Russell to Lord Clarendon, 21 Apr. 1869, f. 43.   **64** Ibid., f. 52.   **65** BLO Clarendon papers, Clarendon to Russell, 25 Jan. 1869.

Equally Gladstone did not share all the views of his foreign secretary and he did rely on both Cullen and Manning as the chief exponents of Catholic attitudes on the disestablishment and disendowment issues. He was also clearly grateful for their support. When the bill was finally passed he wrote to Manning:

> I am much indebted to you on behalf of the Government for the firm, constant and discriminating support which you have afforded our Bill during the arduous conflict now happily concluded. Should you happen to write to Cardinal Cullen, pray be kind enough to ask him to accept a similar tribute of acknowledgement?[66]

Gladstone's purpose was not simply to keep at bay the competing influences upon him as he tried to grapple with the intricacies of Irish and British political life. His stand on the Irish church question was principled but tempered with the harsh realities of public life. Some commentators have treated too lightly the difficulties of enacting this particular piece of legislation. It is surely a mistake to believe, in the light of what we have seen, that the passage of the disestablishment bill was 'one of the smoothest political operations ever carried through the British parliament'.[67]

One might variously estimate the effect of disestablishment on Irish social and political life. It might be seen as the decisive point in the formation of modern party affiliation in British politics,[68] or as an exercise in the constitutional dismantling of a great and complicated vested interest.[69] Alternatively one might think that Gladstone saw in the measure 'the whole answer to Fenianism',[70] or see it as the final triumph of Roman Catholic ultramontanism and so as so rejoice with Cullen that 'the poor Protestants are all very irritated. They never did imagine that England would have abandoned their cause'. One might feel with Queen Victoria that Gladstone had dreamed the whole thing up on the basis of personal ambition,[71] or think that he merely saw it as an end in itself and as a means of cutting down the establishment.[72] Beyond doubt the Church of Ireland under the 1869 act was able to preserve

66 BL Add. MS 44537 Gladstone papers, Gladstone to Manning, 24 July 1869, f. 11. Manning wrote to Cullen the following day passing on the prime minister's remarks and saying that Gladstone had acted with 'great firmness & uprightness'. 67 Gabriel Daly, 'Church renewal 1869–1877', in Michael Hurley (ed.), *Irish Anglicanism, 1869–1969* (Dublin, 1970), p. 23. 68 Ibid., Kevin B. Nowlan, 'Disestablishment, 1800–1869', p. 8. 69 W.E. Vaughan, 'Ireland c. 1870' in Vaughan (ed.), *A new history of Ireland, v: Ireland under the Union 1801–70* (Oxford, 1989), p. 728. 70 F.S.L. Lyons, *Ireland since the famine* (London, 1973), p. 143. 71 Erich Eych, *Gladstone* (London, 1938), p. 195. 72 Nicholas Mansergh, *The Irish question, 1840–1921* (London, 1940), p. 299.

a much greater sense of corporate identity, and preserve a greater share of its wealth, than would have been the case if it had been disestablished in post-partition Ireland rather than in 1869.[73]

However one estimates Gladstone's position, and it is not without some ambiguity, it is, I think, an error to believe that 'the fundamental source of [his] interest in Ireland at this time was neither moral conviction nor Fenianism but votes.[74] In the early months of 1868 there was no certainty that the disestablishment issue would arouse such popular support. Equally Gladstone's championing of the church question might have, in his own words, led 'the Liberal party to martyrdom', as did his later stand on home rule. At least in the short term the church bill and the subsequent land act enabled Ireland, as Manning observed, to have a renewed confidence in parliament. 'You', he told Gladstone, 'have fairly earned this', namely the trust of the Irish people, 'which no other English statesman has yet deserved'.[75] Gladstone was convinced that his church measure was one step on the road of giving political justice to Ireland. His political dispositions were also hedged around with religions convictions. In the first flourish of victory for his legislative measure Gladstone did not forget his deeply religious principles. He wrote to the archbishop of Dublin offering any help he could as a private individual to the newly liberated Church of Ireland.[76]

73 R.F. Foster, *Modern Ireland* (London, 1988), p. 396.   74 R.V. Comerford, 'Gladstone's first Irish enterprise, 1864–70', in *A new history of Ireland*, v, 441–2. 75 Leslie, *Dublin Review* (October, 1919), p. 178.   76 BL Add. MS 44537 Gladstone papers, f. 13.

10

The Catholic chapel and the Catholic community: observance and tradition in nineteenth-century Co. Down

Catholic identity within the Irish context arguably rests on two inextricably linked factors. The first is the practice of Catholicism itself which has been grafted unto the attendant cultural accoutrements of the Gaelic outlook and way of life, albeit tinged with both English and continental influences. The second is the long history since the reformation, of the struggle to survive as a religious and political force against a background of official hostility. In the circumstances of County Down we must also take account of the peculiar complexion of Ulster, and in particular the enormous success and prevalence of Protestantism, especially in its Presbyterian guise, in east Ulster. Presbyterians, of course, did produce some of the more radical and liberal elements in Irish Protestantism,[1] but that community also had its share of some of the most reactionary members of the planter tradition. It is against this background that the Catholic community in the nineteenth century developed its self-understanding, and fostered its relationships with its Presbyterian and Protestant neighbours.

The Catholic community in nineteenth-century Down, while labouring under the constraints common to Irish Catholicism as a whole, was nonetheless acutely aware of its peculiar difficulties as an impoverished and disadvantaged minority in a largely Presbyterian setting. Yet it was dependant on the more benevolent elements within the Protestant communities for its survival and expansion, at least in the public aspects of its life and worship.

The historian of Catholicism in Down works under a number of disadvantages. Many of the extant records are either official ecclesiastical or government papers. Such sources, it could be suggested, skew the perspective on the community in too much of an official direction, and make it difficult to know precisely how 'ordinary' Catholics viewed the events which shaped their lives. In the nineteenth century, hostility between Catholics and Protestants was constantly growing, especially after Catholic emancipation, which led many Protestants to again see Catholicism as a political threat. Many of the public records therefore focus on inter-communal strife, the sheer vividness of which overshadows more subtle complexities of the relationship between the two communities.

1 At a dinner in Belfast in 1828 the Catholic bishop, William Crolly, declared that 'if Presbyterian be a name liberality must be its surname': *Northern Whig*, 10 Jan. 1828.

Finally, County Down is divided between two Catholic dioceses: the united diocese of Down and Connor, which incorporates most of east and north Down, and the diocese of Dromore, which includes large tracks of south and west Down with small out posts in Antrim and Armagh. We must also reckon with the influence of Belfast which, after the famine, had overtaken Dublin as the industrial capital of Ireland and which in ecclesiastical geography is in the diocese of Down. However, in the interests of focusing what follows on Down itself, I have tried as far as possible to abstract the urban reality of Belfast with its particular pastoral difficulties, and I discuss that area only when it is absolutely necessary for a full appreciation of the challenges facing Catholicism in the century as a whole.

The Catholic community in Down in the nineteenth century exhibited many of the general features of Ulster Catholicism. At the beginning of the period it was a relatively weak and disparate group with an underdeveloped sense of religious identity and little political power. By the end of the century the community exhibits what we have come to expect as the marks of a quintessentially Catholic ultramontane nationalist community.[2] S.J. Connolly has argued that this process, at least at a religious level, made fairly rapid progress in the early decades of the century. There are good reasons, however, as we shall see, for concluding that the process was slower in Ulster than in the rest of Ireland.[3] That process, nevertheless, is perhaps one of the most fascinating adjustments in nineteenth-century Irish history. At the same time, the persistence of Catholicism in Down was in many respects a haphazard affair. It was one of two Ulster counties to have the lowest percentage of Catholics in the general population. The concentration of Catholics in particular areas was the result of specific religious factors. Walter Harris, for example, noted in the eighteenth century the prevalence of Catholics in Downpatrick because of the town's proximity to a centre of pilgrimage, St Patrick's well at Struell. By contrast, the north-east of the county had very few Catholics.[4] In Donaghadee, the first Mass since the seventeenth century was celebrated only in 1805, and by 1884 the Catholic electorate in the Ards and Castlereagh area accounted for just six per cent of the total.[5]

2 S.J. Connolly, *Religion and society in nineteenth-century Ireland* (Dundalk, 1985), p. 35.
3 James Doyle, bishop of Kildare and Leighlin, told a select committee on tithes that northern Catholicism was slow to respond to developments within the church in the period after the Union. See *First and second reports from the select committee, Lords, on tithes in Ireland*, HL 1831–2 (663) xxii, p. 278.   4 The same was true of the north-west. In 1812 the parish of Annahilt had only twenty Catholics who had but recently arrived. They worshipped with their co-religionists at Ballynahinch: William Shaw Mason, *A statistical account or parochial survey of Ireland*, 3 vols (Dublin, 1819) ii, 18.
5 Paul Bew and F. Wright, 'The agrarian opposition in Ulster politics', in S. Clark and J.S. Donnelly Jnr (eds), *Irish peasants: violence and political unrest, 1780–1914*

Perhaps not surprisingly, the Catholic community in the early years of the century shared some of the features of its larger Presbyterian neighbour. Patrick MacMullan, bishop of Down and Connor, writing from Downpatrick in 1814 to the authorities in Rome acknowledged that a number of parishes in the diocese maintained what they took to be a right to 'call' their own priests. Thus the parish in Belfast elected a committee of the more prominent members to help in the administration of the congregation, and these individuals were known by the Presbyterian title of 'elders'. MacMullan was determined to resist what he took to be such dangerous tendencies in his flock and was resolved to reassert full episcopal authority.[6] This relative independence of the laity in ecclesiastical affairs was also apparent in Newry, which in the early nineteenth century had the largest population of urban Catholics in Ulster. There Bishop Michael Blake complained to the primate Archbishop Thomas Kelly of Armagh that the church committee in the town had repeatedly refused to pay the salaries of the curates and to supply the other needs for worship. Blake sought to impress upon the committee that they had no rights independent of the bishop. To this end he deprived it of one of its traditional functions, that of collecting money after Mass on Sundays, and instead he organized his own collections. The committee in reaction was to accuse him of insulting the Catholics of Newry.[7]

From the middle decades of the century Belfast was beginning to be an important centre of Catholic population. As early as 1825 Bishop William Crolly petitioned Rome for permission to move the administrative centre of the Down and Connor diocese from Downpatrick to Belfast. A number of Catholics in Belfast were emerging as substantial businessmen. For the most part, however, Catholics in Down were at the lower end of the social spectrum as labourers or as the poorer sort of tenant farmer, although generally speaking they were, in common with Catholics elsewhere in east Ulster, better off than their co-religionists elsewhere.[8] Furthermore, close proximity of Catholics to Protestant ideas resulted in Catholics imbibing something of the Protestant work ethic, and consequently they took less time off to observe religious festivals and holidays than Catholics in other areas, whose practice in this regard was, so we are informed, 'inimical to industry in the southern part of Ireland'.[9]

The freedom of Catholics to practise their religion openly and without

(Manchester, 1983), p. 212.   6 ADDC MacMullan papers B14/3, MacMullan to Revd John Connolly, 12 Oct. 1814.   7 PRONI DIO (RC) 3/1, 28 June 1833, Blake letter book, p. 7.   8 H.D. Inglis, *Ireland in 1834*, ii (London, 1835), p. 215, shows that employment was more constant and wages were up to 4d more per pay that elsewhere in the country.   9 A. Day and P McWilliams (eds), *Ordnance Survey memoirs of Ireland: vol. XII, parishes of Co. Down (iii) 1833–8* (Belfast, 1992), p. 7.

hindrance gave rise to an enormous amount of church building in the period up to the famine. One of the features of such building in rural areas early in the century was that much of the heavier work, such as drawing stone from quarries, was carried out by parishioners themselves free of charge. Cornelius Denvir, bishop of Down and Connor 1836–65, declared in his report to Rome on the state of his diocese in 1845 that there was at least one chapel in every parish and that in the greater number there were two, many of which were substantial and newly built.[10]

The provision of places of worship would not have been possible without Protestant benefactions. The Protestants of Belfast not only gave the land for a new Catholic chapel to be built in 1842, but also contributed a further £800 to the cost of the building. Thomas McGivern, the future bishop of Dromore, when parish priest of Drumgath in the 1870s, obtained from Lord Downshire land for a Catholic cemetery near Rathfriland.[11] A previous marquis had granted Hugh Smith, the parish priest of Lisburn, an acre and a half of land on which to build a church. Similarly, Patrick Curran, the parish priest of Newtownards and Hollywood, and a former tutor to the marquis of Londonderry, used his influence with the Castlereagh family to obtain the site in Newtownards on which he built a Catholic church in 1813. The Londonderry family maintained a benevolent interest in Catholic affairs in the area late into the century; the dowager marchioness built the third church for the Hollywood parish in 1875.[12] Such examples could be multiplied many times over.

Despite a growing confidence about their position in Ulster society, Catholics still harboured a sense of the burden of their history. Addressing a St Patrick's Day banquet in Belfast in 1853, James Killen, the parish priest of Hollywood, said that for nearly 300 years the clergy had suffered persecution, and were willing to suffer again with their people.[13] Such sentiments were not entirely the product of an overactive imagination. Until 1871 a marriage between a Catholic and a Protestant, if conducted by a Catholic priest, was

10 AICR Cullen papers Denvir to Paul Cullen, 20 Dec. 1845.   11 As recorded in his obituary in the *Newry Telegraph*, 27 Nov. 1900.   12 James O'Laverty, *An historical account of the diocese of Down and Connor, ancient and modern*, 5 vols (Dublin, 1880), ii, 142–7. Estyn Evans pointed out that the ornate Gothic style of many such churches demonstrated little concern for continuity with regional tradition. See his *Mourne county* (3rd ed. Dundalk, 1978), p. 201. Contemporary critics questioned the advisability of lavishing scarce resources on such buildings in the face of often overwhelming poverty, a view shared by some Catholic observers. Horace Plunkett, *Ireland in the new century* (Dublin, 1904), p. 107; M.J.F. McCarthy, *Priests and people in Ireland* (Dublin, 1902), *passim*. More recently Liam Kennedy has argued that church building in its own way contributed to some economic development. 'The Roman Catholic Church and economic growth in nineteenth-century Ireland', in *Economic and Social Review*, 10: 1 (1978) 56.   13 *The Ulsterman*, 19 Mar. 1853.

invalid in the eyes of the law. For having performed such a wedding in Loghlinisland, the local Catholic curate, the Revd Hugh Bradley, had a warrant issued against him in 1829 at the behest of the Church of Ireland rector, James Stannus. When the Sisters of Mercy opened their convent in Downpatrick in 1855 there was much opposition. The local newspaper accused them of trying to win converts to Rome, and urged Protestants to greater zeal in visiting the poor and the sick of the area as a means of trying to counter the baneful influence of the nuns.[14] The accusations of prose-lytism became a common trope for Protestant discontent at the presence of the nuns,[15] but the situation improved with the passing of the years. By the time of the death of Mother Borgia, the superior of the convent, in 1864 Protestants turned out in large numbers to mourn her passing.[16]

At the same time bishops and priests stressed the rapid progress the church had made since the turn of the century. By 1835 in the Down portion of the Down and Connor diocese there were 58,405 Catholics worshipping in 37 chapels. For the Dromore diocese the figures were 76,275 worshipping in 34 chapels.[17] While sometimes compared unfavourably with Catholicism elsewhere in the country, measured by such factors as the ratio of priests to people and attendance at Mass, County Down by early mid-century fared better than many areas. In Dromore there were 17 parish priests, including the bishop, and 10 curates, which gives a ratio of one priest to every 2,825 Catholics. In the rest of Down there was one priest for every 2,085 Catholics, one of the best ratios in the whole country.[18]

An analysis of the returns of those attending Mass is broadly in line with work done elsewhere.[19] It is difficult to be absolutely precise since the returns are incomplete, but it is possible to suggest that, in the Dromore diocese, 25,000 people or roughly 32.77 per cent of the Catholic population attended

14 *Downpatrick Recorder*, 5 May 1855.   15 Ibid., 12 April 1856, 12 Dec. 1857 etc. 16 *Catholic directory* (Dublin, 1865), p. 351.   17 *First report of the commission of public instruction Ireland* (45 & 46), HC (1835), pp 18–19.   18 These figure are based on the 1835 House of Commons report, pp 230–9 and pp 243–61. Using the same report Sean Connolly gives a somewhat different picture. Cf. S.J. Connolly, 'Catholicism in Ulster 1800–50' in Peter Roebuck (ed.), *Plantation to partition: essays in Ulster history in honour of J.L. McCracken* (Belfast, 1981), p. 159 table 1. Connolly suggests for Dromore that there was one priest for every 2,934 Catholics. However, in his calculations he fails to take account of the fact that the bishop of Dromore also acted as the parish priest of Newry. His figures for the rest of the county are combined with those of Antrim to give one priest for every 2,654. If, however, we take only the county Down section of the Down and Connor diocese, the ratio is as I have indicated. By 1871 there were still only twenty-eight priests in that part of Down, a figure which had remained fairly constant since 1733, despite the fact that the Catholic population had increased threefold. See A. Knox, *A history of Co. Down* (Dublin, 1875), p. 159.   19 David W. Miller, 'Irish Catholicism and the great Famine' in *Journal of Social History*, 9 (1975), 81–98.

Mass on Sundays and holidays, while in the rest of Down the figure was 19,902 or approximately 34 per cent.[20] To take another indicator of adherence to the Catholic faith, we can see a lively and profound outpouring of piety at a popular level, associated with such pilgrimages as the annual Hilltown gathering to commemorate the killing of a priest and his congregation in 1643, and that to the holy well at Struell. Attempts were made by the official church to channel popular enthusiasm into more orthodox waters, as can be seen in the parish mission movement. These became increasingly popular from the mid-century, and at an emotional level fulfilled something of the same function as 'revival' meetings among Protestants. They were also a means of raising money. At the famous Lisburn mission in July 1853, which attracted worshippers from Down as well as Antrim, admission charges to high Mass ranged from one shilling to sixpence, and the evening services cost the devotees between three and six pence. At times these missions had something of an ecumenical flavour with Protestants of the more 'respectable classes' attending in order to listen to the sermon. Of course, there could also be sectarian overtones to such gatherings. The rioting which was occasioned by the Lisburn mission was blamed by the *Northern Whig* on the parish priest, John McKenna, on the grounds that he had staged the event to coincide with the Boyne commemoration festivities.[21]

There were other indications of reform. Diocesan administration became more formal, with annual or triennial visitations of each parish by the bishop, during which the conduct of the clergy was scrutinized, first communion administered, children and adults confirmed and catechism examined.[22] Measured by external ultramontane criteria, Catholic religious life in Down by the end of the century was in an expansive and exuberant mood. Clerical numbers were increasing; Belfast, Downpatrick and Newry could boast of Catholic schools, orphanages and a hospital. Priests from the Passionist, the Redemptorist and the Jesuit religious orders had made their appearance for the first time in Ulster, either in Belfast or in County Down, the Jesuits only briefly; and the Dominicans re-established themselves in Newry for the first time since the Reformation. The laity were worshipping in churches in unprecedented numbers. There remained, however, a sense of nostalgia for the past. In 1897 Pope Leo XIII issued an encyclical letter on the rosary. In commenting on it, the Belfast *Irish News*, in triumphalist vein, declared that '[i]n all our vicissitudes Irish Catholics can still claim to have preserved in a

20 Ibid., p. 86. Miller indicates that in the environs of Newry, Mass attendance was in the region of 46–51%. 21 *Northern Whig*, 6 July 1853. McKenna's reply rejecting the accusation appeared in *The Ulsterman*, 9 July 1853. 22 Michael Blake gives details of all these practices. See Cullen papers AICR Blake to Cullen, 10 Feb 1846.

great measure the love of their forefathers for the pious and efficacious practice of which the Holy Father writes so eloquently.'[23]

One of the areas in which Catholics made considerable gains was in education. Although by the end of the century Catholic illiteracy rates still tended to be higher than those of Protestants, the general educational standing in the community in Down had made enormous progress. There is some suggestion that Catholic priests in Ulster were less concerned about specifically Catholic provision in education than their colleagues in other areas of the country.[24] Leading churchmen could certainly see some advantages in having Catholic and Protestant children educated together. Before the establishment of St Malachy's College in Belfast in 1833, the bishop, William Crolly, was accustomed to preparing his seminarians for Maynooth by sending them to the Presbyterian Belfast Academical Institution, hoping thereby to inculcate acceptance of individuals of another denominational tradition among his candidates for the priesthood.

On the other hand, the early years of operation of the national school system were marred by opposition from some Ulster Presbyterians, led in many instances by the indomitable Henry Cooke. On several occasions the more redoubtable opponents of the system resorted to violence. In 1836 the Revd James Porter, of the secession Presbyterian Church at Drumlee, allowed his school to be affiliated to the national system. The school was attacked by a Presbyterian mob, and both Porter and his schoolmaster were assaulted.[25] By contrast Catholics in Down were anxious supporters of the system. The first clergyman of any denomination to apply for a grant under the terms of the national school provisions was Thomas Kelly, then Catholic bishop of Dromore and subsequently archbishop of Armagh. Within the first two years of the system's operation, many of the parishes in Down had applied for grants, the applications (as was required) carrying the signatures of both Catholics and Protestants. Perhaps most remarkably of all, the system was also supported in those early years by Paul Cullen, then rector of the Irish College Rome. Subsequently Cullen was to become one of the system's sternest critics.

Michael Blake, who succeeded Kelly as bishop of Dromore, showed some hesitation about the system, but he was soon won over to it largely through assurances given by Daniel Murray, archbishop of Dublin. Blake's main complaint then became the fact that the commissioners were slow to supply the necessary funds, and that his people were thus becoming frustrated since

23 *Irish News*, 4 Oct. 1897.   24 Connolly, 'Catholicism in Ulster', p. 162. Equally there are indications to the contrary, cf. *Catholic directory* (Dublin, 1851), p. 210 and *Report from the select committee on the state of Ireland*, 1825, viii, 363.   25 D.H. Akenson, *The Irish educational experiment* (London, 1970), p. 170.

there was great need of education for the poor of his diocese.[26] Blake's concern for adequate funding was also shared by Cornelius Denvir,[27] bishop of Down and Connor, who was an enthusiastic supporter of the system to the extent of becoming a commissioner of education. He resigned from this post, however, in 1857 owing to pressure from other members of the Irish hierarchy.

It is also clear that, where Catholics had control over schools, they were concerned to ensure that the Board of Education's regulations were duly observed. Robert Stuart Currie, a district inspector of education, remarked in his 1864 report on the convent school in Downpatrick that the Sisters of Mercy were scrupulous in this regard, lest infringement of regulations might 'prevent the school from recommending itself to persons of different religious denominations, or in any way lessen its usefulness and circumscribe its influence'.[28] The glowing testimony Currie gave of the benefits of convent education in Downpatrick contrasts sharply with that of D.C. Richmond, the education inspector for the Armagh and Belfast areas, the latter including north Down, before the Powis commission four years later. Whilst Currie praised the nuns for the quality of their education, Richmond testified to the 'marked inferiority of convent to ordinary national schools'.[29] Although by this stage the bishops were more aggressive in their demands for a Catholic education system spearheaded by nuns and Christian Brothers, Richmond saw such schools in less than benevolent terms. In his view, the Catholic system produced 'true and earnest adherents of the Church, but is opposed to the formation and independence of character which a method of greater freedom tends to produce. In this respect the Christian Brothers and nuns are entirely at one.'[30]

Bishop Denvir's association with the education commission was publicly opposed by a number of priests and prominent lay people in his diocese. By the time he was forced to resign as bishop in 1865, the *Catholic Directory* had drawn attention to what it took to be the unsatisfactory level of provision for Catholic education in the diocese of Down and Connor. This meant, according to the *Directory*, that Catholic children were required to attend national schools 'in which the course of religious instructions highly perilous to the faith of such Catholic children' was given.[31] This also reflected the

---

26 Blake to Murray, 3 and 10 Mar. 1838, in Mary Purcell (ed.), 'Documents: Dublin diocesan archives; Murray papers', *Archivium Hibernicum*, 37 (1982), 81–2. **27** Ibid., Denvir to Murray, 11 Mar. 1838, p. 92. **28** *Downpatrick Recorder*, 13 Aug. 1864. Bishop Blake made a similar point to the education office in Dublin thirty years earlier concerning the convent school in Newry. PRONI (DIO) RC 3/1 Blake letter book, Blake to Thomas Kelly, 26 May 1833. **29** *Report from the commissioners of primary education (Ireland)*, HC (1870) xxviii pt 1, app. 3, p. 557. **30** Ibid., p. 554. **31** *Catholic*

view of Patrick Dorrian, Denvir's coadjutor bishop and successor, that because of Denvir's neglect many Catholic children had to attend Presbyterian schools where there was a danger of proselytism.[32] On the other hand, the Powis commission recorded that Denvir in 1854, and Dorrian's own testimony before it in 1868, had stressed that they were both satisfied that the national system was not used for proselytizing purposes.[33]

It is perhaps possible to detect here not so much antipathy to the system as such but rather a desire on the part of the hierarchy to have a greater influence on Irish society as a whole. For social and economic reasons it was impossible for the church in Down to maintain a comprehensive provision for Catholic education at the elementary level. By 1868 the attendance of Catholic children at schools run by nuns or Christian Brothers was a mere 228. The foundation of institutions for post-primary education in Belfast and Newry earlier in the century was in the first instance to provide for the training of priests. It was probably a growing sense of political power rather than a fear of the consequences of mixed education that determined the increasingly militant attitude of Catholic churchmen to the question.

Writing in 1851 George Crolly, a County Down man and a professor at Maynooth, defended the national school system, and rejected what he took to be the assumption, too often displayed by 'popular newspaper writers', that mixed education was 'essentially bad'. Quoting from a bull of Pope Gregory XVI issued in 1841 he pointed out that during the first ten years of its existence 'the Catholic religion had suffered no injury' from the system.[34]

For his part, Michael Blake specifically rejected the idea that the national schools as such posed any threat to Catholicism. At a meeting of the Catholic hierarchy in 1844, Blake repudiated the opposition of some churchmen who viewed the schools as part of a larger conspiracy against the church and who 'dwelt on the dangers to which the Catholic religion is exposed in Russia and Prussia, as if there were any parity between the government of Great Britain and Ireland and those despotic monarchies'.[35]

From 1845 the bishops also confronted the problem posed to them by the queen's colleges. Cullen writing from Rome informed Blake that that the government's aim of educating Catholics and Protestants in the same universities would be fatal to Catholic interests. Naively he believed that if the

directory (Dublin, 1865), p. 164. **32** AAA Dixon papers, Dorrian to Archbishop Joseph Dixon, 2 June 1864. **33** *Report from the commissioners'*, op. cit., p. 585. **34** George Crolly, *The life of the Most Rev. Doctor Crolly, archbishop of Armagh, and primate of Ireland* [*sic*] (Dublin, 1851), p. lii. Archbishop Crolly had told the pope in 1838 that if the national system was condemned by Rome it would outrage the best government Ireland ever had, and religion would suffer not only in the British Isles but also in the British colonies. **35** Peadar MacSuibhne, *Paul Cullen and his contemporaries with their letters from 1820–1902*, 5 vols (Naas, 1962), ii, 342.

bishops kept aloof from them the government would 'in the end make the colleges Catholic'. For their part, Blake, Crolly and Denvir to varying degrees all supported the queen's colleges while seeking various adjustments to make those institutions more Catholic. Conversely, neither Denvir nor Blake would allow the collection for the Catholic University to be taken up in their dioceses on St Patrick's day 1851. Blake, however, underwent several changes of mind on the colleges' issue. He told Cullen that he was pleased that the pope did not approve of the colleges act. On the other hand, he declared that 'I would not be anxious to see [the pope], the head of a state, in public opposition to the minister of England.' He told Cullen that he simply did not see the necessity of a solemn public condemnation of the colleges by the pope.[36]

It would be misleading, however, to conclude from all this that the episcopal leadership of the Catholic community in Down in the first half of the century was unconcerned about specifically Catholic education provision. The Revd John Keenan founded a school in Newry under the direction of Bishop Thomas Kelly in 1823 which subsequently became St Colman's College. Bishops MacMullan, Lennan and Blake all left money in their wills for the purposes of Catholic education. Furthermore, Blake's opposition ensured that the standard religious textbooks of the national system, *Introductory lessons on Christian evidence* and *Scripture lessons*, were not used in the Newry Model School when it opened in 1849.

It is equally clear that, prior to 1831, Catholics and Protestants enjoyed the benefits of mixed education without too much complaint from either side. By 1824, some 6,000 children in Down were attending schools conducted by various Protestant educational societies.[37] Furthermore, Mason's *Parochial survey* and the *Ordnance Survey memoirs* give abundant evidence of the fact that Catholic and Protestant children were taught together. To give but one random example: in the parish of Killinchy in north-east Down, the Kildare Place Society ran a school which was visited by the clergy of all denominations, all of whom, according to the day book, were satisfied with how the school was conducted. In this instance, the master, John Murray, was a Catholic, and of 181 children taught there 98 were Presbyterians, 3 were Church of Ireland, and 80 were Catholics.[38]

This is not to suggest that there were no complaints arising from mixed education. We have some evidence that organizations such as the Kildare Place Society in some instances did see one function of their schools as a means of converting children from popery. On the other hand, the Catholic

36 AICR Cullen papers, Blake to Cullen, 8 Oct. 1846. **37** *Second report of the commissioners of Irish education inquiry*, HC, 1826–7, xii, pp 36–7. **38** Day and McWilliams, *Parishes of county Down II*, p. 92.

authorities obviously believed that it was possible to minimize and counteract such threats. However, once the government became directly responsible for education in the period after 1831, Catholic churchmen began to become increasingly uneasy that, in conjunction with other government initiatives, they might be used as instruments of state policy for the subversion of Catholicism. Even Bishop Blake in one of his periods of depressed discontent maintained that taken as a whole government policies were intended to cause the 'alienation of the people from their pastors and finally the triumph of heresy and infidelity', the result of which would be 'to enslave our religion and our country to the British government'.[39] One aspect of the issue was the question of government interference in what was seen as a parental and ecclesiastical responsibility. This was to be an enduring consideration. In 1892, when the education bill proposed compulsory attendance at school, the bishops objected, on the grounds that this restricted the freedom of choice of parents with regard to the education of their children. So perplexed was he that Patrick McAlister, bishop of Down and Connor, wanted a papal condemnation of what he saw as an 'infidel system' of compulsory education.[40]

Developments elsewhere also had an influence on the attitude of Irish churchmen to the education question in its various guises. The struggles over education in Italy, France and Germany, a growing skepticism in Rome about all social change in the aftermath of the 1848 revolutions, and the failure of many Roman officials to fully comprehend the position of Ireland as a largely Catholic country within the essentially Protestant United Kingdom, all combined to ensure that the care and subtleties needed to deal objectively and fairly with the Irish education question were not always in evidence.

As with so many other questions facing Irish society, the post-famine period witnessed a hardening of attitude in Catholic demands and expectations. Although Blake and Denvir remained at the helm of Catholic leadership in Down for more than a decade after the famine, both had less flexible assistants, who eventually succeeded them. As the clergy gradually became more ultramontane, they also became more agnostic in regard to both government initiatives and to Protestant influence.

Perhaps, however, the single most important factor conditioning Catholic views in the great debates on education was the increased militancy of the Presbyterian Church. Led in the matter by Henry Cooke, the Synod of Ulster skillfully manipulated the provisions of the 1830 Act and prevailed upon the government to change the system so as to favour Presbyterian interests. The resultant Catholic frustration found expression in an 1859 declaration by bishops. Although they were by now reconciled to the system,

39 AICR Cullen papers, Blake to Cullen, 12 Dec. 1845.   40 AICR Kirby papers, McAlister to Kirby, 14 Feb. 1892.

it was nonetheless objectionable in several respects, particularly in that the 'changes made to its rules from time to time, having been adverse to Catholic interests, have increased the distrust of the Catholic episcopacy'.[41]

Given their disadvantageous numerical position in Down, not even the most militant members of the Catholic community could afford to maintain too great a hostility to their Anglican and Presbyterian neighbours. This might go some way towards explaining the relatively moderate stance taken by most of the leading churchmen in Down on the education question in the nineteenth century. No such constraints operated on Catholic opinions in other regions of the country. Tom Garvin's observation regarding a later period is equally applicable to the circumstances of Catholics in the middle decades of the century. 'Far from Ulster physically and psychologically, the southern counties of Ireland were as insensitive to Protestant fears as they were immune to Orange threats'.[42]

There can be little doubt that the growth of the Catholic presence in areas such as Belfast threatened Protestant sensibilities, and stimulated Protestant hostility to Catholic political pretensions. The struggle over education, and Catholic determination to assert as much control as possible, is perhaps best seen as part of a wider shift in the relationship between the two communities. It is tempting to try to understand inter-community hostilities in Ireland in terms of a simple correlation between Catholic political advance and Protestant fears of domination. However, one cannot neglect the role of specifically religious beliefs in the mutual antagonism between Catholics and Protestants. Upon his nomination as bishop of Down and Connor in 1895 Henry Henry wrote to the rector of the Irish College in Rome that he was deeply conscious of the burden laid upon him 'in this heretical diocese'.[43]

A soiree in the Orange hall in Downpatrick on 6 December 1870 heard the leading County Down Orangeman, Matthew Skillen, denounce the errors and dogmas of Rome. He asked his listeners, how many Masses it would take to get a soul out of purgatory. 'Just as many as it would take snowballs to heat a baker's oven.' He reminded his audience that Orangemen existed to protect the Protestant community against the errors he had just parodied.[44] By contrast, Henry Cooke told a meeting in Belfast in July 1840 that his politics were inseparable from his religion and that he got them both from the bible.[45] William Johnston of Ballykilbeg was yet another political figure able to combine his political and religious beliefs. His biographer assures us that 'a violent hatred of popery' was imbued virtually with his mother's milk and

41 *Catholic directory* (Dublin, 1860), p. 239. 42 Tom Garvin, *Nationalist revolutionaries in Ireland, 1858–1928* (Oxford, 1987), p. 52. 43 AICR Kelly papers, Henry to Michael Kelly, 1 Sept. 1895. 44 *Downpatrick Recorder*, 10 Dec. 1870. 45 A.T. Jackson, *Friends and acquaintances of Henry Cooke* (Belfast, 1985), p. 23.

from this he derived the conviction, from which he never wavered, that the Church of Rome 'was the enemy of freedom'.[46] At the same time Johnston wanted to maintain a distinction between Catholics as individuals and their church. As if to emphasize this, Johnston affected to be astonished when the parish priest of Downpatrick, Bernard McAuley, urged his flock in the 1857 Down by-election to vote for Johnston's opponent, Richard Ker. Johnston declared that his fight was not with Catholics but with 'the Church which degrades and enslaves them'.[47] A distinction doubtless lost on the Catholic community.

In so far as one can separate out the religious and political factors in the relations between the communities, one can discern that Catholics moved from a position of support for the Union at the beginning of the nineteenth century, through a period of disenchantment, to favouring at the end of the century some measure of home rule within the United Kingdom. Arguably, Protestant antagonism to Catholicism was the largest single influence in that process. Nevertheless Catholics remained committed to the established order and valued Ireland's part in the British empire. Such commitment to imperial interests was noticed by Jeremiah O'Donovan Rossa, who was disgusted by the lack of nationalist spirit among Catholics in north Down during his Fenian recruiting tour of Ulster in the 1860s.[48]

In spite of the widespread contact through mixed education, and even some common agitation on the question of land reform, inter-community hostility was an enduring feature of the second half of the century. The inability of many Protestants to differentiate between Catholics who were loyal and those who wanted radical political change was doubtless one factor in the growing sectarianism in east Ulster, whereby Catholicism itself became the focus of hostility. Catholics were, of course, at times equally intolerant. The sentiments, if not all the details, of the Ordnance Survey memorialist in 1838 could have been written at almost any point in the century:

> During the last thirty-five years, Orangeism (under the appellation of loyalty) has prevailed to a considerable extent in this part of the country, from which some of the foulest crimes have originated though chiefly owing to the retaliation of the papists ... Half the murders owing to party zeal. However, it is greatly allayed at present, yet such has been it baleful effects on that portion of society that even the infant

46 Aiken McClelland, *William Johnston of Ballykillbeg* (Lurgan, 1990) p. 5.   47 Ibid., pp 17 and 57. McClelland insists, however, that Johnston remained on friendly terms with his Catholic neighbours.   48 Jeremiah O'Donovan Rossa, *Recollections* (New York, 1892), p. 289.

children of these deluded people are taught to hate each other merely because one is born a protestant and the other a papist.[49]

The resurgent sectarianism in Down in the 1840s was fuelled by renewed tension between the Orange order and revived ribbonism. However, if the sectarian riots in Belfast at various points in the century, the Dolly's Brae affair in 1849, and the riots at Crossgar in July 1857 poisoned the relationship between the two communities, the phenomenon itself was not new. Drilling in Ballynahinch and Newry presaged the hopeless attempts at rebellion in 1803. At a meeting in Belfast in August that year, resolutions were passed condemning the 'despicable number of insignificant traitors' who had taken part in the fiasco at Loughlinisland.[50]

At times of relative political instability, Catholic clergy often remarked, by way of contrast, on the friendliness which existed between the communities. At the jubilee celebrations of his episcopal consecration Patrick Dorrian acknowledged that it had been his great fortune to live in friendship and harmony with Presbyterians and Protestants, who had always dealt fairly with him.[51] This was more than simply the maintenance of friendly individual relations at a time of community distance.[52] There is no doubt, however, that by the 1880s the interests of both communities were so clearly at variance that religious differences were exploited for political ends. This had not always been the case. In the early years of the century the legacy of the United Irishmen did indicate to some degree that it was possible for Catholics and Protestants to share the same ideological platform. We have seen how the social *mores* of both communities were relatively similar. With the coming of the 'second reformation', however, and the agitation over repeal, the stage was set for the two communities to steadily draw apart.[53] Ironically, one of the elements in fostering inter-community strife was the spectacle of public disputations on matters of theology between Catholic and Protestant clergy, such as that in Downpatrick at the end of April 1828 associated with the attempts of the British Reformation Society to open a branch in the town.[54] Sometimes the clergy refused to indulge in such spectacles. Several priests preaching a mission in Newry in March 1853 refused a challenge by

---

49 Day and McWilliams, *Parishes of county Down III*, p. 31. **50** *Belfast News Letter*, 9 Aug. 1803. **51** *Belfast Morning News*, 20 Aug. 1885. **52** A phenomenon identified by K. Theodore Hoppen, *Elections, politics and society in Ireland, 1832–1885* (Oxford, 1984), p. 266. **53** According to Finlay Holmes, the Catholic Church emerged from the Protestant crusade 'stronger and more intolerant of Protestantism than it had ever been before', *Our Presbyterian heritage* (Belfast, 1985). p. 114. **54** The more than 300 pages of these debates can be read in *An authentic report of the discussion which took place at Downpatrick on 22, 23, 24, 28, 29 and 30 April 1828, on six points of controversy between the Church of England and the Church of Rome* (Belfast, 1829).

Protestant parsons to debate the truths of the Christian faith on the grounds that such emotionally charged encounters did nothing to advance the cause of religion.[55]

Another area of contention, and one of the features of the second reformation, was the attempt to induce Catholics to convert to Protestantism. When the Catholic priest George Dempsey, the administrator of Bryansford, tried to embarrass Lord Roden and his parson, the Revd A.W. McCreight, by displaying in Downpatrick the clothes and other articles which they used to try to bribe Catholics into conforming to the established Church, Roden served him with a notice to quit. Roden, who had a reputation of generally being kindly to his Catholic tenants, later dropped the case.[56]

The revival not only consolidated the emergent sense of Protestant identity in Ulster; by the 1880s its effects also had definite political overtones as the Protestant community now set about attempts to resist home rule.[57] By then the alliance between the Church of Ireland and the Presbyterian Church was well cemented. Rome and its clergy were seen as the common enemy of all shades of Protestant opinion.

Not all Catholic observers, however, saw the revival in menacing terms. At the Down assizes in 1859 Chief Baron Pigott, a Catholic, concluded that the revival had 'extinguished party animosity [and] produced the most wholesome moral results',[58] perhaps demonstrating how out of touch senior judges can be. At the beginning of that decade, Protestant resistance to Catholic expansionism was clearly demonstrated in the opposition which was provoked by the restoration of the Catholic hierarchy in England. Even then, however, there were some surprising instances of accommodation. The parishioners of Dromore were joined by Anglicans and Presbyterians when they petitioned the Catholic MP for Lancashire South, Alexander Henry, himself a native of County Down, to vote against Lord John Russell's response to the restoration, namely the ecclesiastical titles act. A similar petition was sent to Sharman Crawford by the Catholics of Garvaghy.[59] Crawford and Lord Castlereagh both spoke against the measure. Castlereagh was rebuked by the *Downpatrick Recorder*, which assured him that he would have to answer to the Protestant electorate of Down for this instance of betrayal of the Protestant interest.

The internal dynamics of Catholicism also contributed to heightened tension. Ultramontane Catholicism had its own distinctive political agenda. The issue here was not so much the espousal of any one political platform but

55 *The Ulsterman*, 12 Mar. 1853.   **56** The details are given in O'Laverty, *An historical account*, i, 59–63.   **57** David Hempton and Mertyl Hill, *Evangelical Protestantism in Ulster society, 1740–1890* (London, 1992), p. 167.   **58** Jonathan Bardon, *A history of Ulster* (Belfast, 1992), p. 344.   **59** *Catholic directory* (Dublin, 1852), p. 251.

rather the tendency to seek control of the political process as a whole. If the Belfast *Ulsterman* at its foundation could declare that its intention was to be a journal which by its honesty, intelligence and national feeling might truly 'represent the Catholics of Ulster',[60] that representation would have to conform to what the clergy determined was truly in the interests of the community. Bishop Henry in later years was bitterly to regret that some of his people were putting nationality before religion by resisting his political posturing in Belfast. Here, of course, the problem had been exacerbated by the Parnellite split. It is a mark of how the church's role had changed that the clergy could confidently predict Parnell's end. Archbishop Michael Logue thus wrote to Tobias Kirby in Rome that 'the north, priests and people, is solid against Parnell. A small clique in Belfast and Newry[61] are trying to make a noise, but nobody heeds them. I am hammering away on the subject on every available occasion.'[62] As part of the same hammering process Bishop Patrick McAlister was determined to counter the pro-Parnellite *Belfast Morning News* in the name of morality. By founding his own newspaper, the *Irish News*, he effectively emasculated the opposition and forced the rival newspaper out of business.[63]

Such clerical politicking was by no means new. The *Newry Commercial Telegraph* had complained sixty years earlier of clerical interference in elections, despite the assurances given in the run up to emancipation that priests would be happy to abandon politics and concentrate on their pastoral duties.[64]

There can be little doubt that the Catholic community in Down in the nineteenth century, for the most part, saw its social salvation as linked to the fortunes and general prosperity of the United Kingdom. In its religious life, the community shared the growing ultramontane and Italianate tastes of mainstream Irish, and indeed British, Catholicism. Like the Catholic community in the other northeast counties of Ulster, it had an almost schizophrenic attitude to Protestantism. Although dependent on the generosity of wealthy Protestants for its rapid growth and development, its very success encouraged alienation between the two communities which progressively obliterated common liberal political objectives.

It is, however, important not to be seduced into too ready an acquiescence in the idea of the inter-community harmony at the beginning of the century as compared with the barely concealed contempt at the end. Even in the more

60 *The Ulsterman*, 17 Nov. 1852.   61 Much in the tradition of the independence of the laity in those two towns, which we witnessed at the beginning of the century. 62 AICR Kirby papers Logue to Kirby, 5 Dec. 1891.   63 Ibid., McAlister to Kirby, 18 April 1891. McAlister asked for the pope's blessing for his paper which would 'serve the cause of religion in Ulster'.   64 *Newry Commercial Telegraph*, 16 Jan. 1835.

tolerant days of 1817 the president of the Belfast Academical Institution, the Revd Dr William Bruce, could write under the pseudonym Zwinglius, that

> Ever intelligent Protestant must know, that this infallible and immac- ulate guide which assumes the title of THE CHURCH, is tainted with errors more numerous than the most ignorant and fanatical Protestant sect, or than all our sects put together.[65]

By contrast, as we have seen, in the middle of the penultimate decade of the century, Patrick Dorrian could attest that throughout his ministry in County Down and in Belfast, he had always lived in friendship with his Protestant neighbours, and he respected their religious convictions although he disagreed with them.[66]

In general, the concern of ecclesiastical authority was to secure the most favourable conditions possible within which to conduct the church's business. What is perhaps significant was the capacity of the Catholic community to shed its residual resemblance to the culture around it, to absorb the extra- neous elements of ultramontanism, and therefore to distance itself from its own past. To that extent one can talk just as much of dislocation from, as of continuity with, its inherited traditions. Such a phenomenon affected both communities. Catholics and Protestants in Down were equally caught up in political and religious developments originating elsewhere. Owing to the historical antagonisms between the two communities, the second reformation and the revival, the struggles over education and the growing political tensions which arose from repeal and home rule, all revived in a more vehement strain inter-religious hostility. One effect of all this was to make Catholicism in the Ulster context more inward-looking and more preoc- cupied with its distinctive characteristics, forcing it in the twentieth century into flirtations with radical politics and violence, as it sought to channel the renewed energies of prejudice and sectarianism.

---

65 *Belfast News Letter*, 27 May 1817.   **66** *Belfast Morning News*, 20 Aug. 1885.

Index